THE TIARA AND THE TEST TUBE

THE TIARA AND THE TEST TUBE

The Popes and Science from the Medieval Period to the Present

Paul Haffner

Gracewing

First published in England in 2014
by
Gracewing
2 Southern Avenue
Leominster
Herefordshire HR6 0QF
United Kingdom
www.gracewing.co.uk

ISBN 978 085244 860 1

Typeset by Gracewing

CONTENTS

CONTENTS....v

PREFACE....vii

ABBREVIATIONS....ix

1 A HISTORY LESSON....1

Stanley Jaki....5

The stillbirths of science....16

The viable birth of science....26

2 POPE SYLVESTER....49

Studying and teaching....50

Mathematics....55

Gerbert's spheres....58

The astrolabe....64

Gerbert's fame and rise....65

3 POPE INNOCENT III AND THE HOSPITALS....73

Ancient medicine....74

The Old Testament....75

The Christian era....78

The Middle Ages....85

Pope Innocent III....92

4 POPE GREGORY XIII AND HIS CALENDAR....................101

The Reform of the Calendar..105

Pontifical Gregorian University..110

Background and History...110

Pope Benedict XVI at the Pontifical Gregorian University.....113

5 THE PONTIFICAL ACADEMY OF SCIENCES...................117

Early history...118

Refounding the Academy...125

Pope Pius XI...126

The Academy today...129

6 THE VATICAN OBSERVATORY...137

Historical roots..138

Foundation of the Specola..149

Recent developments..155

7 POPE PIUS XII AND PROOFS FOR THE EXISTENCE OF GOD...163

The Ontological Argument..167

The Five Ways...169

The Cosmological Argument..171

The Argument from Contingency.......................................173

The Teleological Argument..175

The Esthetical Argument...179

Anthropological arguments..181

The argument from conscience 182
The argument from universal consent....... 183
The argument from human restlessness....... 185
Pascal's Wager 186
Pius XII and proofs for the existence of God....... 187
8 POPE JOHN PAUL II AND HUMAN DIGNITY....... 201
The limits of science....... 202
Realist perception of the cosmos....... 203
Science and ideology....... 208
The Galileo affair....... 214
Evolution and the human person....... 218
Faith and reason....... 221
9 POPE BENEDICT XVI AND THE LOGOS....... 231
Early work....... 231
The Logos and the human person....... 238
Science and rationality....... 240
Science and the Logos....... 248
10 POPE FRANCIS AND THE PERIPHERY....... 261
Early life....... 261
The periphery....... 265
Faith, science and the periphery....... 270
BIBLIOGRAPHY....... 281

Preface

A popular myth put about by secularists is that between the Church and science the relationship has been, and continues to be, a stormy one. Nothing could in fact be further from the truth. An analysis of historical data shows that modern science developed in the Middle Ages in an atmosphere of Christian faith in the creation. Pope Sylvester II was a brilliant mathematician whose discoveries led to the number system we use today. Pope Innocent III founded a hospital in Rome which was the basis for the modern city hospital system world-wide. The civil calendar in use today owes its existence to Pope Gregory XIII. The Pontifical Academy of Sciences and the Vatican Observatory are both highly-respected institutions which continue to contribute to scientific progress.

This book then proceeds to examine four modern Popes have contributed in a special way to the dialogue between faith and science: Pope Pius XII who renewed the proofs for the existence of God in the light of modern science, Pope St John Paul II who reaffirmed the crucial importance of the dignity of the human person in science, Pope Benedict XVI who proposed the rational basis for creation in terms of the doctrine of the Logos, and Pope Francis who sees science in terms of the existential periphery to be evangelised.

Rome, 11 July 2014
Feast of St Benedict

ABBREVIATIONS

AAS =	*Acta Apostolicae Sedis*. Commentarium officiale. Typis Polyglottis Vaticanis, 1909–.
CCC =	*Catechism of the Catholic Church*. LEV, Vatican City 1992.
CCL =	*Corpus Christianorum series latina*. Tournai: Brepols, 1954–.
DP =	*Discourses of the Popes from Pius XI to John Paul II to the Pontifical Academy of Sciences*. 1936–1986. Vatican City: Pontifical Academy of Sciences, 1986.
DS =	H. Denzinger. *Enchiridion Symbolorum, Definitionum et Declarationum de rebus fidei et morum*. Edizione bilingue a cura di P. Hünermann. EDB, Bologna 1995.
OR =	*L'Osservatore Romano*, daily edition.
PG =	J. P. Migne. *Patrologiae cursus completus*, series graeca. 161 voll., Paris 1857–1866.
PL =	J. P. Migne. *Patrologiae cursus completus*, series latina. 221 voll., Paris 1844–1864.
SC =	*Sources Chretiennes*. Paris: Cerf, 1942–.

1

A HISTORY LESSON

Great cultures, where the scientific enterprise came to a standstill, invariably failed to formulate the notion of physical law, or the law of nature. Theirs was a theology with no belief in a personal, rational, absolutely transcendent Lawgiver, or Creator. Their cosmology reflected a pantheistic and animistic view of nature caught in the treadmill of perennial, inexorable returns. The scientific quest found fertile soil only when this faith in a personal, rational Creator had truly permeated a whole culture, beginning with the centuries of the High Middle Ages. It was that faith which provided, in sufficient measure, confidence in the rationality of the universe, trust in progress, and appreciation of the quantitative method, all indispensable ingredients of the scientific quest.

S. L. Jaki, *Science and Creation*

THE PRESENCE OF science in our lives and its many technological applications are so familiar to us that we take them for granted. Over the past century, society has changed more profoundly and more rapidly than during any other period in history. Transport by land, sea and air, space travel, computer technology, telecommunications, the information superhighway, antibiotics, are only some examples of the scientific revolution which has taken place. Mankind has advanced greatly in its understanding of the universe from atoms to galaxies; the Human Genome Project which seeks to map all human genes should herald a new era in medical understanding of the human body and in treating disease. These rapid developments have given rise to a variety of questions which have a bearing upon the theology of creation.

The discovery of electricity completely changed our lives, as well as the invention and development of motor cars and air planes. In the medical realm, the discovery of antibiotics and anti-viral agents has meant that diseases which once were often fatal, like pneumonia, can now be cured. In the realm of daily living vast progress has been made in the last thirty years, particularly in computer science and technology bringing speedier and more efficient communications. However, our understanding of the universe has also developed greatly.

Just over one hundred years ago, scientists thought that their understanding of the world was practically complete. But then, early in the twentieth century, the discovery of relativity theory and the development of quantum mechanics once again opened new frontiers in the physical world. The atom which seemed like a tiny billiard ball was then split, thus revealing hitherto unknown subatomic particles and forces. Our journey also into the cosmos as a whole has revealed the vastness, complexity and yet beauty of a universe which we are still uncovering. Similarly, the voyage of discovery into the biological realm has also involved the breaking of new frontiers. The father of modern genetics is really an Augustinian priest, Gregor Mendel, from the latter part of the nineteenth century whose studies into the laws of heredity in plants paved the way for great progress in the twentieth century. Now the human genome project has mapped the genetic profile of the human being in such a way that many diseases which up to now have been incurable may one day be cured. Clearly this remarkable scientific progress has not been without its problems. Technology has not always applied scientific discoveries for the best, and applications have not always been shared with humanity in such a way that the less fortunate could have also benefited from these developments.

Yet we do not find anything comparable in the great civilizations of the past: the development of science seems historically to be an exclusive feature of Western civilization. In ancient cultures we certainly find some highly-developed social structures, large cities, men and women of great culture, magnificent architecture, wood and metal processing, the art of pottery and also philosophy, theatre and literature. However there was nothing like science as we know it today. They seemed to have all that is needed to develop a scientific understanding of the world, but they did not manage to do so.

It is necessary to distinguish between primitive science, namely the knowledge that is acquired with empirical tools, and modern science, which is based on a detailed understanding of how the cosmos works, analysing matter through mathematics. Basically this is a unique discovery, achieved by our civilization of Western Europe.

Measurements were made to high accuracy, both in the construction of buildings like the pyramids of Egypt and for surveying agricultural land. The motions of the stars and planets were recorded by the Babylonians, but there was no comprehensive understanding of the way these motions can be calculated by solving the equations of dynamics. The Greeks speculated about the ultimate constituents of matter, but did not know whether they exist or if they do what is their size and structure or how they interact with each other and how their properties can be related to those of everyday matter. Above all, there is no conception of the way all the infinite variety of phenomena, astronomical, electrical, dynamical, chemical and atomic, can be understood as the manifestations of a unified structure that can be expressed in a very few differential equations.

Before starting the examination of how the Popes impact on science, it would be in order to define what we mean by science, albeit briefly. Science is an intellectual activity carried on by human persons in order to investigate the natural world in which humans live and to discover the ways in which this information can be organized into meaningful patterns. A primary aim of science is therefore to collect facts or data. An ultimate purpose of science is to discern the order that exists between and among the various data. Science is an intellectual human activity that is concerned with integrating and coordinating, in a systematic way, new information with an existing and ever-expanding reservoir of information. This integrating gives a more complete description and explanation of the natural world in which we live. This increasing body of knowledge available to scientists and society is supplied from many different fields of exploration. As a result of the intellectual activities associated with science, we conclude that science is a way of obtaining objective knowledge. Science is a process seeking principles of order in the universe. Thus, science becomes a way of objectively knowing about the physical, chemical, and biological worlds in which humans live and the myriad interrelationships which exist in the cosmos. The result of the organized, intellectual activities called science is the obtaining, by humans, of an intelligible picture of the natural world in which they live.

Science has works on a number of presuppositions, which may be evident but not proven by science itself. First science assumes the existence of a theory-independent, external world, and the orderly nature of this external world. It presumes the knowability of the external world, the existence of truth, and the laws of logic. Science assumes the reliability of our cognitive and sensory faculties to serve as truth gatherers and as a source of justified true beliefs in our intellectual environment. It rests upon the adequacy of language to describe the world, and the existence of values used in science (like "test theories fairly and report test results honestly"). Science also assumes the uniformity of nature and induction, and the existence of numbers.[1]

Stanley Jaki

An interesting and important question in this great scientific development over the past century concerns how it all came about in the first place. It is true that one discovery builds upon another. For example, the invention of computers is inconceivable without the prior discovery of electricity. Many scholars would say that the early moves in the development of modern science go all the way back to the Middle Ages.[2] Fr Stanley L. Jaki OSB discovered this fundamental historical paradigm of the history of science, namely that the Middle Ages represent the cradle of science. This period therefore represents the starting point in our examination of the relationship between the Popes and science.

Györ—a Roman, medieval, baroque and modern industrial town—where Jaki was born on 17 August 1924, and where he grew up, instilled into him a keen appreciation for history. There is a scientific root in his family's background. His mother's uncle, Gusztáv Szabó, was Rector of the *József Nádor Müszaki Egyetem* (Hungarian Institute of Technology) in Budapest in the 1930's. Jaki's elder brother, also a Benedictine and a graduate of the Pázmány Péter (now Eötvös Lóránt) University in Budapest, for decades taught physics and mathematics in two preparatory schools of the Benedictine Order in Hungary. He himself had outstanding teachers in mathematics and physics at the Jedlik Gymnasium, a Preparatory School run by the Benedictine Order in his native town of Györ. For three years during his student years, the Yearbook of the Gymnasium carried a book-length essay by one of the physics teachers on the life and work of Anyos Jedlik (1804–1888), a Hungarian Benedictine and the co-discoverer of the dynamo, who was also the predecessor of Lóránt Eötvös in the chair of physics at the Pázmány Péter University in Budapest.

Upon his graduation from the Jedlik Gymnasium in June 1942, he entered the Benedictine Order and, on 13 May 1944 (which was to become the Feast of Our Lady of Fatima), he made his religious profession. After completing his undergraduate training in philosophy and theology, he was sent to Rome in 1947 to complete his theological studies with a doctorate in systematic theology at the Pontifical Institute of Sant'Anselmo, so that he could return to Pannonhalma Archabbey (which celebrated its millennium in 1996) and teach theology. On 29 June 1948 he was ordained priest.

Following the defence of his doctoral thesis in late November 1950, he was not allowed by his Order to return to Hungary, a country subject at that time to cruel Stalinist oppression. Nor was he allowed to remain in Europe, although he was fluent in French. The young Dom Stanley accepted an invitation to the United States of America, to Saint Vincent's Archabbey, Latrobe, Pennsylvania, to teach systematic theology in its major interdiocesan seminary and French in its College. From Autumn 1951 until early 1954, he taught the tracts *De Deo Uno, De Deo creante, De homine et gratia* and *De novissimis.* As these tracts often touch on scientific questions, he wished to study such themes in depth for the benefit of his students. First he delved into outstanding popularizations of science such as those written by Eddington and Jeans. He realized that a thorough training in science was necessary, so that during these years he attended courses at the same Saint Vincent's College in mathematics, as well as American history and literature, to gain his bachelor of science degree in 1954. During these years he also studied the two famous allocutions of Pope Pius XII to the Pontifical Academy of Sciences.[3] These dealt with the proofs of God's existence in the light of modern science and were a very important influence on Jaki, who became interested in a proof of the existence of God from considerations of physical entropy in the universe.

However, on 9 December 1953 Stanley Jaki underwent a severe tonsillectomy with complications that deprived him for ten years of the effective use of his vocal chords.[4] He had to give up teaching in February 1954 and left Saint Vincent's in July 1954. He was then permitted to pursue advanced studies in physics, and, in September 1954 enrolled at the graduate school of Fordham University. There he encountered the prominent physics professor and Nobel Prize winner Victor F. Hess,[5] famous for his discovery of cosmic rays, who himself had been afflicted with a chronic ailment of his vocal chords, as a result of radon and thoron inhalation, during his pioneering work in radioactivity. An affinity developed between the two also because both came from an Austro-Hungarian background. Jaki obtained his master of science degree in July 1955, did another year of course work for the doctorate and started his research in September 1956. Contrary to his wishes he could not choose for his topic a subject in theoretical thermodynamics, such as the question of entropy in the universe. He was urged to undertake, under the mentorship of Dr Hess, an experimental project, the development of a new method for measuring the distribution of radon and thoron at the earth-air interface. In 1957, Jaki defended his thesis, which in 1958 he co-published with Dr Hess.[6]

Meanwhile, in the late summer of 1957, along with other refugee Benedictines, Jaki set up the Woodside Priory school in Portola Valley, California. He could not manage to teach because of his vocal chords, so he became bursar, with plenty of opportunity to read in the history and philosophy of science at the nearby Stanford University. Jaki wrote a dozen or so articles in those years for the *Katolikus Szemle*, a Hungarian quarterly Catholic review published in Rome.[7] These articles are an early expression of his interest in astronomy, cosmology, fundamental particle physics, extraterrestrial life, the origin of life and the medieval origins of science. As the dry climate in Portola Valley caused chronic discomfort for his throat, he was allowed to return to the notoriously humid East Coast, partly because he obtained a fellowship at Princeton University (1960–1962). There he took part in various graduate seminars in the history and philosophy of science.

Because of his health, Stanley Jaki was, in his own words, *damnatus ad litteras*, or condemned to write. In the autumn of 1961, the idea of *The Relevance of Physics* started to take shape in Jaki's mind. The work was ready by the autumn of 1964, and was published by the University of Chicago Press in late 1966. Years later Jaki learned that Professor Herbert Feigl was one of the three scholars who had read the typescript for the University of Chicago Press. In his report, Feigl stated that "the author displayed outstanding scholarship on every page".[8] Professor Heitler (renowned for his work on quantum mechanics) recommended the work as "compulsory reading for all scientists, students, and professors".[9]

In 1965, Stanley Jaki joined the Faculty of Seton Hall University at South Orange, New Jersey, and from 1975 until his death in 2009, he was Distinguished Professor at Seton Hall University. During the academic year 1967–68, he was also associated with the Institute for Advanced Study in Princeton, New Jersey. Originally, Jaki wanted *The Relevance of Physics* to include a chapter on physics and psychology and another on physics and sociology. However, the work was already long enough, and so the material was included in *Brain, Mind and Computers,* first published in 1969.[10] This work won Jaki the Lecomte de Nouy Prize for 1970.

Stanley Jaki was the first Catholic priest chosen to deliver the Gifford lectures, and is one of about ten Americans to have done so, following Josiah Royce, William James, Alfred North Whitehead, John Dewey, Reinhold Niebuhr and Paul Tillich. Jaki gave these lectures in 1974–75 and 1975–76, at the University of Edinburgh. The invitation for the Gifford Lectures was issued to Jaki in May 1973 on the strength of his now very impressive list of publications which earned him a world reputation as an historian and philosopher of physics.

In 1980, Jaki was elected Hoyt Fellow at Yale. Since 1985, he has been *membre correspondant* of the *Academie Nationale des Sciences, Belles Lettres et Arts* of Bordeaux. International recognition for his work on science and religion came on 12 May 1987, when Stanley Jaki received the Templeton Prize for Progress in Religion. The brochure for the presentation ceremony stated that: "Professor Stanley Jaki has offered the world in a series of highly original and learned works a reinterpretation of the history of science, which throws a flood of light on the relation of science and culture, and not least the relation of science and faith."[11] In 1997, Jaki was awarded the Széchenyi Medal of the Széchenyi Társaság (Hungary). He also held memberships in Sigma Xi (The Scientific Research Society), the History of Science Society, the Olbers Gesellschaft (Bremen), and the Hellenic Society for Humanistic Studies (Athens).

Stanley Jaki delivered guest lectures at over fifty major universities, colleges and research institutes in North America, Europe and Australia, and was an invited lecturer at over thirty congresses, symposia and colloquia. These included the Olbers Lectures (Bremen, 1970), the Gifford Lectures at Edinburgh (1974–75 and 1975–76), the Fremantle Lectures at Oxford University (1977), the McDonald lectures at the University of Sydney (1980). He has been the McDermott Lecturer, University of Dallas (1983), the Wethersfield Institute Scholar (1986, 1987, 1992), the Farmington Institute Lecturer, Oxford University (1988, 1989) and the Forwood Lecturer, University of Liverpool (1992). In addition, Jaki has lectured in France, Belgium, the Netherlands, Germany, Italy, Spain, Greece, Hungary, Sweden, Japan, and Australia.

In 1983, he gave a paper at the International Conference on Science in Islamic Polity at Islamabad, on "The Physics of Impetus and the Impetus of the Koran."[12] In 1987 he delivered the first Wethersfield Institute Lectures, followed in 1988 and 1989 by two series of lectures at Corpus Christi College, Oxford, under the sponsorship of the Farmington Institute. In December 1988 he was invited lecturer at the Southeast-Asia Bishops Conference on Science and Religion in Hong Kong. In 1989, he gave lectures at the Pontifical Gregorian University and the Pontificio Ateneo Romano della Santa Croce in Rome, and at the Soviet Academy of Sciences in Moscow. In the same year he received an honorary doctorate from Marquette University, one of a string of such honours that have been conferred on him. In May 1990 he presented an invited paper, "Ecology or Ecologism?" at the Pontifical Academy of Sciences at its Symposium, held jointly with the Royal Swedish Academy of Sciences, on the fate of rain forests.[13] He participated in the World Congress of Catholic Physicians, New York (1998), and the International Giordano Bruno Conference, Rome (2000).

Stanley Jaki is the author of over one hundred books and several hundred articles, many of which have been translated into various languages, including French, Italian, Spanish, Hungarian, Polish, Russian and Chinese. In several instances, Jaki has translated a work into English, in order to expose the author's errors. This is the case with the translation with a commentary on the Renaissance pantheist Giordano Bruno's *The Ash Wednesday Supper*. Similarly, with his translation of Kant's *Universal Natural History and Theory of the Heavens*, Jaki examines Kant's weaknesses in science and his strange notions about extra-terrestrial life. In many of his other works, Jaki points out the falsity of Kant's idealism which places reality in ideas perceived by the mind rather than in the external objective world. He also brings to the attention of modern Catholics the dangers of mixing Kantian thought into Thomistic philosophy, in what is known as transcendental Thomism. This hybrid kind of philosophy only diminishes the realism of Aquinas' vision and paves the way for confusion in theology. In his translation of J. H. Lambert's *Cosmological Letters of the Arrangement of the World Edifice*, Jaki has offered scholars of the history of science the first translation of a classic of the history of cosmology. While most of his articles have been written for Catholic journals, several have also been written for those of other

Christian traditions, showing that Jaki is a respected figure in the world of learning as a whole.

In September 1990, Pope John Paul II named Stanley Jaki honorary member, with full rights and privileges of ordinary members, of the Pontifical Academy of Sciences. He was formally invested as a Pontifical Academician at the Plenary Meeting of the Academy on 29 October 1990. In his acceptance speech on that day, he highlighted what has been his chief work:

> This great honor of becoming a member of the Pontifical Academy of Sciences comes in a context this Plenary Session of the Academy on Science and Culture—which is of special satisfaction to me, a theologian and physicist who has focused, for the past thirty years, on the history and philosophy of physics. Physics, the most exact form of all sciences, becomes part of human culture not only through its discoveries—theoretical and technological—but all too often, and even more so, through the philosophy in terms of which physics is evaluated and in terms of its historical development ... In all that research my guiding light has been Pierre Duhem, ... in the analysis of physical theories and in discovering an unsuspected continent (medieval physics) of the history of science.[14]

As regards the history and philosophy of science, Jaki would have been the first to admit that Pierre Duhem (1861–1916), the French physicist and philosopher and historian of science, was an important influence on him. After completing his doctorate in physics in 1957, Jaki realized that the real problems concerning the relation of science and religion belonged mostly to the history and philosophy of physics. In 1961, Jaki read the biography of Duhem by his daughter, Hélène.[15] He felt a true "meeting of minds" and was intrigued by Duhem's work stressing the importance of the medieval period for the growth of science. Jaki was stimulated by Duhem's defence of Christian culture, and published a considerable number of works dealing with Duhem.[16] In particular, *Uneasy Genius*, a work of about half a million words, situates much of Duhem's historical, philosophical and religious thought in the context of his life. Duhem's argument that the ancient Greeks failed in science because of their belief in eternal cycles was developed by Jaki on a vast scale in his *Science and Creation*.[17] There he accounts for the "stillbirths of science" (a momentous phrase coined by Jaki) in all major ancient cultures on the basis of the absence, in all of them, of belief in creation out of nothing and in time. Duhem had dealt in that respect only with the Greeks.

For Pierre Duhem, physics was incomplete and imperfect in its knowledge of things and he held, in the actual practice of science, a strong separation between physics and metaphysics.[18] Physics, the sole object of which is sensory evidence,[19] is a discipline with intrinsic incompleteness; in Duhem's view, this arises from the fact that there could never be a strict one-to-one correspondence between the mathematical formalization of the laws which grouped sensory data, and reality. This incompleteness of science is a theme which Jaki has explored extensively. It is important to indicate both his influence within Jaki's works and also Jaki's radical novelty and difference from Duhem.

As regards philosophy, Jaki considers himself in the line of the methodical realism of Etienne Gilson.[20] He also follows Gilson in placing basic epistemological propositions in their historical contexts. Again, with Gilson, he stresses that common-sense truths are not a derivative of commonly-held opinions. In the history and philosophy of science, Jaki is regarded as a "revisionist" by those who overstress the contribution of the Renaissance and Enlightenment to science at the expense of the medieval period. Jaki also regards Chesterton[21] and Maritain[22] as important thinkers for a realist perspective upon the cosmos.

In addition to his critique of the various forms of empiricism and idealism, ancient and modern, Jaki argued that the history of science has repeatedly been used unfairly and inaccurately as an anti-Christian ideological tool, especially by a long line of French anticlerical propagandists, from the Encyclopedists to George Sarton and Alexander Koyré. No short summary can do justice to the insight, detail, and philosophical power and importance of Jaki's body of work on these issues and the relations between science, philosophy, ethics, religion, and culture.

Stanley Jaki also explored in detail the thought of John Henry Cardinal Newman (1801–1890) so contrasting a variety of common misperceptions of the famous English churchman, especially those approaches that diminish Newman's deep appreciation of the supernatural. For Jaki, Newman's chief challenge today, as in his times, aims at the defence of the supernatural. Jaki shows that such a defence was, for Newman, far more than a simple intellectual enterprise: for him the supernatural was above all a spiritual challenge of the profoundest sort. Jaki has explored numerous key topics drawn from Newman's writings, and shows that much as the topics of original sin, angels, miracles, Anglo-Catholicism, conversion, and the papacy may differ from those of assent, science, evolution, and history, they all bespeak Newman's total engagement with the concretely-given supernatural.[23] In an age of an ecumenism often heedless of basic and unchangeable parameters, Newman's insistence on the grievous sin of staying in schism, to say nothing of the sin of plain heresies, can hardly be attractive.[24] In an age of dubious innovations in Catholic ecclesiology, Newman's emphasis on such firm doctrines as the four Notes of the Church, as well as of a Church which, in his eyes, was the One True Fold of salvation, can appear very uncomfortable to such innovators.[25]

As to theology, Jaki was strongly influenced by his studies from 1947 until 1950 at the Pontificio Ateneo Sant'Anselmo, Rome, under C. Vagaggini, who greatly stressed that there is a true science not only about the general, but also about the particular, concrete and individual. He did so precisely with an eye to the rise of the various empirical sciences including historiography. Under Vagaggini, systematic theology was steeped in the history of dogma, with a proper appreciation of the historical role of Saint Thomas Aquinas. Jaki is quite empirical (but not empiricist) in his sifting of historical material, and combines the qualities of an historian and philosopher of science with those of a theologian. Most importantly, Jaki, who went to Rome with a deep sense of loyalty for the Magisterium, refused to be swayed by incipient anti-papal currents that were carried towards the Tiber from the banks of the Rhine, the Seine, the Meuse, and the Rhone. P. E. Hodgson, a Catholic nuclear physicist at Oxford University remarked that the central strand in Jaki's work is respect for all facts, historical and physical, a respect for objective knowledge across its full spectrum, of the material world as known by scientists, of the God we know through the material world and through His revelation, of the teaching of His Incarnate Son, of the authority vested by Christ in Peter and his successors and of the teaching they give us in His Name.[26] His books on the papacy like *And on This Rock* and *The Keys of the Kingdom*, are an assurance that his interpretation of science is an indirect homage to the infallible teaching authority of Peter's successors.[27]

Father Jaki died, following a heart attack, on 7 April 2009, in the Intensive Care Unit of the *Clinica de la Conception* in Madrid. He was in Spain to visit friends on his way back to the USA, after delivering a lecture in Rome on his latest book, at the Renaissance-era Casina (Garden House) of Pope Pius IV, headquarters of the Pontifical Academy of Sciences. He had also delivered some lectures in Rome, for the Master program in Faith and Science, at the Ateneo Pontificio Regina Apostolorum, and at the Pontifical North American College. Fr Stanley Jaki was survived by two brothers, both Benedictine priests, Fr Zénó Jaki and Fr Teodóz Jaki, who live at the Archabbey of Pannonhalma. His Requiem Mass was celebrated on 29 April 2009 by the Archabbot Asztrik Várszegi OSB, and Bishop László Bíró concelebrated, along with numerous other members of the clergy. Attending the rite were the two brothers of Father Jaki, Teodóz and Zénó, both Benedictine monks, his sister Erzsébet, and the President of the Hungarian Academy of Sciences, Szilveszter E. Vizi. Father Jaki is buried at the Archabbey, in the crypt of the Chapel of Our Lady.

The stillbirths of science

In his analysis of the stillbirths and unique viable birth of science, Jaki approaches history in a way which is consistent with his approach to reality in general: the way of moderate realism. It corresponds to taking a middle ground between regarding history as almost everything (an error analogous to that of materialism) and taking history for practically nothing (an error analogous to that of idealism). He therefore rejects historicism, which is the positivist approach to history, as well as the evolutionist view of history in which the passage of time is without purpose. According to him "both metaphysics and historical reality must be taken seriously and in their entirety," and all the more so because the history of science contains a decisive truth to be uncovered:

> One must show readiness to look for a lesson in all its phases, in the most developed as well in the most embryonic, and in particular to try to see whether a consistent lesson can be found in the entirety of the historical process.[28]

One fundamental historical question stands out in bold relief, namely why science only came to its viable birth during the high Middle Ages. Modern experimental science was rendered possible as a result of the Christian philosophical atmosphere of the Middle Ages. Although a *talent* for science was certainly present in the ancient world (for example in the design and construction of the Egyptian pyramids), nevertheless the philosophical and psychological climate was hostile to a self-sustaining scientific process. The stillbirths of science in all ancient cultures and its one viable birth in the Middle Ages constitute the fundamental paradigm of the history of science.[29]

As Jaki recounts, although some scientific elements were first in evidence a little before 2000 BC, the subsequent three thousand years of scientific endeavour were marked by a pattern of repeated historical blind alleys. Science came to "an aborted birth in seven great cultures: Chinese, Hindu, Maya, Egyptian, Babylonian, Greek and Arabic."[30] In other words, science suffered stillbirths in the cultures of ancient China, India, Egypt, Babylonia. It also failed to come to fruition among the Maya, Incas, and Aztecs of the Americas. Even though ancient Greece came closer to achieving a continuous scientific enterprise than any other ancient culture, science was not born there either. Science did not come to birth among the medieval Muslim heirs to Aristotle. According to Jaki, underlying all those stillbirths is an interplay of two conceptual factors that are ultimately but two sides of the same coin or currency, which is not convertible into belief in a transcendental Creator who set autonomous consistent laws to the universe created by Him. These two factors depict the universe as a huge organism about which one can only predict that it would go through endless repetitive cycles of birth, death and rebirth.

As one may expect, therefore, there is a major difference between Jaki's approach and that of Joseph Needham concerning the failure of the ancient Chinese in matters scientific. The difference emerges very sharply in Jaki's evaluation of Needham who, as befits a hybrid thinker trying to be Christian (Anglican) and materialist (Marxist) at the same time, saw much good in the organismic approach which set the tone of thought about nature, both in Confucianism and Taoism. As one may expect, Needham took lightly the endorsement by Taoists as well as Confucians of the doctrine of eternal recurrence. Jaki also exposes Needham's tactic of praising and damning in the same breath Christian belief in a truly transcendental Creator and Lawgiver, although something akin to that belief, in Needham's own admission, might have made it possible for the early Chinese to conceive the notion of genuine scientific laws.

Jaki handles the same problem in quite a different manner. He shows how early Chinese science had drawn strength from the belief in a personal Creator and in a universe with laws, but science was undermined in the pantheistic, organismic, cyclic world-view which eventually prevailed. He lists in detail the various organismic metaphors (mostly based on the human body) in terms of which Chinese sages tried to understand the universe. In the Confucian view of the cosmos, a strong parallel was drawn between the parts of man's body and the parts of the universe; the latter was conceived as cyclic with respect to time. In the Taoist view of reality, nature was an all-encompassing living entity animated by impersonal volitions, and man was a ripple on the great rhythmic undulations of the *yin* and the *yang* (the two basic forces of the cosmos), with little sense of purpose. There were endless returns in nature, no real beginning, and the universe was essentially unfathomable.

In the second century after Christ, Buddhism entered China from India and further reinforced an "already strong preoccupation with cycles dominating the cosmos."[31] The Chinese possessed the raw materials of science in printing, gunpowder and magnets, and yet there was no intellectual ferment and no real scientific progress. The cyclic conception of reality inhibited this growth, as the awareness of the causal connection between events was stymied for the Chinese. As Jaki notes: "the ensuing resignation of the Chinese into practical mediocrity, though not into despair and despondency, was a matching counterpart of their moderate preoccupation with the exact period of the great cosmic cycle, the Great Year."[32] Jaki further shows that, even in modern China, the philosophical atmosphere is hardly one conducive to science. Despite an apparent rejection of the wisdom of ancient China, the cultural revolution of Mao Tse-tung "drew heavily on ancient Confucian and Taoist aphorisms, as if they represented the spirit of modern science."[33] Confirmation of Jaki's views can be found in the catastrophic impact of the "cultural revolution" on science in Maoist China.

Jaki finds a dramatic illustration of the stifling impact of belief in the Great Year on the prospect of science in ancient India, the birthplace among other things of such seminal scientific insights as the decimal notation, including the place value for zero. Despite these insights, there was an inability to develop them into a self-sustaining system of scientific investigation. The ancient Hindus were greatly preoccupied with their cyclic notion of the cosmos, to assign an exact figure to the length of the Great Year, dominated by the Kaliyuga or the world-age of decay. They remained victims of the despair resulting from their perception that "the eternal recurrence was a treadmill out of which there was no point in trying to escape."[34] This worldview weakened the search for truth about the physical world in the form of "theoretical generalization leading to the formulation of quantitative laws and systems of laws."[35] Jaki noted a similar effect in the preference among ancient Hindus for viewing the universe as a huge divine body.

Despite the paucity of records, evidence can also be seen of a hopeless world-view in the culture of the pre-Columbian Americas. The Aztec gods were personifications of various periodically-changing forces and phenomena in nature. Organismic and cyclic notions ousted a reliable notion of space, time and causality. Nature was a source of fear and fatalism. The Incas could not break out of a cyclic cosmic view. Although the Maya had arithmetic, they failed to get beyond addition and subtraction. Again, the Maya held a cyclic notion of time, in which the universe had no beginning: they failed to go forward and interpret nature in a truly scientific way. In Jaki's words, the fact "that they had not been successful in this respect illustrates that the emergence of science is a more extraordinary event than many children of the atomic age would imagine."[36]

The Egyptians espoused a cyclic notion of time, and the whole world was considered as an animal, yielding for them an organismic, animistic, rhythmic cosmos. Even Akhenaton's (Amenophis IV's) "monotheism" (around 1370 BC) could not change that worldview, trapped as it was in the morass of a pantheistic, animistic matrix. In some practical areas, such as the listing of certain drugs and their attention to the pulse-beat, the Egyptians failed to produce a coherent scientific enterprise owing to their superstitious and magical view of man and the cosmos. The stillbirth in Egyptian science is all the more striking because of such great technical achievements as the pyramids. The lack of development of scientific and historical reflections is no coincidence, for "science and historiography are but different types of a causal and rationally confident probing into the space-time matrix in which external events, physical and human, run their irrevocable courses." Instead, the ancient Egyptians held to an animistic cyclical world-view resting on the "watery-abyss" as the ultimate entity. Jaki concludes: "From its dark, pantheistic depths and from its utterly unpredictable stirrings there could not emerge an unambiguous and effective pointer suggesting the presence of clear, rational laws in the universe."[37]

The Babylonians were also trapped in an animistic and cyclic world-view which was not a fertile soil for the development of scientific enterprise. Their gods, representing various forces in nature, were unpredictable, capricious and violent. Every part of nature had a will of its own, according to the Sumerians, Babylonians and Assyrians. The Babylonians observed the heavens in order to discover the course of human events on earth. In the organismic and cyclic Babylonian cosmology, there was no true beginning or first principle: all lacked consistent explanation and exuded pessimism, as exemplified in the classic Babylonian cosmology, *Enumah Elish*. A major proof of the anti-scientific impact of that cosmogony is seen in Jaki's presentation of its crudely animistic details.[38] There the actual world order is so uncertain as to call for a yearly expiatory ceremony, the Akitu festival, whose participants tried to ward off cosmic disorder by immersing themselves in a ritual orgy. Clearly, it is not difficult for Jaki to show that in such a milieu the practical talents of the Babylonians in collecting astronomical data, so useful later for the Greeks, and in developing practical algebra, could not have been expected to rise to a truly scientific level. Babylon and Assur enjoyed a long period of peace, the Sumerians and Assyro-Babylonians had intellectual strength, industrial power, curiosity and patience; yet their culture did not yield science. Jaki's reasons are these: the ancient Mesopotamian culture lacked confidence in the ability to investigate, predict, influence or control a world which was a wilful, animistic struggle between order and chaos; hence there was no self-sustaining scientific activity.

In ancient Greece, science came much closer to a viable birth than it did in other ancient cultures: astronomy, algebra and geometry were better developed than in other ancient cultures. Ancient Greek science went beyond the phase of description, observation and classification (this stage being exemplified by Aristotle's biology or Galen's medicine) and "moved up to the stage where the entire body of knowledge was a derivative of some fundamental postulates."[39] Yet Jaki notes a curious progress in Greek science: a very creative (yet short) period (450–350 BC), followed first by an extended period of elaboration (350 BC–150 AD) and then by a long stagnation coming to an end around 600 AD. Such is the story of the stillbirth of science in ancient Greece where efforts to give science a viable birth by formulating the correct laws of motion invariably failed to reach the right target.

Since the proper understanding of motion is inseparable from a correct notion of time, the clue to the stillbirth of science in ancient Greece can logically be sought in the reflections of Greek sages on their basic framework of time-perception, the idea of the Great Year. According to Jaki, who notes that the Greek world view was "steeped in the idea of eternal cycles",[40] this idea posed a circular barrier to the Greek mind which failed to appreciate the linear flow of time implicit in inertial motion. In Aristotle's world view everything general, including ideas, recurred cyclically, and this undermined the concept of time. Aristotle's vision of the cosmos also bespoke necessity: this discouraged *a posteriori* empirical investigation of the cosmos.

The Stoics tried to escape the clutches of the prospect of eternal recurrences, yet their belief in these remained alive even in the Hellenistic centuries: in their world-view, process rather than being dominated. Jaki stresses that the foundation of knowledge is the stability of reality rather than its flux. The Great Year was a circular barrier for the Greek mind and deprived it of insights and aspirations which were necessary for the growth of science. Jaki further argues that infinitesimal calculus could not develop within the ancient Greek ambience, for much the same reason: for this development to take place it was necessary that time be "no longer considered as a mirror image of eternal recurrences, but rather as an uninterrupted one-dimensional flow of events."[41]

For Epicurus, the gods were not subject to cycles, so that the stars did not rigidly rule human events, yet he retained a cyclic view for the world as such. In trying to escape the absolute necessitarianism of Aristotle's cosmology, he made chance a basic factor, which, as a counterpart of atomism, deprived the Epicurean universe of rationality and consistency. As Jaki shows through many quotations from ancient Greek philosophical writings, the cyclic notion of cosmic existence is "the very foundation of the three main cosmologies developed by the Greeks, the Aristotelian, the Stoic and the Epicurean (atomistic)."[42] In this cyclic, and often pantheistic universe, matter and processes were eternal. This encouraged the view of man as a mere "bubble on the inexorable sea of events whose ebb and flow followed one another with fateful regularity."[43] Despondency was one of the natural reactions to this state of affairs. The other was smugness, or the belief that the present epoch was like riding the crest of cultural history. The latter illusion was held by Aristotle. Some of his little remembered but revealing statements to that effect, as quoted by Jaki, counter the Marxist claim that the failure of science in ancient Greece was mainly due to socio-economic factors.[44] For all their groping in the dark concerning the rise of science, the Greeks never quite found the light-switch.

Despite the fact that by the early ninth century the Arabs had acquired all of the available Greek learning, they did not really advance it, apart from some progress made in the fields of optics and geometry. They certainly fell far short of the level where science, through the formulation of the correct laws of motion, became a self-sustaining enterprise in coping with a physical world in which everything is always in motion. The case of the Arabs, according to Jaki, is all the more noteworthy because, unlike the Greeks and other ancient cultures, they were monotheists with a firm belief in creation. Yet it is precisely some aspects of this belief of theirs that hampered them in their scientific endeavours.

According to Jaki, there were two essential reasons for this. First, there was "the Koran's over-emphasis on divine will in relation to divine rationality." For the orthodox school of Moslem thought (the *Mutakallimun*, exemplified by Al-Ashari and Al-Ghazzali), "the notion of a consistent physical law was not acceptable because it seemed to derogate from Allah's sovereign will, which appears rather capricious in not a few pages of the Koran."[45] The laws of nature were downplayed, since God's will was seen as so omnipotent as to amount to arbitrariness or mere capriciousness. Only in fields such as optics or mathematics (where there was need for little empirical investigation of events or processes) did the Arabs make some progress. Their chemistry, a field which deals with processes, was laced with superstition. Yet there is a second reason why science failed to take off in the Arab world. Those who were not such orthodox Moslems (the *Mutazalite* school represented by such figures as Avicenna and Averroes) followed Aristotle to such an extent that they took on board the pantheism and necessitarianism involved in the ancient Greek world-picture. This led to a schizophrenic split between their belief in God and their philosophy. Being so wholeheartedly Aristotelian, these Mutazalites had cast away the belief in the Creator "that could have helped them to steer clear of the pantheistic shallows of the Greek world-view including the notion of the Great Year."[46]

The Arabs' failure will seem all the more tantalizing if one considers that Avicenna (who died in 1037) came very close to the idea of inertial motion. This is especially poignant since, as Jaki notes, "much of the Greek scientific and philosophical corpus reached the Latin West through Muslim mediation."[47] Since the scientific formulation of inertial motion fell to a Christian medieval scholar, Jean Buridan, it then becomes almost imperative to suppose that, as Jaki remarks in another context, there was a factor in the Christian faith in creation that was missing in its Moslem counterpart. This factor was belief in the Incarnation that acted as a powerful safeguard against the lure of pantheism. According to Jaki, "the crucial insight in Buridan's discussion of impetus is a theological point which is completely alien to Avicenna's thinking."[48] Even a devout Moslem like Al-Biruni was ambivalent about a world finite in time with a beginning and an end, and did not affirm creation out of nothing or the rationality of the cosmos. In short, the Moslem notion of the Creator was insufficient to overcome cyclic, pantheistic, animistic, organismic and magical elements.

The viable birth of science

Since science suffered a stillbirth even in early medieval Arab civilization and since it was a self-sustaining enterprise by the late seventeenth century, this implies that its viable birth should be sought in a relatively brief period. The "received" view has now been for the last three hundred years that science arose like a phoenix during the Renaissance whose spokesmen rescued Greek science from a thousand-year-long neglect. Jaki argues that this view has derived "derived partly from the reformer's scorn for medieval Catholicism and partly from the hostility of the leaders of the French Enlightenment to anything Christian."[49] Both groups had a vested interest in painting the Catholic Middle Ages as dark as possible.

As a result neither the secularist nor the Protestant world of scholarship was ready to take notice of the monumental studies of Pierre Duhem, beginning with his two-volume Les origines de la statique (1905–1906) and continued with his three-volume *Etudes sur Léonard de Vinci* (1906–1913). As Jaki shows in his magisterial studies on Duhem, those two works had more than amply revealed the crucial debt owed by Copernicus and Galileo (and indirectly by Newton) to some medieval scholars at the Sorbonne. Studied slighting of those works anticipated a similar attitude towards the publication, in the 1950s, of the last five volumes of Duhem's ten-volume *Le système du monde*, possibly the greatest scholarly feat by a single individual in modern times. This was the series which first showed the medieval period not as a dark age for science but rather its very cradle. In fact, as Jaki shows, the almost forty-year delay of the publication of *Le système du monde* is a proof of that "scholarly" resistance to plain evidence.[50] Jaki's criticism does not spare, in that respect, Catholic scholarship which has still to realize the crucial importance of Duhem's heroic efforts.[51] For Jaki it is emphatically not "a freak happening of history that science was born in a Europe that was living through its centuries of faith."[52]

The key point, according to Jaki, is that Jean Buridan anchored his impetus theory (which implies a beginning for any particular motion) in the beginning of all motion in the first moment of creation. Buridan's creative scientific thinking owed much to his keen awareness of the solemn definition, at Lateran IV, of the age-old doctrine of creation out of nothing and in time. Also most important for Buridan was the condemnation, on 7 March 1277, by Etienne Tempier, Bishop of Paris, of 219 "Aristotelian" propositions, some of which seemed to restrict the freedom of the Creator to create the universe solely in its actual form. The overall aim was to "safeguard the abilities and exclusive rights of the Creator against any compromise dictated by a narrow rationalism."[53] Bishop Tempier outlawed such notions as the perennial recurrence of things every thirty-six thousand years, a view of the world as eternal, the view that the celestial orbs are like organs in a human body, and the idea that stars determine individuals from the moment of their birth. The decree showed that Christians were willing to distinguish, within the received Greek corpus, what was contrary to a Christian belief in Creation from what could be accepted in Greek philosophy and cosmology. Jaki stresses that Bishop Tempier's decree "expressed rather than produced that climate of thought."[54]

These statements of the teaching authority of the Church expressed an atmosphere in which faith in God the Creator had penetrated the medieval culture and given rise to philosophical consequences. The cosmos was seen as contingent in its *existence* and thus dependent on a divine choice which called it into being; the universe is also contingent in its *nature* and so God was free to create this particular form of world among an infinity of other possibilities. Thus the cosmos cannot be a necessary form of existence, and so has to be approached by *a posteriori* investigation. The universe is also rational, and therefore a coherent discourse can be made about it. Indeed the contingency and rationality of the cosmos are like two pillars supporting the Christian vision of the cosmos.

> The contingency of the universe obviates an *a priori* discourse about it, while its rationality makes it accessible to the mind though only in an *a posteriori* manner...; the rise of science needed the broad and persistent sharing by the whole population, that is, an entire culture, of a very specific body of doctrines relating the universe to a universal and absolute intelligibility embodied in the tenet about a personal God, the Creator of all.[55]

Jean Buridan was clearly imbued with the spirit of the tradition set by that decree of the Bishop of Paris. He was professor of philosophy at the Sorbonne around 1330, and, as Jaki notes, the first modern physicist. Buridan rejected the Aristotelian notion that the universe and the motion of the stars were eternal; moreover, he stated that the motions of the heavenly bodies were subject to the same laws as bodies on earth. In his impetus theory, a moving body had impetus imparted to it by a source of motion. In Aristotelian physics, the mover had to remain in continuous contact with the moved object; with Buridan this was no longer the case, for, by virtue of an impetus imparted to it, the object moved off on its own. The individual case was a small replica of the impetus which God imparted to the heavens in the beginning of all motions. Buridan's work prefigured Newton's first law of motion. Buridan's great disciple Nicole Oresme (1323?–1382), later Bishop of Lisieux, continued and made known the work of his teacher.

Within that climate of thought, it was possible for Oresme to treat with impressive calm the possibility of the earth's motion. Oresme's unhesitating rejection of the Aristotelian doctrine of eternal recurrence also reflects, to quote Jaki, "the robust confidence of an overwhelmingly Christian ambience for which the once-and-for-all process of cosmic existence was almost as natural a conviction as the air one breathed."[56] Because the Middle Ages were steeped in the doctrine that the world had an absolute beginning in time, there was an appreciation of the meaning of dynamic motion. The process was not, of course, simple and straightforward, as Jaki is wont to note. In the medieval tracts there was a great deal of mixing of "insights and rumours, of sound principles and fantastic tales, of critical sense and baffling credulity, of reason and magic."[57]

Duhem's chief interest in medieval science had been that of a physicist looking for the conceptual and historical sources of the basic form, the principle of virtual velocities, of the true laws of motion. It remained for Jaki, in whom the physicist and historian of physics is coupled with the theologian, to point insistently at the theological matrix of the original formulation of the impetus theory. Jaki's position on the tradition of the Parisian school is nuanced, noting that Augustinian and Franciscan schools of theology were behind Tempier's condemnation of the 219 theses, and these had a voluntaristic tendency.[58] Jaki's theological interest thus provided a much needed corrective to Duhem's one-sided esteem of Ockham, who went so far along the road suggested by the decree of Bishop Tempier as to put in jeopardy the "inherent and coherent rationality" of God's creation.[59] It was not long before Ockham upset the philosophical balance by making the nominalist distinction between "God's absolute will and ordained will."[60] It left him free to cavort in paradoxical phrases celebrating inconsistency, such as the statement that there could be starlight without any stars. By overemphasizing God's absolute will, Ockham prevented the unicity of God from being accessible to the mind via reason alone. Thereafter, as Jaki notes, "the recognition of the unity of material beings, or a unitary vision of the universe, so indispensable for science, was also beyond the mind's powers."[61]

Jaki also diverges from Duhem concerning his interpretation of St Thomas Aquinas. The latter's benevolent approach to Aristotle did not result in a diluting, however slightly, of that all-important Christian tenet that God was able and free to create any kind of universe, or not to create at all. For Jaki, Duhem overlooked the great importance of Thomas' insistence on the full rationality, that is, consistency, of creation by an infinitely rational God. It was the Thomistic balance that alone made possible the view, so important for the future of science that, to quote Jaki, "the contingency of the universe obviates an a priori discourse about it, while its rationality makes it accessible to the mind though only in an a posteriori manner."[62] In the medieval vision of the cosmos, above all exemplified by St. Thomas, the two massive pillars of importance for

Christianity and for science are the rationality and the contingency of the universe.

If properly heeded, that insistence, as Jaki argues, could have forestalled two mistaken developments: one was the Ockhamist, and subsequently Reformed, emphasis on contingency in the wrong-headed sense that God could not set consistently valid laws in the universe. The other was the Renaissance sympathy accorded to the Greek idea of the Great Year, beneath which lay hidden a cosmic view riveted in the abolition of all distinct contours.[63] The surface problem here was an uncritical neo-Platonism. The most instructive case for Jaki, in this latter respect, is the pantheistic thinking of Giordano Bruno, whose claim to "scientific expertise" is demolished by Jaki in a special monograph.[64] Bruno, who held the universe to be infinite in time and cyclic, first found an echo among the anti-scientific and crypto-pantheistic protagonists of German idealism and *Naturphilosophie,* a fact traced out by Jaki in careful detail.[65]

Jaki also shows that during the Renaissance it was Nicholas of Cusa, Leonardo da Vinci, Copernicus, Tycho Brahe, Benedetti, and Kepler who represented not only the best in science but also attested "the inspiration and safeguard which faith in the Creator provided for scientific endeavour during an age that witnessed a hardly concealed desire on the part of many to bring about a 're-naissance' of classical paganism."[66] Nicholas of Cusa was able to employ such Platonic notions as the world-organism to illustrate harmony in the cosmos, because from the start, he was clear about the Christian sense of creation. However, when faith was lacking there was a real regression from civilized Christian culture to a pagan view of the cosmos.

Jaki regards Galileo as a conscious and Newton as an unconscious heir to that scientific tradition which commenced with Buridan and Oresme.[67] He also shows that Newton's epistemology was a subconscious, or at least an inarticulated middle ground between Francis Bacon's empiricism and Descartes' rationalism.[68] For Galileo, Boyle, Newton and others "the world was rational only because the Creator was supremely rational."[69] Jaki insists that it was only in this conceptual matrix that the viable birth of science became a full reality.

The next and most instructive phase which Jaki elaborates in the interaction between the fortunes of science and the Christian doctrine of creation relates to the thought of Kant. Jaki unfolds in detail the little-remembered fact that Kant endorsed something closely equivalent to the Great Year in his youthful, and scientifically largely worthless, cosmological work.[70] He also shows the equally ignored fact that the later Kant emphatically endorsed pantheism in a context that was antiscientific to a shocking extent. Kant, as Jaki points out, held a different perspective on God and the cosmos, as he tried to make it appear that reason was denied access to God, the soul and the universe; indeed he regarded the universe as a "bastard product of the metaphysical cravings of the intellect"[71] which was thus no longer a stepping stone to the existence of the Creator. Kant's main aim was to secure for man his autonomy vis-à-vis God; here he was partly inspired by his reading of Rousseau.

Owing to his a priori approach, Kant held that "the infinite perfection of God must evidence itself in an infinite creation." The notion of the universe as a perpetuum mobile "foreshadowed Kant's gradual shifting into pantheism." In the *Allgemeine Naturgeschichte* (1755), Kant had stated that the teleological way was a valid proof of God's existence, but later, in 1763, Kant rejected the cosmological and teleological arguments in *Der einzig mögliche Beweisgrund zu einer Demonstration des Daseins Gottes* (The only possible argument for a demonstration of the existence of God).[72] The only proof accepted by Kant at that time was the ontological way which, as Jaki notes, "did not lead to a really existing God."[73] In Kant's idealism the *noumenon* or *Ding an sich* was inaccessible to the intellect and hence the impetus of knowing the real world, which is the motivation for science, was threatened.

After Kant, the idea of the Great Year, which had for two centuries almost disappeared from the printed page, made its return through German idealism.[74] The old pagan notion of eternal recurrence found a further spokesman in Nietzsche, who opposed those scientists involved with the formulation of the entropy principle, as he feared this would have undermined his idea of the eternity of cyclic progression in the universe. Once more Jaki discredits these thinkers by showing in detail the nullity of their claim that they had any competence, let alone great competence in science.[75]

Such is a brief outline of the historical landscape, which Jaki presents with massive documentation as a proof on behalf of a twofold proposition. On the one hand, science suffered stillbirths in all ancient cultures, as they were dominated by a cyclic world-picture and by pantheism, doctrines antithetic to the Christian doctrine of creation. On the other hand, science achieved a viable birth in a cultural matrix which had already been steeped for centuries in that very Christian doctrine. In other words, the philosophical consequences of this belief were able to penetrate the mentality of the scientist, so as to become almost second nature.

In the Middle Ages, ideas about the created universe had developed which were greatly conducive to scientific enterprise. This world vision included the idea that the cosmos is good, and therefore attractive to study. Also the universe was considered to be single entity with inner coherence and order, and not a gigantic animal which would behave in an arbitrary fashion, as was often believed in antiquity. The world was considered to be endowed with its own laws which could be tested and verified; it was not magical or divine. Further, the cosmos was seen to be rational and consistent, so that what was investigated one day would also hold true the next. The world picture also involved the tenet that cosmic order is accessible to the human mind, and can be investigated experimentally, not just by pure thought. In addition to these ideas, medieval Christendom also was imbued with the concept that it was worthwhile to share knowledge for the common good.

During this fertile period of scientific growth, there was a harmonious relationship between science and Christianity, and indeed most of the earliest scientists were devout believers, like Saint Albert the Great, renowned for his investigations in the physical and chemical realms, and Saint Hildegard of Bingen, known for her pioneering work in the biological and ecological areas. Other unknown early scientists worked on such areas as the development of clocks. Before the rise of science, human activity followed biological time and solar time, regulated by the natural succession of night and day. In contrast scientific time involves high numerical accuracy. Monasteries needed to have a way of measuring time with reasonable accuracy so as to regularize the hours of prayer, work and study and while they followed biological time at first, gradually they developed sand and water clocks. By the twelfth century, highly sophisticated mechanical clocks had been built, and these produced a profound effect on civil society as well. At the heart of scientific activity lies the measurement of time.

Therefore, harmony between faith and science preceded disharmony. For instance, the Galileo affair, which took place after science had been born in a Christian setting, is sometimes used to obscure the many examples of harmonious and fruitful collaboration between the Church and science. In fact, Galileo himself was an example of a devout Christian and a great scientist. Moreover, even in the Galileo case "the agreements between religion and science are more numerous and above all more important than the incomprehension which led to the bitter and painful conflict that continued in the course of the following centuries."[76] It is true that in the Galileo affair, as in other misunderstandings, a healing of memories is needed. What can be learned from the Galileo situation is the necessity to delineate with increasing clarity the respective fields of competence, methods and value of the conclusions of science and theology, according to their respective nature. In particular, the Holy Scriptures do not teach us scientific details about the physical world but rather the fact that it was created.[77]

However, it is also true that the Galileo affair has been so highlighted as to obscure the many examples of harmonious and fruitful collaboration between the Church and science. Indeed there have been many cases where devout Christians have made a prodigious contribution to science, including Nicolaus Copernicus, the astronomer (+1543), Gregor Mendel (+1884), the author of Mendel's law of heredity, and Bishop Niels Stensen (+1686), the great geologist and anatomist who discovered the duct (*Ductus Stenonianus*) which carries saliva from the parotid gland to the mouth.

Church authorities have often expressed the essential and basic harmony between science and religion. Over one hundred years ago, the First Vatican Council put it this way: "Truth cannot contradict truth".[78] In 1936, Pope Pius XI enunciated what must be the first principle of relations between science and religion when he wrote "science as a true understanding of reality can never contradict the truths of the Christian faith".[79] Fifty years later, at the celebration of the fiftieth anniversary of the Pontifical Academy of Sciences, Pope John Paul II stated that "there is no contradiction between science and religion".[80]

While science and religion enjoy their own fields of competence, there can be fruitful collaboration between them. Scientific discovery uncovers more and more of the material cosmos, both in the realm of the very small atomic world and the very large astrophysical universe. More and more can be seen and is understood in the biological sphere. The complexity, beauty and intricacy of the universe thus unveiled are a stimulus towards adoration of the Creator who made this cosmos, and who guides it in His Providence. Scientific progress has helped to exorcise superstition, another service for which religion is grateful. At the same time, religion can assist science not to close its eyes to a larger canvas. At this present time, it can guide scientists and technologists to use their discoveries for the real good of mankind. Such guidance is needed so that the right decisions are made regarding the applications of advances in genetics, and other matters which touch the beginning and end of human life, so that the immense value of human life is always respected and never manipulated or damaged. Religion can assist in the sharing of scientific progress with all sectors of the community, especially with the less fortunate ones. Science and technology have brought untold benefits to mankind, for which we should be thankful and which we must use for the best. In Christ's words: "When someone is given a great deal, a great deal will be demanded of that person; when someone is entrusted with a great deal, of that person even more will be expected" (Luke 12:48). Much has been entrusted to humanity through scientific growth, and thus more will be expected in loving response to the Creator.

Jaki links the stillbirths in science with the doctrine concerning original sin.[81] The weakening of the intellect was the cause of false visions of the cosmos, involving eternal cycles and a necessary universe. The psychological climate of such ancient cultures was often either hopelessness or complacency,[82] and either case resulted in a failure to arrive at a belief in the existence of God the Creator, and an inability to produce a self-sustaining scientific enterprise.

The redemptive Incarnation guarantees the Christian vision of Creation and has effected a process of conversion not only in individuals, but in culture as a whole. This conversion to Christianity has had material as well as spiritual benefits for, "even in the secular history of mankind the Gospel has acted as a leaven in the interests of liberty and progress".[83] Thus Christian faith, although primarily connected with eternal life, has a real effect on the here and now. This idea has its basis in the scriptures where Christ says to his followers that setting their hearts first on God's Kingdom will have beneficial effects not only in heaven, but also here upon earth: "Set your hearts on his Kingdom first, and on his righteousness and all these other things will be yours as well" (Mt 6:33). The followers of Christ are promised something of a recompense in this life (despite persecutions) as well as the reward in the life to come: "And everyone who has left houses, brothers, sisters, father, mother, children or land for the sake of my name will be repaid a hundred times over and also inherit eternal life" (Mt 19:29).[84] One specific "reward" which Christian faith in God the Creator has brought about is a reinforcement of the realist vision of the universe which was germane to the unique rise of science. The healing power of Christ has changed human society for the better, and scientific progress is but one example of the advance in human culture, as a fruit of divine Providence.

Nevertheless, there are those who would claim that the scientific progress stimulated by Christianity has in fact brought in its wake many problems and much evil.[85] If Christianity is responsible for the unique birth of science, is it not also to be blamed for the technological ills which beset the world of today? A distinction needs to be made here between scientific discovery and its technological application. Now the reason why there is a moral crisis concerning technological application of various products of science (for example, discoveries in nuclear physics and in bio-engineering) is that while the philosophical framework conducive to scientific discovery has been handed on as an implicit (and often subconscious) body of principles, nevertheless because Western society is no longer (in many parts) explicitly Christian, it lacks the courage and the apparatus to tackle such moral questions. The application of science therefore rests upon purely political or economic criteria which can only be described as utilitarian, without proper regard for the good of the human person and his environment.

A few vaguely Christian ideals have therefore been inherited by a secularized and secularizing society where there is a lack of radical Christian culture and vision to back up the vague ideals. Agnostics feel frustrated because they are unable to link up the implicit cultural principles with a synthetic Christian vision, and some Christians feel inadequate because they do not see the way forward very clearly. Progress lies in seeing that since science grew up in a Christian milieu, its applications were, at first, put to use according to a Christian ethic arising from Christian faith in God the Creator who had left these moral laws imprinted upon creation. While the human person has the capacity to read the natural law written upon his or her heart, even aside from Revelation, nevertheless, because of the Fall, the human will is adversely affected in making moral decisions. Furthermore, Revelation does not merely reinforce the natural law, but shows a more perfect way. Christ reveals to mankind perfect Man as well as true God; through the Incarnation and Redemption, grace is given to guide man towards this ideal revealed by and in Christ.[86] Hence the need for a specifically Christian morality to provide criteria which guide mankind away from purely greedy or destructive applications of science. Since they do not contain their own explanation within their own fields, science, language and history all need to be referred to metaphysics, before any dialogue between faith and science can be made or before any consistent ethical discourse can be pursued.

The Judaeo-Christian vision of creation is diametrically opposed to that series of eternal returns which is to be found in most ancient and modern pagan systems. The fact that the eternal Word became incarnate of the Virgin Mary at a specific moment within history guarantees the uniqueness of Christ's redemptive act:

> Another contribution of orthodox, dogmatic Christianity is ... a strong appreciation of time as actually experienced. That the Incarnation took place at a fixed point of time, marked by the invariable reference to Pontius Pilate in all credal formulas, could but enhance the perception of the uniqueness of each moment and therefore of history. Since such uniqueness is inconceivable within the recurrence of cyclic ages, the Incarnation added further emphasis to a linear perception

> of time, which had been an integral part of Old Testament salvation history.[87]

The Christian idea of a linear progressive cosmos is further guaranteed by the truth that at another specific point in time, Christ will come again in glory to bring all history to its eschatological completion.

Christ took human nature to Himself, which also demonstrates His absolute supremacy over the material realm. While the Word exists from all eternity, His human nature began in time with the Incarnation, meaning that matter is not eternal. Hence the dogma of the Incarnation closes the door to pantheism which is almost always present in eternal cyclic cosmic visions. The doctrine of Christ the only-begotten Son of the Father excludes the possibility that any other entity is also begotten by the Father. Hence the cosmos does not have the status of a begotten entity, but is in a very real sense put in its place: 'In the Christian perspective the exaltedness of the universe remained intact as it is lowered through that infinite distance which is between Creator and Creature'.[88] The expression that Christ and the Holy Spirit are one in substance with the Father also excludes the idea that the cosmos could enjoy this privilege. St Paul transfers to Christ and His Church the concepts of *body* and *fulness* (Col 1:15–20) as a bolster against pantheism.[89] The doctrine that the work of creation is carried out *through* Christ is a shield against the Gnostic error that the cosmos emanated from God.

The doctrine of Christ, true God and true Man, safeguards those truths concerning the nature of the human person. St Ambrose, St Jerome, and St Gregory Nazianzen affirmed against Apollinaris of Laodicea that Christ's human nature included a human soul using the well-known axiom "what is not assumed is not saved".[90] Christ must have had a human soul as this guaranteed the continuity of His human nature between Good Friday and Easter Sunday and in particular for the descent into hell, which the Creed affirms. The completeness of Christ's human nature is thus also an affirmation that the nature of all human beings consists of body and soul. The doctrine that Christ assumed a human nature like ours in all things but sin, strongly reinforces the goodness and dignity of the human being: Human nature, by the very fact that it was assumed, not absorbed, in Him, has been raised in us also to a dignity beyond compare. For, by His Incarnation, He, the Son of God, has in a certain way united Himself with each man. Christ thus reveals the fullness of truth concern the human person: He "reveals man to himself".[91]

The Incarnation of the Word is also a guarantee of purpose and Providence within the cosmos. The Christian approach excludes an idea of Providence which is merely fate as in pagan systems, or the impersonal cosmic force featured in science fiction. Instead, purpose is rooted in the economy of salvation of the Father who has revealed Himself in the Son and guides us in the power of His Holy Spirit. Cosmic meaning is rooted in the Providence of God's plan as it has specifically been revealed to us in Christ: "He has let us know the mystery of His purpose, the hidden plan He so kindly made in Christ from the beginning to act upon when the times had run their course to the end" (Ep 1:9–10). Thus there is no longer a possibility of a fatalistic, chaotic or chance vision of cosmic events.

> Thanks to the Word, the world of creatures appears as a "cosmos", an ordered universe. And it is the same Word who, by taking flesh, renews the cosmic order of creation.[92]

Notes

1 See W. L. Craig & J. P. Moreland, *Philosophical Foundations for a Christian Worldview* (Downers Grove, IL: InterVarsity Press, 2003), p. 348.

2 See, for example, E. Grant, *The foundations of modern science in the Middle Ages: Their religious, institutional, and intellectual contexts*. Cambridge history of science (Cambridge: Cambridge University Press, 1996); A. C. Crombie, *Robert Grosseteste and the origins of experimental science, 1100-1700* (Oxford: Clarendon Press, 1953); Idem, *Science, optics, and music in medieval and early modern thought* (London, Ronceverte, WV, U.S.A.: Hambledon Press, 1990); Idem, *Styles of scientific thinking in the European tradition: The history of argument and explanation especially in the mathematical and biomedical sciences and arts* (London: Duckworth, 1994); Idem; *The history of science from Augustine to Galileo* (New York: Dover Publications, 1995); Idem, *Science, art, and nature in medieval and modern thought* (London, Rio Grande, Ohio: Hambledon Press, 1996).

3 Pope Pius XII, *Discourse to the Pontifical Academy of Sciences*, 21 February 1943, in *DP*, pp. 50–59; Idem, *Discourse to the Pontifical Academy of Sciences*, 22 November 1951, in *ibid.*, pp. 73–84.

4 Cf. "Brain, Mind and Computers" in *Journal of the American Scientific Affiliation* 24/1 (1972), p. 12.

5 Cf. *The Teacher: Dr. Victor Hess. The Student: Rev. Stanley Jaki* 1985(13), pp. 10–11.

6 *A Study of the Distribution of Radon, Thoron, and Their Decay Products above and below the Ground* 1958(1), pp. 373–390.

7 For the details see P. Haffner, *Creation and scientific creativity: A study in the thought of Stanley L. Jaki* (2nd ed.) (Leominster: Gracewing, 2009), pp. 249–253.

8 University of Chicago Press, unpublished letter to S. L. Jaki (20 October 1965).

9 W. Heitler, Review of *The Relevance of Physics* 1966(1) in *American Scientist* 55 (1967), p. 352.

10 *Brain, Mind and Computers* (Washington, DC: Regnery Gateway, 1989).

11 AA.VV., *Templeton* (Nassau, Bahamas: Lismore Press, 1987), p. 4.

12 See S. L. Jaki, "The Physics of Impetus and the Impetus of the Kuran" in *Modern Age* 29 (1985), pp. 153–160.

[13] See S. L. Jaki, "Ecology or Ecologism" in G. B. Marini-Belolo (ed.), Man and His Environment. Tropical Forests and the Conservation of Species (Vatican City State: Pontifical Academy of Sciences, 1994), pp. 271–293.

[14] S. L. Jaki, *Acceptance speech on becoming a member of the Pontifical Academy of Sciences*, 29 October 1990, in N. Dallaporta (ed.), *Science in the Context of Human Culture*, Part 1 (Vatican City: Pontifical Academy of Sciences, 1994), p. 47.

[15] H. Duhem, *Un savant français Pierre Duhem* (Paris: Plon, 1936).

[16] Among these works are: *Uneasy Genius: The Life and Work of Pierre Duhem* (Dordrecht/Boston/Lancaster: Martinus Nijhoff, 1984); *Premices Philosophiques.* Edition with introduction in English of Pierre Duhem's early essays on the history and philosophy of physics (Leiden: E. J. Brill, 1987); *The Physicist As Artist: The Landscapes of Pierre Duhem* (Edinburgh: Scottish Academic Press, 1988).

[17] S. L. Jaki, *Science and Creation: From Eternal Cycles to an Oscillating Universe* (New York: Science History Publications; Edinburgh: Scottish Academic Press, 1986).

[18] Cf. Jaki, *Uneasy Genius*, p. 326.

[19] Cf. *ibid.*, p. 337.

[20] At Jaki's urging, Philip Trower translated Gilson's small epistemological treatise *Le réalisme méthodique* (1935) into English (Front Royal, VA: Christendom Press, 1990) with an Introduction by Jaki.

[21] See S. L. Jaki, *Chesterton: A Seer of Science* (Urbana/Chicago: University of Illinois Press, 1986).

[22] See S. L. Jaki,"Maritain and Science" in *The New Scholasticism* 58 (1984), pp. 267–292.

[23] See S. L. Jaki, *Newman's Challenge* (Grand Rapids, MI: Wm. B. Eerdmans, 2000).

[24] See S. L. Jaki, *Newman to Converts. An Existential Ecclesiology* (Pinckney, MI: Real View Books, 2001); Idem, *Apologetics as Meant by Newman* (Port Huron, MI: Real View Books, 2005).

[25] See S. L. Jaki, *The One True Fold: Newman and His Converts* (Royal Oak, MI: Real View Books, 1998).

[26] P. E. Hodgson, "The Significance of the Work of Stanley L. Jaki" in *The Downside Review* 105(1987), p. 273.

[27] See S. L. Jaki, *And on This Rock: The Witness of One Land and Two Covenants* (Front Royal, VA: Christendom Press, 1997), *The Keys of the Kingdom: A Tool's Witness to Truth* (Pinckney, MI: Real View

Books, 2001). See also *Why Believe in the Church?* (Pinckney, MI: Real View Books, 2002); "Newman's Logic and the Logic of the Papacy" in *Faith and Reason* 13/3 (1987), pp. 241-265; Edition with Introduction and notes of J. H. Newman, *Conscience and Papacy* (Pinckney, MI: Real View Books, 2002).

28 S. L. Jaki, *The Road of Science and the Ways to God* (Chicago/Edinburgh: University of Chicago Press/Scottish Academic Press, 1978), p. 319.

29 Cf. *ibid.*, p. 243. Although Jaki adopts the term *paradigm*, also used by T. S. Kuhn, his position differs from Kuhn's; for this difference, see *ibid.*, p. 241, where Jaki states that Kuhn's is a heavily tilting balance when he acknowledges that world views and metaphysical beliefs are essential ingredients in any paradigm constitutive of science and pays no further attention to them.

30 S. L. Jaki, "The Last Century of Science" in *Proceedings of the Second International Humanistic Symposium* (Athens: Hellenic Society for Humanistic Studies, 1973), p. 259. See chapters 1–6 and 9 of Jaki, *Science and Creation.*

31 Jaki, *Science and Creation*, p. 33.

32 S. L. Jaki, "The History of Science and the Idea of an Oscillating Universe"in *The Center Journal* 4 (1984), p. 140. The Great Year is the length of time in years for an entire cosmic cycle to elapse (analogous with the time period of an oscillation in physics).

33 S. L. Jaki, *The Savior of Science* (Washington, DC: Regnery Gateway, 1988), p. 30.

34 Jaki, "The History of Science and the Idea of an Oscillating Universe", p. 141.

35 Jaki, *Science and Creation*, p. 14.

36 *Ibid.*, p. 62.

37 *Ibid.*, p. 80.

38 Jaki, *Science and Creation*, pp. 92–92. See also S. L. Jaki, *Cosmos and Creator* (Edinburgh: Scottish Academic Press, 1980), pp. 62–65.

39 S. L. Jaki, "The Greeks of Old and the Novelty of Science" in *Arete Mneme: Konst Vourveris. Vourveris Festschrift* (Athens: Hellenic Humanistic Society, 1983), p. 267.

40 Jaki, "The History of Science and the Idea of an Oscillating Universe", p. 143.

41 Jaki, *Science and Creation*, p. 118.

42 Jaki, "The History of Science and the Idea of an Oscillating

Universe", p. 144.

43 Jaki, *Science and Creation*, p. 130.

44 Cf. Jaki, "The Greeks of Old and the Novelty of Science", p. 267.

45 S. L. Jaki, "Science and Christian Theism: A Mutual Witness" in *Scottish Journal of Theology* 32 (1979), p. 567.

46 Jaki, "The History of Science and the Idea of an Oscillating Universe", p. 145.

47 S. L. Jaki, "The Physics of Impetus and the Impetus of the Koran" in *Modern Age* 29 (1985), p. 155. However, the majority of the translators of Greek texts into Arabic in the early Abbasid translation movement were Christians. A significant translator was Patriarch Timothy I of the Assyrian Church of the East. He lived in the generation after John of Damascus, and he transferred his see from ancient Ctesiphon in Persia to the new centre, Baghdad. Patriarch Timothy, who ruled his church for 43 years, translated Aristotle's Topics for the caliph al-Mahdi, in whose court he conversed with other Aristotelian philosophers on knowledge and the doctrine of God. See S. H. Griffith, *The Church in the Shadow of the Mosque: Christians and Muslims in the World of Islam* (Princeton: Princeton University Press, 2007), pp. 110–115.

48 Jaki, "The Physics of Impetus and the Impetus of the Koran", p. 157.

49 S. L. Jaki, "On Whose Side Is History?" in *National Review* (23 August 1985), pp. 43–44.

50 See S. L. Jaki, *Reluctant Heroine. The Life and Work of Hélène Duhem* (Edinburgh: Scottish Academic Press, 1992); Idem, "Science and Censorship: Hélène Duhem and the Publication of the Système du Monde" in *Intercollegiate Review* 21 (Winter 1985–1986), pp. 41–49.

51 S. L. Jaki, *Pierre Duhem: Homme de science et de foi* (Paris: Beauchesne, 1991), pp. 129–146.

52 S. L. Jaki, "The Role of Faith in Physics" in *Zygon* 2 (1967), p. 195.

53 Jaki, *Science and Creation*, pp. 229–230.

54 Jaki, *Science and Creation*, p. 230; cf. Jaki, *The Savior of Science*, p. 51.

55 Jaki, *The Road of Science and the Ways to God*, pp. 38, 33.

56 Jaki, *Science and Creation*, p. 237.

57 Jaki, *Science and Creation*, p. 223.

58 Jaki finds that Duhem over-emphasized the rôle of these Augustinian and Franciscan schools of theology. See Jaki, *Uneasy Genius*, p. 435.

[59] Jaki, *Cosmos and Creator*, p. 80.

[60] *Ibid.*.

[61] Jaki, *The Road of Science and the Ways to God*, p. 42.

[62] *Ibid.*, p. 38.

[63] Cf. *Science and Creation*, pp. 248–250. In *The Road of Science and the Ways to God*, p. 48, Jaki states how the Renaissance was not, in many ways, conducive to the growth of science: “Astrology, magic, cabbala, and skepticism, of which Renaissance literature had an unusually large share, were as many illusory stars to lure the fragile ship of science into deadly shallows and to prevent it from reaching waters sufficiently deep for clear sailing and real advance.”

[64] See S. L. Jaki, Translation from the Italian, with an Introduction and notes, of Giordano Bruno, *The Ash Wednesday Supper* (The Hague/Paris: Mouton, 1975), pp. 22–23; Jaki was the first to translate this work of Giordano Bruno into English. See also Idem, *Giordano Bruno. A Martyr of Science?* (Pinckney, MI: Real View Books, 2000).

[65] S. L. Jaki, *The Relevance of Physics* (Chicago: University of Chicago Press, 1966), pp. 45–50.

[66] Jaki, *Science and Creation*, p. 268.

[67] See Jaki, *Uneasy Genius*, pp. 394–395, 413–414, 426–428. Cf. also Idem, “God and Man’s Science: A View of Creation” in L. Morris (ed.), *The Christian Vision: Man in Society*. (Hillsdale, Mich.: Hillsdale College Press, 1984), p. 42; *The Savior of Science*, pp. 47–50, where Jaki traces the debt of Newton and Galileo to Buridan and Oresme.

[68] See Jaki, *The Road of Science and the Ways to God*, chapter 6, “Instinctive Middle”, especially p. 87, where Jaki states: “The middle road to which Newton was driven back again and again by his scientific creativity was of a piece with his explicit conviction about the validity of going mentally from the realm of phenomena to the existence of God.”

[69] S. L. Jaki, “God and Creation: A Biblical-Scientific Reflection” in *Theology Today* 30 (1973), p. 117.

[70] S. L. Jaki, Translation, with Introduction and notes, of Immanuel Kant, *Universal Natural History and Theory of the Heavens*. (Edinburgh: Scottish Academic Press, 1981), pp. 33–34.

[71] S. L. Jaki, “From Scientific Cosmology to a Created Universe” in *Irish Astronomical Journal* 15 (1982), p. 255.

[72] See Jaki, Introduction to translation of Kant, *Universal Natural History and Theory of the Heavens*, pp. 33–36.

[73] Jaki, *The Road of Science and the Ways to God*, p. 116.

[74] Jaki, "The History of Science and the Idea of an Oscillating Universe", p. 148.

[75] Jaki, *Science and Creation*, pp. 319–330.

[76] Pope John Paul II, *Discourse to the Plenary Session of the Pontifical Academy of Sciences to commemorate the centenary of the birth of Albert Einstein*, 10 November 1979. Referring in a note to the life and works of Galileo, the Pastoral Constitution of Vatican II *Gaudium et spes* 36.1 stated: "We cannot but deplore certain attitudes (not unknown among Christians) deriving from a short-sighted view of the rightful autonomy of science; they have occasioned conflict and controversy and have misled many into opposing faith and science."

[77] See Pope John Paul II, *Discourse to the Plenary Session of the Pontifical Academy of Sciences*, 31 October 1992, paragraphs 6 and 12. In particular, the Pope cited the adage of Cardinal Baronius: "Spiritui Sancto mentem fuisse nos docere quomodo ad caelum eatur, non quomodo caelum gradiatur." (The Holy Spirit wishes to teach us how to go to heaven, but not how the heavens move).

[78] First Vatican Council, Dogmatic Constitution *Dei Filius* on the Catholic Faith, chapter IV in *DS* 3017.

[79] Pius XI, Motu Proprio *In multis solaciis* in *AAS* 28(1936), p. 421.

[80] Pope John Paul II, *Discourse on the occasion of the Fiftieth Anniversary of the Pontifical Academy of Sciences*, 28 October 1986, §3.

[81] See Jaki, *The Savior of Science*, pp. 21–22.

[82] See *ibid.*, p. 42.

[83] Vatican II, *Ad Gentes Divinitus*, 8.

[84] Cf. also Mk 10:29–30; Lk 18:29–30; 1 Tm 4:8. See also Vatican II, *Gaudium et Spes*, 38.2: "Constituted Lord by His resurrection and given all authority in heaven and on earth, Christ is now at work in the hearts of all men by the power of his Spirit; not only does He arouse in them a desire for the world to come but He quickens, purifies and strengthens the generous aspirations of mankind to make life more humane and conquer the earth for this purpose."

[85] See, for example, the classic article of Lynn White which was the basis for a critique of Christianity by ecologists, who claimed that the Judaeo-Christian idea of man's sovereignty over nature brought about an aggressive abuse of the environment. L. White,

"The Historical Roots of Our Ecological Crisis" in *Science* 155 (1967), pp. 1203–1207.

86 See Vatican II, *Gaudium et Spes*, 22; 1 Tm 2:5.

87 P. Haffner, *Creation and Scientific Creativity: A Study in the Thought of S. L. Jaki* (Leominster: Gracewing, 2009), p. 189.

88 Jaki, *The Savior of Science*, p. 73.

89 See *ibid.*, p. 74.

90 See St Gregory Nazianzen, *Letter 101 to Cledonius* in *PG* 37, 181–184.

91 Vatican II, *Gaudium et Spes*, 22.

92 Pope John Paul II, Apostolic Letter *Tertio Millenio Adveniente*, 3.2.

2

POPE SYLVESTER THE MATHEMATICIAN

In otio, in negotio, et docemus quod scimus, et addiscimus quod nescimus.

Gerbert of Aurillac, *Epistola 44*

GERBERT OF AURILLAC was born a peasant, and died as Pope Sylvester II, the first French Pope. He was born in Belliac in old Auvergne, near the present-day commune of Saint-Simon, Cantal, France about the year 946 and from an early age was endowed with a love of learning and intellectual perseverance.[1] The fact that nothing is known of his parents would certainly suggest that they were poor people and did not enjoy any special status. Gerbert was educated at the monastery of Saint-Gerald at Aurillac, a Benedictine monastery which had been founded around sixty years before Gerbert entered it in 963. There he studied under the monk Raymond de Lavaur, who Gerbert later praised for the high quality of his teaching in a letter to the monastery:

> It is from you all in general that I remember having acquired the benefits of my education, but more particularly from father Raymond. If I have acquired any knowledge it is, after God, to him more than to any other mortal that I owe it.[2]

Christian Cluniac enthusiasm pervaded the monastery of Saint Gerauld at Aurillac in which Gerbert was reared. The famous Odo, abbot of Cluny, was previously abbot of Saint

Gerauld, and during Gerbert's formative years it was an important centre for the Cluniac revival of spiritual earnestness in monastic life. Thus Gerbert's early education was received in one of the best monasteries of the tenth century, under the guidance of two remarkably spiritual men, Abbot Gerauld and the monk Raymond, Gerbert's teacher, who later succeeded Gerauld as abbot.[3] At the monastery, Gerbert learnt literature, theology, history, and philosophy, but would not have studied any mathematics and only a very little logic. He was singled out among the other students for scholastic training as a teenager.

The year 967 was one of great importance for Gerbert, since in that year he gained the opportunity to learn mathematical skills which were almost totally lacking throughout Europe. In that year Count Borrell II of Barcelona visited Aquitaine and, as he was returning to Barcelona, he came to the Benedictine monastery of Saint Gerauld at Aurillac. The abbot of the monastery, Gerauld, asked Count Borrell whether there were scholars of the arts in Spain and, when he replied that there were many men of learning, Gerauld persuaded Count Borrell to take one of his students back to Barcelona with him so that he might profit from the learning there. The brothers at the monastery decided that Gerbert was the one who might benefit most, so he accompanied Count Borrell to Barcelona.

Studying and teaching

Gerbert set out in 968, and lived in Barcelona at the cathedral school of Vich, close to Barcelona, for three years. Bishop Atto was in charge of the cathedral school of Vich and he was officially Gerbert's teacher during these years. The path of Gerbert's scholastic learning led him from Aurillac to the Spanish Marches (*la Marca Hispánica*), which existed on the border of Islamic Spain and

Latin France.[4] While studying here under the direction of Atto, Gerbert was fortunate to see the early influences of Islamic science in his learning of the *quadrivium*, or "the four ways": music, arithmetic, geometry, and astronomy.

Gerbert had an interest in studying and teaching the *trivium* and *quadrivium*. These are the seven subjects of the liberal arts. The trivium is more basic and consists of grammar, rhetoric, and dialectic. After learning the trivium, a student is taught the quadrivium which includes arithmetic, music, geometry, and astronomy. When Gerbert taught the trivium he began with Latin grammar by having his students study Cicero, the poets Virgil and Terence, the satirist Juvenal, and other classic Literature. He then led his students to rhetoric by having them practice the art of oratory. To teach dialectics, Gerbert read aloud from a series of books, mostly by Boethius, and gave his students his explanations.[5] He imparted the basic principles of Aristotelian logic. The fact that Gerbert incorporated Aristotle's other texts on logic into his teaching syllabus gave logic a new impetus, witnessing to the new philosophical interest in this topic.[6] Many teachers of Gerbert's time stopped with the trivium. There were very few people capable of teaching the complexity of the quadrivium. Gerbert was qualified to teach these subjects because he had obtained rare knowledge from the Arabs, especially in mathematics and astronomy.[7]

Teaching the trivium and the quadrivium stimulated Gerbert's interest in furthering his studies of Islamic mathematics and astronomy so much that he travelled into Muslim Spain to study in Córdoba, Toledo, and Sevilla. In these cities Gerbert was exposed to the teachings of Arab scholars and their system of mathematics, astronomy, and law. Those cities, particularly Toledo, served as centres for Western Islamic astronomy and most importantly the production of astrolabes.

Count Borrell had signed a treaty with the Muslim caliph of Cordoba in 940. For more than 35 years, the Muslim and Christian kingdoms of Spain were at peace. Trade and scientific exchanges flourished. The Royal Library in Cordoba, just west of the Great Mosque, contained 40,000 books. Many of the caliph's books came from Baghdad, known for its House of Wisdom, where for 200 years works of mathematics, astronomy, physics and medicine had been translated from Greek, Persian and Hindu and further developed by Islamic scholars. During Gerbert's lifetime, the first of these science books were translated from Arabic into Latin through the combined efforts of Muslim, Jewish and Christian scholars. Many of the translators were churchmen, and some became Gerbert's lifelong friends.[8] The question remains open as to how far Gerbert was influenced by Moslem Spain, then at the peak of its brilliance under al-Hakam II ibn Abd al- Rahman (961–976). Although Gerbert is silent upon the subject of his Spanish studies, there is the testimony of his friends in the Spanish March with whom he occasionally corresponded.

One such friend was Guarin, who tried to persuade Gerbert to come back to Spain after he was driven out of Bobbio. Guarin made at least one journey up to Saint Gerauld's at Aurillac, where he left a book on the multiplication and division of numbers edited by Joseph the Spaniard. Gerbert very much wanted this book and wrote Abbot Gerauld for a copy.[9] Impatient at the delay he wrote soon afterwards to another of his Spanish friends, Bonifilius, apparently a former fellow student under Atto, requesting from him a copy of the same book.[10] This was in 984, when Bonifilius had become the bishop of Girone. A third Spanish acquaintance of Gerbert was a certain

Lupitus of Barcelona, to whom he wrote requesting "the book on astronomy which was translated by you".[11] It is logical to assume that this book was a translation from the Arabic, and as such partly indicates the nature of Arab influence upon Gerbert.

Modern French scholars have gone to great lengths to clarify the thesis that Gerbert learned his mathematics from the writings of Boethius and not from the Moslems. It is of course true that the works of Boethius were included in the curriculum of his school at Rheims and that Gerbert held the great Roman in the highest regard. However, it was in the Spanish March, according to Richer, whose testimony cannot be discounted, that Gerbert studied mathematics, and his contacts there provided him with at least two volumes that were probably more closely related to Arabic learning than they were to Boethius.[12]

In 969, Count Borrell and the bishop of Vic made a pilgrimage to Rome, taking young Gerbert with them. He met and impressed Pope John XIII (965–971) and the emperor Otto I (962–973), who was visiting there also. Gerbert's expertise in music and astronomy particularly attracted the attention of Pope John XIII.[13] The pope persuaded Otto to take Gerbert on as tutor for his young son, who was to become Otto II (973–983). After some years employed at this task, Otto gave Gerbert leave to go to study advanced logic at the outstanding cathedral school of Rheims. Gerbert studied logic at Rheims with Gerannus and taught him the arts of the *quadrivium* in return.[14]

The depth of Gerbert's learning soon attracted the attention of Archbishop Adalbero (967–987), who had recently undertaken a series of reform measures at Rheims. Eager to raise the intellectual stature of his diocese, Adalbero instructed Gerbert to bring students to Rheims to be instructed in the liberal arts.[15] Gerbert served as head of the cathedral school of Rheims from 972 to 980 and again from 984 to 989 or 991. At Rheims, Gerbert made major reforms to the curriculum, re-introducing the hitherto neglected art of music, and expanding the scope of instruction in arithmetic, geometry, and astronomy.[16]

He is also the first known teacher in the Latin West to employ the complete corpus of Boethian logical works to teach dialectic. In rhetoric, rather than limiting his instruction to standard late antique or early medieval compilations of rhetorical lore, he sought out and acquired copies of the most important texts of classical antiquity, including Quintilian's *Institutio oratoria*, Cicero's *De oratore*, and the commentary on Cicero's *De inventione* by the fourth-century Neoplatonist (and later Christian) scholar Marius Victorinus. The results of his efforts to promote the study of Ciceronian rhetoric at Rheims are clear. Before Gerbert there is no evidence that the *De inventione* was studied or even known at Rheims; there is no trace of a manuscript, and neither Archbishop Hincmar (845–882) nor the cathedral canon and historian Flodoard (894–966), the two most prolific writers associated with Rheims before Gerbert, show any acquaintance at all with the text. Two decades after Gerbert's arrival at Rheims, however, the monk Richer, of the monastery of St Rémi at Rheims, could write a history of the West-Frankish kings in which he quotes the *De inventione* and demonstrates a clear understanding of the rhetorical terminology and doctrines of this text. He wrote treatises on the abacus and the sphere, and possibly a text on the astrolabe.

Gerbert's students spread his knowledge far and wide, leaving Gerbert's impact on the world. The school of Rheims where Gerbert taught developed into a precursor of the modern university and students from France, Germany, and even Italy came to his school.[17] Gerbert taught many sons of noblemen so that they would be prepared for court life. In the 24 years he was teaching at Rheims, Gerbert taught "thirteen future bishops or archbishops, six abbots of important monasteries, Emperor Otto III's chancellor, the secretary to Emperor Henry II, the future Pope Gregory VI, and King Hugh Capet's son Robert the Pious who would rule France from 996 to 1031".[18] All of these students came from different places in the world, taking back with them what Gerbert had taught. The cathedral school in Chartres was founded by one of Gerbert's students, Fulbert, who became the bishop of Chartres in 1007. Fulbert's school was so successful because it was known in Europe as a centre of liberal arts, which include the *trivium* and *quadrivium* upon which Gerbert was such an expert.

Mathematics

One of Gerbert's colossal contributions to Europe and to the universities of today was his knowledge of and advancements in mathematics, which is part of the *quadrivium.* Gerbert showed a great understanding of the abacus. This device, discovered by the Chinese, was used to calculate arithmetic long before Gerbert's time.

Gerbert learned of Hindu-Arabic digits and applied this knowledge to the abacus, but without the numeral zero.[19] According to William of Malmesbury (c. 1080–c. 1143), Gerbert got the idea of the computing device of the abacus from a Spanish Arab. The abacus that Gerbert reintroduced into Europe had its length divided into 27 parts with 9 number symbols (excluding zero, which was represented by an empty column) and 1,000 characters in all, crafted out of animal horn by a shieldmaker of Rheims. His motive was to construct a practical teaching device. As Richer explained:

> In geometry he expended no less labor in his teaching. As a beginning he had a shieldmaker construct an abacus, or a table for measuring. Its length was divided into twenty-seven parts, on which he arranged nine signs expressing all the numbers. He made 1000 characters of horn, which, placed in the twenty-seven compartments of the abacus, gave the multiplication or the division of each number, dividing and multiplying their infinite numbers with such quickness that, as for their multiplication, one could get the answer quicker than he could express it in words.[20]

Thus Gerbert could perform speedy calculations with his abacus that were extremely difficult for people in his day to think through in using only Roman numerals. With Gerbert's reintroduction, the abacus became widely used in Europe once again during the eleventh century.[21]

Gerbert was the first Christian to teach mathematics using the nine Arabic numerals. An actual copy of Gerbert's abacus board was discovered in 2001. Its counters were marked with nine different signs proving he introduced the Arabic numerals to France.[22] However, Europeans did not adapt Arabic numerals immediately after Gerbert introduced them, but "they only became common in the thirteenth century".[23] The numerals one through nine looked too much like what pagans used, so monks rejected them at first, in fear that they may have a connection to magical arts.[24] The number system would have been even less popular had it included zero, because people "rejected the infinitely large, the infinitely small, and the void".[25]

However, none of this stopped Gerbert from introducing the concept of these Arabic numerals. He was fascinated by the numerals and experimented with them until they made more sense. When he first discovered the numeral's simplicity he was very excited. For example, instead of writing thirty-seven as "MXXXVII", it could simply be written as "37".[26] If Gerbert had never discovered the Arabic numerals and introduced them to Europe, we may still be using Roman numerals today. Despite many scholastic scholars being against the new system, these numerals and calculations involving them eventually spread, and this has had a lasting impact.

Gerbert was also educated in the field of astronomy. Astronomy is one of the more complicated subjects of the *quadrivium* and once again, his study of the subject led to people accusing Gerbert of sorcery.[27] The reason for this may be that in Gerbert's time, astrology and astronomy were closely woven into a single body of knowledge, where astrological thought involved fortune telling and divination. The skill Gerbert demonstrated in this area, one that was so foreign to everyone else, made it easy for him to be accused of learning the black arts. Gerbert, however, agreed with those who taught that "God himself had set His seal of approval upon astronomy when He made use of the stars in the heavens to mark the birth of His Son."[28]

Gerbert's innovations in the medieval classroom went beyond reading aloud from newly adopted texts and expounding these with interpretations and ideas that went outside the usual instructional boundaries. Rather Gerbert put his students into action by *doing* what they were learning about. Students calculated, observed the sky, presented oral speeches and sounded musical instruments. To involve students actively with these matters that did not come up in everyday life, Gerbert expended a great deal of effort in devising visual aids, instruments and tools. While Gerbert's initial instructional model was a wood ball, his subsequent designs did away with that solid core, to emphasize the spatial relationships linking an earth-bound observer to the celestial surroundings.[29]

Gerbert sought to further students' understanding through their interactions with instruments, where they manipulated something, observed, and interpreted on their own. For him to be able to compose instruments that had this educational function, took a double research effort on his part: both into the subject matter, and into the ways of rendering it accessible to learners. Gerbert innovated in teaching through investigating the whole world, discerning relationships among all its apparent parts and creating means by which these relationships were what brought his students into active contact with the world.[30] For Gerbert, "the pupil's victory is the master's glory".[31]

Gerbert's spheres

He pursued his dynamic studies and eventually this led to the reintroduction of the armillary sphere in Europe. The armillary is a model of the earth and its relation to the heavens, used as a visual aid for mathematical astronomical instruction and teaching.[32] Gerbert learned about this device and how to use it from his Arab teachers and eventually he was able to locate the north and south poles in their slanting rotation and distinguish the arctic polar circle, the equator, and the tropic of cancer. He used the armillary as a small model of a very large concept to demonstrate to his students the paths of the planets and stars. He also made sighting tubes to observe stars and constructed globes recording their positions.

The details of Gerbert's armillary sphere are revealed in letters from Gerbert to his former student and monk Remi of Trèves and to his colleague Constantine, the abbot of Micy, as well as the accounts of his former student Richer.[33] Richer described Gerbert's use of the armillary sphere as a visual aid for teaching mathematics and astronomy in the classroom, as well as how Gerbert organized the rings and markings on his device:

> First [Gerbert] demonstrated the form of the world by a plain wooden sphere ... thus expressing a very big thing by a little model. Slanting this sphere by its two poles on the horizon, he showed the northern constellations toward the upper pole and the southern toward the lower pole. He kept this position straight using a circle that the Greeks called *horizon*, the Latins *limitans*, because it divides visible stars from those that are not visible. On this horizon line, placed so as to demonstrate practically and plausibly ... the rising and setting of the stars, he traced natural outlines to give a greater appearance of reality to the constellations ... He divided a sphere in half, letting the tube represent the diameter, the one end representing the north pole, the other the south pole. Then he divided the semicircle from one pole to the other into thirty parts. Six lines drawn from the pole he drew a heavy ring to represent the arctic polar circle. Five divisions below this he placed another line to represent the tropic of Cancer. Four parts lower he drew a line for the equinoctial circle [the equator]. The remaining distance to the south pole is divided by the same dimensions.[34]

Richer stated that Gerbert studied the stars during the night and discovered that they coursed in an oblique direction across the night sky.[35]

Interestingly, Gerbert divided his sphere into 60 degrees instead of 360, making the lateral lines of his sphere equal to six degrees of those employed for the same purpose today. In this way, the polar circle on Gerbert's sphere was located at 26 degrees, just very few degrees off from the actual 23° 28'. Furthermore, this account illustrates that his positioning of the Tropic of Cancer was nearly exact, while his positioning of the equator was exactly correct.[36]

Richer also describes a sphere which Gerbert constructed to make the planets more easily recognizable:

> He succeeded equally in showing the paths of the planets when they come near or withdraw from the earth. He fashioned first an armillary sphere. He joined the two circles called by the Greeks *coluri* and by the Latins *incidentes* because they fell upon each other, and at their extremities he placed the poles. He drew with great art and accuracy, across the *colures*, five other circles called parallels, which, from one pole to the other, divided the half of the sphere into thirty parts. He put six of these thirty parts of the half-sphere between the pole and the first circle; five between the first and the second; from the second to the third, four; from the third to the fourth, four again; five from the fourth to the fifth; and from the fifth to the pole, six. On these five circles he placed obliquely the circles that the Greeks call *loxos* or *zoe*, the Latins *obliques* or *vitalis* (the zodiac) because it contained the figures of the animals ascribed to the planets. On the inside of this oblique circle he figured with an extraordinary art the orbits traversed by the planets, whose paths and heights he demonstrated perfectly to his pupils, as well as their respective distances.[37]

Fortunately, the construction of Gerbert's last and most ingenious sphere is described not only by the pupil Richer but also by Gerbert himself in a letter to a colleague, Constantine, abbot of Micy. The two descriptions supplement each other and clearly reveal Gerbert's most original and effective teaching device. Richer portrays the object in this manner:

> He made yet another sphere composed of circles, in the interior of which he placed no circles; but he fashioned above, upon iron and copper wires, the forms of the constellations. For an axis he used a tube through which one looked at the north pole, and when one looked at this pole the machine corresponded to the sky and all the stars corresponded to the marks of the sphere. This machine was so miraculous that even those who were ignorant of the science, if a single constellation were known to them on the sphere they could find the others themselves, and that without the aid of a teacher. This is how he produced knowledge in his pupils.[38]

It would be difficult to construct such a sphere from this brief account given by Richer. Gerbert's description, written to Constantine in response to a request for such information, sheds light upon the above paragraph from Richer:

> A sphere, my brother, concerning which you inquire for encircling the heavens and demonstrating the stars, is made round in all parts: then a line drawn around the middle is divided equally into sixty parts. Then where you have decided upon the beginning of the line, fix one foot of a compass. Place the other foot on the mark where six parts of the aforesaid line are enclosed, and when you have swung the compass around you include twelve parts. Without moving the first foot, the second foot is extended up to the mark on the first line where the eleventh part ends, and then it is drawn around so that twenty-two parts are encompassed. In like manner the foot is stretched forth to where

fifteen parts of the aforesaid line are included, and by turning the compass, thirty parts are enclosed, and the middle of the sphere, having thirty parts, is cut off by the revolution of the compass.

Then moving the compass to the other half of the sphere, you should fix the first foot there, making sure that you station it exactly opposite [the first pole], and you will follow the above rules for measuring and encircling of these parts. Then the circles which you have drawn will be five in number, the middle one being divided equally into sixty parts.

Then take one of these hemispheres and hollow it out, and where you had fixed the other foot of your compass upon the aforesaid line bore a hole so that the circumference line runs through the middle of the hole. In the poles of the spheres, where you had placed the first foot of the compass, make a single hole, so that the middle of those holes sets bounds to the aforesaid hemisphere. Now there will be seven holes, in each of which you should put single tubes a half foot long: and the two extremities will be placed opposite each other so that both ways you will be able to see as through one tube. However, lest the tubes wobble, you can make an iron semicircle measured and perforated in the same way as the hemisphere, so that the upper ends of the tubes cohere; which differs in this way from organ pipes, that they are all equal in thickness, lest it diminish the brightness by which you contemplate through them the celestial bodies. The semicircle should be made fully two fingers wide, so that the whole hemisphere has thirty parts in length, keeping an equal proportion of the division through which the hole receives the tubes.

> Then some night when our north pole is visible, take the hemisphere model out under the sky, so that through each tube, whose limits we have described, you can clearly distinguish and study the same north pole. If you are in doubt as to which star is the pole, fix a tube in such a position so that it does not move all night, and upon that star which you suspect to be the pole: now if it is the pole, you will be able to see it all night: if any other, its location will shortly afterwards not appear visible through the tube.
>
> Accordingly, the hemisphere being stationed in the aforesaid manner so that it cannot be moved in any way, first you will be able to measure through the lower and upper tube the north pole, through the second the arctic circle, through the third the summer [Cancer], through the fourth the equator, through the fifth winter [Capricorn]. However, for the south pole, which is under the earth, no sky appears to be gazed at but only earth through any tubes.[39]

Gerbert's astronomical advances progressed even further. He also produced a sophisticated sundial, musical instruments, water clocks, and a steam-powered organ.[40] Gerbert is also credited for making an astrolabe and writing about its use. The astrolabe was invented in Greece, and once again, Gerbert used his foreign studies to bring to Europe new knowledge. The astrolabe was used to measure elevation, compute latitudes, and determine when the sun rises and sets.[41] Without Gerbert's astronomical advances, astronomy may have stayed an "evil" subject, and we may have never known what we know of the subject in universities today.

Gerbert was a fervent scholar and teacher as well as a religious authority. His incorporation of Arabic scientific and mathematic principles even caused legends to spring up about this remarkable man.[42] However, it cannot be denied how important his work was to Western European medieval thought of the late tenth century. With the exception of brief stays in Rome, Bobbio, and at the court of the Holy Roman Emperor Otto II, Gerbert taught first the trivium and then the quadrivium in Rheims until replacing the archbishop Adalbero, his mentor and fellow reformer, in 989.[43] Here, he focused heavily on classical sources and his knowledge of Islamic practices learned in Spain and integrated them into contemporary Western European traditions to create a classroom environment not previously seen before. Rheims also served as a place where Gerbert constructed and used instruments such as the abacus, armillary sphere, and celestial sphere in his instruction.[44]

The astrolabe

Gerbert was probably the author of a description of the astrolabe that was edited by Hermannus Contractus some 50 years later. Since the astrolabe was known and studied in al-Andalus before 978, the possibility that Gerbert acquired knowledge of the astrolabe in 967–970 is still open. The astrolabe was used and studied in al-Andalus already during the reign of al-Hakam II ibn Abd al-Rahman (961-976).[45] The astrolabe's use varied from location to location, but was pivotal in Western and Eastern Islamic surveying, calculating geometric and trigonometric functions, determining specific dates and times for religious rituals, evaluating astrological signs, as well as general astronomy. Drawing from the Mediterranean classical Greek sources, Muslims preserved and improved the function of the astrolabe from Ptolemy through John Philoponus.[46] From Baghdad to Damascus to Cairo to

Toledo, the astrolabe served a special role in observatories and mosques. It is then possible to surmise that in his time spent in Islamic Spain, Gerbert not only came in contact with, but became learned with this instrument while studying with Islamic scholars. When he returned from Spain he probably brought with him copies of Llobet of Barcelona's (late tenth century AD) Latin translations of Arabic manuals on astronomy, astrology and the astrolabe. Gerbert remained in close contact with Spanish scholars, requesting additional books and translations. He introduced the astrolabe to his students at Rheims. Knowledge of the astrolabe spread quickly throughout Europe.[47]

In Rheims, he constructed a hydraulic-powered organ with brass pipes that excelled all previously known instruments, where the air had to be pumped manually. The basis for this is the God-given order in the cosmos which is reflected in mathematical order.[48]

Gerbert's fame and rise

Thereafter, Gerbert's fame as a teacher spread rapidly, attracting attention as far away as Saxony, where the schoolmaster Otric of Magdeburg heard of his reputation as a philosopher and sent one of his students to investigate.[49] When Otric's informant brought back an erroneous report about Gerbert's taxonomy of the branches of knowledge, Otric became convinced that Gerbert was misleading his students with false doctrines and reported his discovery to scholars at the court of Otto II. Otto, doubting the validity of Otric's charges, arranged a disputation between the two men at Ravenna when Gerbert arrived in Italy with Archbishop Adalbero in 981.[50]

The ties that Gerbert had made with Otto during his trip to Rome with Borrell and Hatto in 970 now bore fruit. After witnessing Gerbert's victory over Otric in the disputation at Ravenna, Otto appointed Gerbert abbot of the wealthy and prominent monastery of Bobbio in northern Italy.[51] Gerbert's stay at Bobbio was short-lived, however. Finding himself opposed at every turn by predatory magnates and refractory monks, he left Bobbio in late 983 and returned to Rheims, where he took up the position of scholasticus once more. He served in that capacity until 989, when, upon the death of his friend and patron Archbishop Adalbero, he became secretary to Arnulf, the newly elected archbishop, having been passed over for the position himself. When Arnulf was deposed at the synod of Saint-Basile de Verzy in June of 991 after betraying the city of Rheims to his uncle, the Carolingian pretender Charles of Lotharingia, Gerbert was installed as his successor. Arnulf's supporters did not accept his deposition from office, however, and their challenges to Gerbert's legitimacy ultimately made his position untenable. In 997 he left Rheims for good and fled to the court of Otto III, who appointed him his personal tutor. Shortly thereafter in 998, Pope Gregory V (996–999), Otto III's cousin, appointed him Archbishop of Ravenna. In 999, Gerbert was elected pope, adopting the name Sylvester II.

When Stephen (975–1038) became King of Hungary in 997 he desired to make Hungary a Christian nation, so he sent Abbot Astricus to Rome to petition Pope Sylvester II for royal dignity and for the power to establish episcopal sees. Sylvester acceded to his wishes, recognizing the Magyar nationality and endowing the famous kingly crown on Stephen. His crowning took place on 17 August 1001. The Crown of St Stephen has become the proud symbol of Hungarian nationhood and is part of its coat-of-arms.

Gerbert's time as pope was extremely difficult and he was unable to bring peace and prosperity as he wished:

> Greatness did not bring him happiness; power, in his case, was not crowned with achievement. He found that the unfortunate circumstances of the time, the animosity of the Romans towards him, and the swift approach of death were more than able to paralyze his own worthy projects and high endeavours, and the powerful protection of the Emperor.[52]

He was the first Frenchman to become pope and the Romans certainly considered that the Papacy should not go to a "foreigner". A revolt in the winter of 1001 saw both Emperor Otto III and the pope forced out of Rome. Otto III never returned to Rome, and having twice unsuccessfully tried to take the city, he died on the third attempt in 1002. Gerbert returned to Rome soon after the death of Otto III, although he never regained his strength, and died in 1003. He is buried in the basilica of St John Lateran.

Pope Sylvester left a permanent heritage. The enlightened zeal of Gerbert in the cause of studies effected a real revival of intellectual activity. What had been carried out under Charlemagne in the promotion of liberal arts by Alcuin, and what Saint Bruno had effected in the same direction under Otto the Great for the Germans, was accomplished for the newly rising kingdom of France by Gerbert. The range of subjects with which he dealt was much more liberal and comprehensive, and the influence of his work was perhaps deeper than that of either Alcuin or Bruno. Gerbert may be described as the father of the schoolmen.[53]

In one sense Gerbert was also a direct ancestor of the papal and Church reform movements of the eleventh century. His influence upon the young emperor Otto III is well established. Equally significant were Gerbert's two pupils, Heribert and Adelbald, whose strategic posts in the imperial service helped them further Gerbert's educational ideas and reform principles. Heribert was raised to the archbishopric of Cologne the year Gerbert was elevated to the papacy. In Cologne, from 999 to 1021, he furthered Gerbert's reform principles. Adelbald, on the other hand, was a first-rate mathematician. Insofar as these two men, close to the emperor, influenced Henry II along the lines of renewal, Gerbert effectively lay behind the imperial reform policies in Italy and Germany. Thus Gerbert became an important figure in the Lotharingian reform movement which so fundamentally influenced Henry II. The reforming movements converge in a very real way at Rome in the eleventh century under Pope Gregory VII.[54]

Notes

1 Wide disagreement exists among Gerbert scholars as to the date of his birth, ranging from 938 to 950. French scholars chose the earliest possible date for their celebration, but a later date, 946, has more to be said for it from the sources. See O. G. Darlington, "Gerbert, the Teacher" in *American Historical Review* 52/3 (1947), p. 456.

2 Gerbert, *Epistola* 194.

3 See Darlington, "Gerbert, the Teacher", p. 457.

4 *Ibid.*, p. 460. The Spanish March (Spanish: Marca Hispánica), also known as the March of Barcelona was a buffer zone beyond the former province of *Septimania,* created by Charlemagne in 795 as a defensive barrier between the Umayyad Moors of Al-Andalus, the Duchy of Gascony, the Duchy of Aquitaine and the Frankish Kingdom.

5 See N. M. Brown, *The abacus and the cross: The story of the Pope who brought the light of science to the Dark Ages* (New York: Basic Books, 2010), p. 73.

6 O. Pedersen, *The First Universities: Studium Generale and the Origins of University Education in Europe* (Cambridge: CUP, 1997), p. 109.

7 R. Erdoes, *AD 1000: Living on the Brink of Apocalypse* (San Francisco: Harper & Row Publishers, 1988), p. 25.

8 See Brown, *The abacus and the cross.*

9 Gerbert, *Letter* 19.

10 Gerbert, *Letter* 25.

11 Gerbert, *Letter* 21.

12 Darlington, "Gerbert, the Teacher", p. 461.

13 See Richer of St. Rémi, *Historia* III, 44: "Et quia musica et astronomia in Italia tunc penitus ignorabantur, mox papa Ottoni regi Germaniae et Italiae per legatum indicavit illuc huiusmodi advenisse iuvenem, qui mathesim optime nosset, suosque strenue docere valeret". Richer was Gerbert's former student and a French nobleman, who served as a monk in Rheims. The manuscript of Richer's *Historiarum Libri Quatuor*, neither circulated nor copied in his own day or subsequently, was found by Pertz in the library of Bamberg in 1833. It was the original, written and amended by Richer himself. No copies exist.

14 While it is possible to understand Richer's use of the word *logica* here as a reference to dialectic alone, three chapters later he clearly uses it to refer to both dialectic and rhetoric, a usage that originated with Plato and was transmitted to the Middle Ages by Isidore of Seville. See Richer of St. Rémi, *Historia* III, 45, 48.

15 For a summary of Adalbero's reforms to the monasteries in the diocese of Rheims, see Michel Bur, "Saint-Thierry et le renouveau monastique dans le diocèse de Reims au Xe siècle," in *Saint-Thierry, une abbaye du VIe au XXe siècle: Actes du Colloque international d'histoire monastique Reims-Saint-Thierry*, 11 au 14 octobre 1976, ed. Michel Bur (Saint-Thierry, 1979), pp. 44–49.

16 See Richer of St. Rémi, *Historia* III, 49–54.

17 See Brown, *The abacus and the cross*, p. 68.

18 *Ibid.*

19 C. Seife, *Zero: The Biography of a Dangerous Idea* (New York: Penguin Books, 2000), p. 77.

20 Richer of St. Rémi, *Historia* III, 54.

21 See J. D. Buddhue, "The Origin of Our Numbers" in *The Scientific Monthly* 52/3 (1941), p. 266.

22 Brown, *The abacus and the cross*, p. 79.

23 Pedersen, *The First Universities*, p. 119.

24 H. P. Lattin, *The peasant boy who became pope: Story of Gerbert* (London: Abelard-Schuman, 1958), p. 59.

25 Seife, *Zero: The Biography of a Dangerous Idea*, p. 77.

26 Lattin, *The peasant boy who became pope*, p. 60.

27 See *ibid.*, p. 57.

28 Erdoes, *AD 1000: Living on the Brink of Apocalypse*, p. 39.

29 E. Cavicchi, "Reflections on the Teaching of Gerbert of Aurillac" in *Orbe Novus* 1(2010), p. 13.

30 *Ibid.*, p. 16.

31 Gerbert, *Letter* 196.

32 An armillary sphere is a model of objects in the sky (in the celestial sphere), consisting of a spherical framework of rings, centred on Earth, that represent lines of celestial longitude and latitude and other astronomically important features such as the ecliptic. As such, it differs from a celestial globe, which is a smooth sphere whose principal purpose is to map the constellations.

33 See Darlington, "Gerbert, the Teacher", pp. 464, 467–472.

34 Richer of St. Rémi, *Historia* III, 50.

35 See *ibid.*

36 See Darlington, "Gerbert, the Teacher", p. 468.

37 Richer of St. Rémi, *Historia* III, 52.

38 *Ibid.*, III, 53.

39 A. Olleris, ed., *Oeuvres de Gerbert* (Clermont and Paris, 1867), pp. 479–480. English translation from Darlington, "Gerbert, the Teacher", pp. 469–470.

40 Erdoes, *AD 1000: Living on the Brink of Apocalypse*, p. 89.

41 Erdoes, *AD 1000: Living on the Brink of Apocalypse*, p. 39.

42 A. M. Flusche, *The life and legend of Gerbert of Aurillac: The organbuilder who became Pope Sylvester II* (Lewiston, NY: Edwin Mellen Press, 2006), p. 24.

43 The trivium often complements the quadrivium in higher scholastic learning, though some people were learned in just one. This derives from the idea of the "Seven Liberal Arts" of late antiquity and was also called *artes liberales* in Latin. The trivium consisted of Grammar, Rhetoric and Dialectic and had to be completed before one could learn the quadrivium.

44 Flusche, *The life and legend of Gerbert of Aurillac*, pp. 25–26.

45 See M. Zuccati, "Gerbert of Aurillac and the astrolabe: an open historical problem" in *Orbe Novus* 1(2010), pp. 114–123.

46 See J. T. Dellinger, "Gerbert—The Veritable Ptolemy and Al-Hakam II of Tenth-Century Western Europe", p. 3. The oldest surviving treatise on the astrolabe comes from the mathematician and philosopher John Philoponus (ca. 490–574 AD). In 530 he wrote wrote a work entitled *On the use and construction of the astrolabe and the lines engraved on it.* See D. Hayton, *An Introduc-*

tion to the Astrolabe (2012), p. 6.

47 See Hayton, *An Introduction to the Astrolabe*, p. 9.

48 See C. Sigismondi, "Gerberto e la misura delle canne d'organo" in *Archivum Bobiense* 29 (2007), pp. 355–396. Gerbert of Aurillac in his Mensura Fistularum explained how to compute the length of organ pipes. The method is shown on two octaves, starting from a fistula of length L=16 units and radius 1 which is equivalent to a monochord of length $\lambda = 18$. The adopted acoustic correction for the first octave to the Pythagorean lengths is $L=\lambda-\alpha \cdot r$ with $\alpha=2$. The lower octave starts from L=36-2=34 units. The proportion 16:34=34:x is used for obtaining the next diapason. All lengths of the notes of this second octave follow this proportion and no longer need the additional acoustic correction. Gerbert found the same multiplicative law for computing the lengths of the pipes and monochords, opportune constants allow to switch from monochord (12) to lower organ octave (14+1/3+1/144+1/288) to the higher one (13 + ½).

49 See Richer of St. Rémi, *Historia* III, 55.

50 See *ibid.*, III, 56.

51 See *ibid.*, III, 55–65.

52 W. P. H. Kitchin, "A Pope-Philosopher of the Tenth Century: Sylvester II (Gerbert of Aurillac)" in *The Catholic Historical Review* 8/1 (1922), pp. 42–54.

53 See H. K. Mann, *Lives of the Popes*, vol. V (London: KeganPaul, 1910), p. 24.

54 See Darlington, "Gerbert, the Teacher", p. 475.

3

Pope Innocent III and the Hospitals

Just as the founder of the universe established two great lights in the firmament of heaven, the greater light to rule the day, and the lesser light to rule the night, so too He set two great dignities in the firmament of the universal Church, the greater one to rule the day, that is, souls, and the lesser to rule the night, that is, bodies. These dignities are the papal authority and the royal power. Now just as the moon derives its light from the sun and is indeed lower than it in quantity and quality, in position and in power, so too the royal power derives the splendour of its dignity from the pontifical authority.

Pope Innocent III, *Letter to the prefect Acerbius and the nobles of Tuscany*, 1198

Before the advent of Christianity there were a few hospital-like centres in some regions. While among savage tribes the sick and feeble were often put to death, more humane practices are found among civilized peoples. One of the earliest centres on record for the care of the sick was founded around 300 BC in Ireland, by Princess Macha. It was called *Broin Bearg* (house of sorrow), and was used by the Red Branch Knights and served as the royal residence in Ulster until its destruction in AD 332.[1] In India, the Buddhist King Azoka (252 BC) established a hospital for men and animals. The Mexicans in pre-Columbian times had various institutions in which the sick and poor were cared for.

Ancient medicine

In a general way, an advance in medical knowledge implies that more was done to relieve suffering, but it does not necessarily prove the existence of hospitals. From ancient papyri we learn that the Egyptians employed a considerable number of remedies and that the physicians held clinics in the temples. Similar customs prevailed in Greece; the sick resorted to the temple of Æsculapius where they spent the night (*incubatio*) in the hope of receiving directions from the god through dreams which the priests interpreted. Lay physicians (*Æsculapiades*) conducted dispensaries in which the poor received treatment. At Epidaurus the Roman senator Antoninus erected (A.D. 170) two establishments, one for the dying and the other for women lying-in; patients of these classes were not admitted in the Æsculapium.

The ancient Greeks practised a very simple form of medicine and Greek temples included places where the sick could sleep and receive help. The Romans are believed to have established some military hospitals. The Romans in their treatment of the sick adopted many Greek usages. Æsculapius had a temple on the island in the Tiber (291 BC), where the church and monastery of St Bartholomew now stand. In the ancient Roman temple, the same rites were observed as among the Greeks. Municipal physicians were appointed to treat various classes of citizens, and these practitioners usually enjoyed special privileges and immunities. Provision was made in particular for the care of sick soldiers and slaves, the latter receiving attention in the *valetudinaria* attached to the estates of the wealthier Romans. But there is no record of any institution corresponding to our modern hospital. It is noteworthy that among pagan peoples the care of the sick bears no proportion to the advance of civilization. Though Greece and

Rome attained the highest degree of culture, their treatment of the sick was scarcely equal, certainly not superior, to that which was found in the oriental nations. Both Greeks and Romans regarded disease as a curse inflicted by higher powers and rather sought to propitiate the malevolent deity than to organize the work of relief. On the other hand the virtue of hospitality was quite generally insisted on; and this trait, as will presently appear, holds a prominent place in Christian charity.

The Old Testament

While the Bible is not a scientific or medical textbook, it is only reasonable that if God truly did inspire the books that compose the Bible, there is also valuable knowledge also on a natural level. The ancient Jewish regulations of the Old Testament were a stimulus to medical knowledge and care.

A look into the medical practices from ancient Egypt and those found in the Pentateuch, however, reveals that Moses did not necessarily rely on "wisdom" of the Egyptians (which, in many cases, consisted of life-threatening malpractice). While some medical practices in the Pentateuch are similar to those found in ancient Egyptian documents, the Pentateuch exhibits a conspicuous absence of those harmful malpractices that plague the writings of the Egyptians. Moses penned the most advanced, flawless medical prescriptions that had ever been recorded. Furthermore, every statement that pertained to the health and medical well-being of the Israelite nation recorded by Moses could theoretically still be implemented and be completely in accord with every fact modern medicine has learned in regard to germ spreading, epidemic disease control, communal sanitation, and a host of other medical and scientific discoveries.

Among the ancient documents that detail much of the Egyptian medicinal knowledge, the Ebers Papyrus ranks as one of the foremost sources; this papyrus was discovered in 1872 by a German Egyptologist named Georg Ebers.[2] It consists of a gamut of medical remedies purported to heal, enhance, and prevent.

> Altogether 811 prescriptions are set forth in the Papyrus, and they take the form of salves, plasters, and poultices; snuffs, inhalations, and gargles; draughts, confections, and pills; fumigations, suppositories, and enemata.[3]

Among the hundreds of prescriptions, disgusting treatments that caused much more harm than good can easily be found. For instance, under a section titled "What to do to draw out splinters in the flesh," a remedy is prescribed consisting of worm blood, mole, and donkey dung".[4] It is easy to note that dung "is loaded with tetanus spores" and "a simple splinter often resulted in a gruesome death from lockjaw".[5] Remedies to help heal skin diseases included such prescriptions as: "A hog's tooth, cat's dung, dog's dung, aau-of-samu-oil, berries-of-the-xet-plant, pound and apply as poultice."[6] Various other ingredients among a plethora of remedies concocted included "dried excrement of a child", "hog dung", and "a farmer's urine".[7] One recipe to prevent hair growth included lizard dung and the blood from a cow, donkey, pig, dog, and stag.[8]

In addition, it seems that the Egyptians were among the first to present the idea of "good and laudable pus". Due to the idea that infection was good and the pus that resulted from it was a welcomed effect, "well-meaning doctors killed millions by deliberately infecting their wounds".[9] Needless to say, the modern-day reader would not want to be a patient in an ancient Egyptian clinic! While some of the Egyptian medicine actually did include prescriptions and remedies that could be helpful, the harmful remedies and ingredients cast a sickening shadow of untrustworthiness over the entire Egyptian endeavour in the light of modern medicine.[10]

The first five books of the Old Testament are not essentially devoted to the description and analysis of medical prescriptions. They are not ancient medical textbooks. These books do, however, contain numerous regulations for sanitation, quarantine, and other medical procedures that governed the daily lives of the Israelite nation. Missing entirely from the pages of these writings are the harmful remedies and ingredients prescribed by other ancient civilizations. In fact, the Pentateuch exhibits an understanding of germs and disease that much "modern" medicine did not grasp for 3,500 years after the books were written.

Blood always has been a mysterious and special substance whose vast mysteries and capabilities have yet to be fully explored. Doctors in the twenty-first century transfuse it, draw it, separate it, package it, store it, ship it, and sell it. Although modern-day scientists have not uncovered completely all of the wonders of blood, they have discovered that it is the key to life. Without this "liquid of life", humans and animals would have no way to circulate the necessary oxygen and proteins that their bodies need in order to survive and reproduce. Haemoglobin found in the red blood cells carries oxygen to the brain, which in turn uses that oxygen to control the entire body. A brain without oxygen is like a car without gas or a computer without electricity. Blood makes all of the functions in the body possible.

Thousands of years before the lethal practice of bloodletting was conceived, mankind had been informed by God that blood was indeed the key to life. In Leviticus 17:11, we read: “For the life of the flesh is in the blood.” Today, we understand completely the truthfulness of this statement. How did an ancient shepherd like Moses come to know such information? How could Moses have known almost 3,500 years ago that life was in the blood, while it took the rest of the scientific and medical community thousands of years (and millions of lives) to grasp this truth?

In reality, entire books could be written on the Old Testament’s amazing medical accuracy.[11] Many physicians who have compared Moses’ medical instructions to effective modern methods have come to realize the astonishing value and insight of the Old Testament text. As Dr Macht once wrote: “Every word in the Hebrew Scriptures is well chosen and carries valuable knowledge and deep significance”.[12] Such is certainly the case in regard to the medical practices listed in its pages. Indeed, the accurate medical practices prescribed thousands of years before their significance was completely understood provide excellent evidence for the divine inspiration of the Bible.

The Christian era

In the New Testament, Jesus Christ placed a particular emphasis on care for the sick and outcast, such as lepers. He and His Apostles went about curing the sick and anointing of the sick. According to the Gospel of Matthew, Jesus identified so strongly with the sick and afflicted that He equated serving them with serving Him:

> For I was hungry and you gave me food, I was thirsty and you gave me drink, I was a stranger and you made me welcome, lacking clothes and you clothed me, sick and you visited me, in prison and you came to see me. Then the upright will say to him in reply, “Lord, when did we see you hungry and feed you, or thirsty and give you drink? When

> did we see you a stranger and make you welcome, lacking clothes and clothe you? When did we find you sick or in prison and go to see you?" And the King will answer, "In truth I tell you, in so far as you did this to one of the least of these brothers of mine, you did it to me." (Mt 25:35–40)

He had instructed His disciples to go out and heal the sick: "Cure the sick, raise the dead, cleanse those suffering from virulent skin-diseases, drive out devils. You received without charge, give without charge" (Mt 10:8). The Church, adhering to this command of Jesus, during the course of her history, which by now has lasted two millennia, has always attended to the sick and the suffering. In His Sermon on the Mount and in parables such as *The Good Samaritan,* Jesus called on followers to worship God, act without violence or prejudice and care for the sick, hungry and poor. Christ Himself gave His followers the example of caring for the sick by the numerous miracles He wrought to heal various forms of disease including the most loathsome, leprosy. He also charged His Apostles in explicit terms to heal the sick (Lk 10:9) and promised to those who should believe in Him that they would have power over disease (Mk 16:18). Like the other works of Christian charity, the care of the sick was from the beginning a sacred duty for each of the faithful, but it devolved in a special way upon the bishops, presbyters, and deacons. The same ministrations that brought relief to the poor naturally included provision for the sick who were visited in their homes.

During His ministry on earth Jesus had raised people from the dead and cured a large number of persons and a variety of illnesses. These were accepted as miraculous cures, and for a while after His death and Resurrection, His apostles also healed miraculously in the name of God.

St Peter healed a cripple at the Beautiful Gate. He said, "I have neither silver nor gold, but I will give you what I have: in the name of Jesus Christ the Nazarene, walk!" (Ac 3:6). The sick were even taken out into the streets and laid on beds and sleeping-mats in the hope that at least the shadow of Peter might fall across some of them as he went past (Ac 5:15). St Peter healed Aeneas, a paralytic who had been bedridden for eight years (Ac 9:33–35). He also raised Tabitha from the dead (Ac 9:40–41). Although mention is occasionally made of anointing (Jm 5:15), laying on of hands (Mk 16:18), fasting (Mk 9:29), drinking of wine (1 Tm 4:23) and even the use of a simple eye preparation (Jn 9:6; Rev 3:18), the healing process was based on the notion that faith could cure illness. In James 5:14–15 the sick are advised to visit the Church elder who will effect cure by way of prayer and anointing. St Paul referred to Luke as the beloved physician (Col 4:14). Central to the New Testament's understanding of illness is the development of a Christian theology of suffering. Whilst living in an imperfect world damaged by sin, the Christian should expect and accept suffering and know that not all illnesses would be cured. Indeed the concept of illness being caused by sin figures prominently in the Gospels (Jn 9:2).

The Graeco-Roman world in which Christianity appeared was often cruel and inhumane. The weak and the sick were despised. Abortion, infanticide and poisoning were widely practised. The doctor was often a sorcerer as well being a healer and the power to heal equally conferred the power to kill. Among the pagans of the classical world only the Hippocratic band of physicians had a different attitude to their fellow human beings. They swore oaths to heal and not to harm and to carry out their duty of care to the sick.

It was the Christians of the Roman Empire who began to change society's attitude to the sick, disabled and dying, by their radically different outlook. In many ways, Christianity and medicine are natural allies; medicine gives men and women unique opportunities to express their faith in daily practical caring for others, embodying the commands of Christ: "whatever you did for one of the least of these brothers of mine, you did for me" (Mt 25:40).

Stories of Christian caring had enormous impact, even before Constantine's decree of toleration. Pope Clement, a Christian leader in Rome at the end of the first century of the Christian era, records how the Christian community was already doing much to relieve the plight of poor widows. In the second century when plague hit the City of Carthage, pagan households threw sufferers onto the streets. The entire Christian community, personally led by their bishop, responded. They were seen on the streets, offering comfort and taking them into their own homes to be cared for.

In his *Ecclesiastical History*, Eusebius refers at several places with appreciation and admiration to Christian physicians; he tells how the Phrygian physician Alexander died a martyr's death;[13] he recounts how "the splendid physician Zenobius" died courageously of the wounds dealt him in his sides,[14] and praises Bishop Theodotus as "very skilled in the healing of bodies", and supreme "in his power of healing minds".[15] Hieronymus mentions in his work on famous men the names of Flavius and of Bishop Basilius of Ancyra, a man "skilled in medicine", whilst the ecclesiastical historian Philostorgius praises Aetius, an able physician who would never take a fee.[16]

Among those martyred under Diocletian were Saints Cosmas and Damian; they were twins born to Christian parents in Cilicia, part of today's Turkey, in the third century. Saints Cosmas and Damian lived in the region around the border between modern day Turkey and Syria. They practised as physicians in the seaport of Ægea, then in the Roman province of Syria, now Ayas, on the Gulf of İskenderun, and gained a great reputation. They accepted no pay for their services and were, therefore, called *anargyroi*, "the silverless". In this way they brought many to the Catholic Faith. Over 48 miracles were credited to the holy twins, including, amongst others, the development of remedies against plague, scabs, scurvy, kidney stones and bed-wetting. Their most famous miracle involved the miraculous replacement of a diseased leg of a white patient with the leg of a recently-deceased black man.

When the persecution of Diocletian began, the Prefect Lysias had Cosmas and Damian arrested in 287, and ordered them to deny their faith in Christ. They refused and underwent a series of tortures, including crucifixion, from which, miraculously, they remained unscathed. The torturers, weary of what they realized was the impossible task of forcing apostasy from their mouths, finally beheaded them both. Their three brothers, Anthimus, Leontius, and Euprepius died as martyrs with them. The execution took place 27 September, probably in the year 287. At a later date, a number of legends grew up about them, connected in part with their relics.

The remains of the martyrs were buried in the city of Cyrus in Syria; the Emperor Justinian I (527–565) sumptuously restored the city in their honour. Having been cured of a dangerous illness by the intercession of Cosmas and Damian, Justinian, in gratitude for their aid, rebuilt and adorned their church at Constantinople, and it became a celebrated place of pilgrimage. At Rome Pope Felix IV (526–530) erected a church in their honour, the mosaics of which are still among the most valuable art remains of the city. Their feast is celebrated in the Latin Church on 26 September, and on 17 October in the Greek Church. Cosmas and Damian are regarded as the patrons of physicians and surgeons and are sometimes represented with medical emblems. They are invoked in the Canon of the Mass and in the Litany of the Saints.

However, it was not until Constantine granted the first Edict of Toleration in AD 311, that Christians were able to give public expression to their ethical convictions and undertake social reform. From the fourth-century to present times, Christians have been especially prominent in the planning, siting and building of hospitals, as well as fundraising for them. Cities with significant Christian populations had already begun to change prevailing attitudes, and were already beginning to build hospices (guest houses for the sick and chronically disabled).

A few decades after Constantine, Julian, who came to power in AD 355, was the last Roman Emperor to try to re-institute paganism. In his Apology, Julian said that if the old religion wanted to succeed, it would need to care for people even better than the way Christians cared.

As political freedom increased, so did Christian activity. The poor were fed and given free burial. Orphans and widows were protected and provided for. Elderly men and women, prisoners, sick slaves and other outcasts, especially the leprous, were cared for. These acts of generosity and compassion impressed many Roman writers and philosophers.

It is believed that the first church hospitals were constructed in the East. The fact that the first hospitals were founded in the East accounts for the use, even in the West, of names derived from the Greek to designate the main purpose of each institution. Of the terms most frequently met with the *Nosocomium* was for the sick; the

Brephotrophium for foundlings; the *Orphanotrophium* for orphans; the *Ptochium* for the poor who were unable to work; the *Gerontochium* for the aged; the *Xenodochium* for poor or infirm pilgrims.

An early hospital may have been built at Constantinople during the age of Constantine by St Zoticus. In AD 369, St Basil of Caesarea founded a 300-bed hospital. This was the first large-scale hospital for the seriously ill and disabled. It cared for victims of the plague. There were hospices for the poor and aged isolation units, wards for travellers who were sick and a leprosy house. It was the first of many built by the Christian Church. Fabiola was a Christian noble woman and Roman matron of rank belonged to the patrician Roman family of the *gens Fabia*.[17] Under the influence of St Jerome, Fabiola converted to Christianity and devoted her life to the practice of Christian asceticism and charitable work. Fabiola is distinguished by the foundation of the first public hospital in western Europe. As St Jerome describes:

> She was the first person to found a hospital, into which she might gather sufferers out of the streets, and where she might nurse the unfortunate victims of sickness and want. Need I now recount the various ailments of human beings? Need I speak of noses slit, eyes put out, feet half burnt, hands covered with sores? Or of limbs dropsical and atrophied? Or of diseased flesh alive with worms? Often did she carry on her own shoulders persons infected with jaundice or with filth. Often too did she wash away the matter discharged from wounds which others, even though men, could not bear to look at. She gave food to her patients with her own hand, and moistened the scarce breathing lips of the dying with sips of liquid.[18]

Pope Symmachus (498–514) built hospitals linked with the basilicas of St Peter, St Paul, and St Lawrence.[19] During the pontificate of Vigilius (537–555), Belisarius founded a *xenodochium* in the Via Lata at Rome.[20] Pope Pelagius II (578–590) converted his house into a refuge for the poor and aged. Pope Stephen II (752–757) restored four ancient *xenodochia*, and added three others.

The Middle Ages

In the so-called Dark Ages (476–1000) rulers influenced by Christian principles encouraged building of hospitals. Charlemagne, along with his other reforms, made wise provision for the care of the sick by decreeing that those hospitals which had been well conducted and had fallen into decay should be restored in accordance with the needs of the time. He further ordered that a hospital should be attached to each cathedral and monastery.

The famous Benedictine Abbey of Cluny, founded in 910, set the example which was widely imitated throughout France and Germany. Besides its infirmary for the religious, each monastery had a hospital (*hospitale pauperum*, or *eleemosynaria*) in which externs were cared for. These were in charge of the *eleemosynarius*, whose duties, carefully prescribed by the rule, included every sort of service that the visitor or patient could require. As he was also obliged to seek out the sick and needy in the neighbourhood, each monastery became a centre for the relief of suffering. Among the monasteries notable in this respect were those of the Benedictines at Corbie in Picardy, Hirschau, Braunweiler, Deutz, Ilsenburg, Liesborn, Prüm, and Fulda; those of the Cistercians at Arnsberg, Baumgarten, Eberbach, Himmenrode, Herrnalb, Volkenrode, and Walkenried, No less efficient was the work done by the diocesan clergy in accordance with the disciplinary enactments of the councils of Aachen (817, 836), which prescribed that a hospital should be maintained in connection with each collegiate church. The canons were obliged to contribute towards the support of the hospital, and one of their number had charge of the inmates. As these hospitals were located in cities, more numerous demands were made upon them than upon those attached to the monasteries.

In Great Britain and Ireland, the care of the sick, like other works of charity, was for a long time entrusted to the monastic orders. Each monastery, taking its pattern from those in Continental Europe, provided for the treatment both of its own inmates who fell ill and of infirm persons in the neighbourhood. In the *Penitential of Theodore* (668-690) we read that the monastery is free to receive the sick.[21] According to Harduin a large hospital was founded at St Albans in 794. A little later (796) Alcuin writing to Eanbald II, Archbishop of York, exhorts him to have in mind the foundation of hospitals where the poor and the pilgrims may find admission and relief. The temporal rulers also were generous in this respect. In 936 King Athelstan returning from his successful campaign against the Scots, made certain grants to the Culdees or secular canons of St Peter's Cathedral, York, which they employed to found a hospital. This was known at first as St Peter's, afterwards as St. Leonard's from the name of the church built in the hospital by King Stephen. It provided for 206 bedesmen and was served by a master, thirteen brethren, four seculars, eight sisters, thirty choristers, and six Servites. Archbishop Lanfranc in 1084 founded the hospital of St. Gregory outside the north gate of Canterbury and endowed it with lands and other revenues. It was a large house, built of stone and divided into two sections, one for men and the other for women.

An important place was held by women in the Italian medical schools of the Middle Ages. Moreover, in the convents for women, room was found for intellectual pursuits, and important works on medicine were written by St Hildegard (1098–1178), a Benedictine abbess from near Bingen-on-the-Rhine. Hildegard was the most important medical writer of her time. She catalogued both her practical expertise and its theoretical basis in two works: *Physica,* whose nine books focus on the scientific and medicinal properties of various plants, stones, fish, reptiles, and animals; and *Causae et Curae,* an exploration of the human body, its connections to the rest of the natural world, and the causes and cures of various diseases.[22] These works document a variety of medical practices, and serve as a valuable witness to areas of medieval medicine that were often not as well documented because their practitioners (mainly women) did not often write in Latin. Among the practices that Hildegard discusses in *Causae et Curae* is the use of bleeding and home remedies for many common ailments. She also focuses many of her remedies on common agricultural injuries such as burns, fractures, dislocations, and cuts.

The School of Salerno is regarded as the oldest medical school of the West. Salerno on the Mediterranean Sea, originally probably a Doric colony, was from the sixth to the eleventh century under the rule of the Lombards, and from 1075 to 1130 under that of the Normans. In 1130 it became a part of the Kingdom of Naples and Sicily. The origin of the school is obscure, but, although it was not primarily a religious foundation, a large number of priests were engaged there as teachers of medicine. Women and non-Christians were admitted to these studies. Salerno was destined to cultivate for a long time Greek medical science in its pristine form, until the twelfth century saw the school come under Arab influence. One of its oldest physicians was Alpuhans, later (1058–85) Archbishop of Salerno. With him worked the Lombard Gariopontus (+ 1050), whose *Passionarius* is based upon Hippocrates, Galen, and Caelius Aurelianus. Contemporary with him was the female physician Trotula who worked also in the literary field, and who is said to have been the wife of the physician Joannes Platearius. Perhaps the best known literary work of this school is the anonymous *Regimen sanitatis Salernitanum* a didactic poem consisting of 364 stanzas, which has been translated into all modern languages. It is said to have been dedicated to Prince Robert, son of William the Conqueror, upon his departure from Salerno in 1101.

An important change in the intellectual tendency of the *Civitas Hippocratica*, as this school called itself, was brought about by the physician Constantine of Carthage (Constantinus Africanus), a man learned in the Oriental languages and a teacher of medicine at Salerno, who died in 1087 a monk of Monte Cassino. While hitherto the best works of Greek antiquity had been known only in mediocre Latin translations, Constantine in the solitude of Monte Cassino began to translate to translate Greek authors from the Arabic (like the *Aphorisms* of Hippocrates and the *Ars parva* of Galen), as well as those Arabic writer which were accessible to him (Isaak, Ali Abbas). As he brought to the knowledge of his contemporaries first-class Greek authors, but only secondary Arab writers, the study of the former became more profound, while on the other hand an interest was awakened in the hitherto unknown Arabic literature. His pupils were Bartholomaeus, whose *Practica* was translated into German as early as the thirteenth century, and Johannes Afflacius (*De febribus et urinis*). To the twelfth century, when Arabian polypharmacy was introduced, belong Nicolaus Praepositus (about 1140), whose *Antidotarium*, a collection of compounded pharmaceutical formulae, became a model for later works of this kind, and Matthaeus Platearius, who, towards the end of the century, wrote a commentary on the above-named *Antidotarium* (*Glossae*) and a work about simple drugs (*Circa instans*).

Similar productions appeared from the hand of an otherwise unknown Magister Solernitanus. Maurus, following Arabian sources, wrote on uroscopy. Petrus Musandinus (author of *De cibis et potibus febricitantium*), the teacher of Pierre Giles of Corbeil (*Ægidius Corboliensis*), who later became a canon and the physician-in-ordinary to Philip Augustus of France (1180–1223), even at this time began to complain about the decay of the school. Its first misfortune dates from the death of King Roger III (1193), when the army of King Henry VI captured the city. The establishment of the University of Naples by Frederick II in 1224, the preponderance of Arabian influence, and the rise of the Montpellier school, all exerted so unfavourable an influence that by the fourteenth century Salerno was well-nigh forgotten.

Salerno was the oldest school having a curriculum prescribed by the state. In 1140 King Roger II ordered a state examination to test the proficiency of prospective physicians, and Frederick II in 1240 prescribed five years of study besides a year of practical experience. When we consider the proximity of Northern Africa, that the neighbouring Sicily had been under Saracenic rule from the ninth to the eleventh century, and that the Norman kings, and to a far greater degree Frederick II, gave powerful protection to Arabian art and science, it seems wonderful that this oasis of Graeco-Roman culture endured so long. Down to the twelfth century this school was ruled by a purely Hippocratic spirit, especially in practical medicine, by its diagnosis and by the treatment of acute diseases dietetically. Arabian influence makes itself felt first of all in therapeutics, a fact which is easily explained by the proximity of Amalfi, where the Arabian drug-dealers used to land. Local conditions (resulting from the Crusades) explain how surgery, especially the treatment of wounds received in war, was diligently cultivated. In Rogerius we find a Salernitan surgeon armed with independent experience, but showing, nevertheless, reminiscences of Abulhasem. His *Practica Chirurgiae* dates from the year 1180.

Bologna was the principal home of scholastic medicine, and, as early as the twelfth century, a medical school existed there. The most famous physician there was Thaddeus Alderotti (Th. Florentinus, 1215–95), who even at that time gave practical clinical instruction and enjoyed great fame as a physician. Among his pupils were the four Varignana, Dino and Tommaso di Garbo, and Pietro Torrigiano Rustichelli—later a Carthusian monk—all well-known expounders of the writings of Galen. Indirect disciples were Pietro de Tussignana (+ 1410), who first described the baths at Bormio, and Bavarius de Bavariis (died about 1480) who was for a long time physician to Pope Nicholas V. Bologna and the study of anatomy Bologna has stained incomparable glory from the fact that Mondino de Liucci (about 1275-1326), the reviver of anatomy, taught there. There, for the first time since the Alexandrian period (nearly 1500 years), he dissected a human corpse, and wrote a treatise on anatomy based upon personal observation—a work which, for nearly two and a half centuries, remained the official textbook of the universities. Although Mondino's work which appeared in 1316, contains many defects and errors, if nevertheless marked an advance and incited men to further investigation.

Padua, the famous rival of Bologna, received a university in 1222 from Frederick II. Padua came into existence through a secession from Bologna. Bologna was soon surpassed by the daughter institution, and, from the foundation of the University of Vienna in 1365 until the middle of the eighteenth century, Padua remained a shining model for the medical school of Bologna. The first teacher of repute was Pietro d'Abano (Petrus Aponensis, 1250–c.1320), known as the "great Lombard"— an honorary title received during his residence at the Universlty of Paris. On account of his excessively liberal opinions and his derision of Christian teaching in his *Conciliator differentiarum,* his chief medical work, he was accused of heresy. From this period also date the *Aggregator Brixiensis* of Guglielmo Corvi (1250–1326), a work in even greater demand in later times, and the *Consilia* of Gentile da Foligno (+1348), who, in 1341, performed the first anatomical dissection in Padua.

The fame of the school of Padua was greatly advanced by the family of physicians, the Santa Sophia, which about 1292 emigrated from Constantinople, and whose most famous members were Marsilio (+1405) and Galeazzo (+ 1427). The latter, one of the first teachers in Vienna (about 1398–1407), and later professor at Padua, wrote in Vienna a pharmacopoeia which indicates absolutely independent observation in the field of botany. His antithesis and contemporary was Giacomo dalla Torre of Forli (Jacobus Foroliviensis, +1413), professor at Padua, known for his commentary on the *Ars parva* of Galen. Giacomo de Dondi (1298–1359), author of the *Aggregator Paduanus do medicinis simplicibus,* tried to isolate a salt from the thermal waters of Abano, near Padua. As anatomist and practitioner Bartholomaeus de Montagnana (+1460) was important, and the grandfather of the unfortunate Savonarola, Giovanni

Michele Savonarola (1390–1462), author of the *Practica Major*, worked along similar lines.

In France, Montpellier shone as a medical school, dating from the twelfth century. Like Salerno, Montpellier developed great independence as far as the other schools were concerned, and laid the greatest stress upon practical medicine. With the decay of Salerno, Montpellier gained in importance. The chief representative of this school is the Spaniard, Arnold of Villanova (1235–c.1312). His greatest merit is that, inclining more towards the Hippocratic school, he did not follow unconditionally the teachings of Galen and Avicenna, but relied upon his own observation and experience, while employing in therapeutics a more dietetic treatment as opposed to Arabian tenets. To him we are indebted for the systematic use of alcohol in certain diseases. Other Montpellier representatives of purely practical medicine are Bernard of Gordon (+ 1314; *Lilium medicinae*, 1305) a Scot educated in Salerno; Gerardus de Solo (about 1320; *Introductorium juvenum*); Johannes de Tornamira (end of the fourteenth century, *Clarificatorium juvenum*), and the Portuguese Valeseus de Taranta (*Philonium pharmaceuticum et chirurgicum*, 1418). The medical school of Paris, founded in 1180, remained behind Montpellier in regard to the practice of medicine.

Pope Innocent III

Probably the most important work that the Popes did for medical science in the Middle Ages was their encouragement of the development of a hospital system throughout Christendom. The story of this movement is not only interesting because it represents a coordination of social effort for the relief of suffering humanity, but also because it represents the provision of opportunities for the study of disease and the skilled care of the ailing such as can come in no other way. Those who are familiar with the history of medicine, and especially of surgery, know that a great period of progress in these departments came during the thirteenth century. The following two centuries indeed represent an epoch of surgical advance such as was probably never surpassed and only equalled by the last century.

The reasons for this great development in surgical knowledge are properly understood only when we come to realize that there was a corresponding development in hospital organization. These two features of medicine always go hand in hand. The hospitals, as might be expected, preceded the surgical development, and owed their great progress at this time mainly to the Popes. The city hospital as we have it at the present time, that is, the public institution meant for the reception of those suffering from accidents, from acute diseases of various kinds, and also for providing shelter for those who have become ill and have no family or friends to take care of them, is an establishment dating from the beginning of the thirteenth century. It will doubtless be a surprise to most people to be told that the modern world owes this beneficent institution to the fatherly watchfulness, the kindly foresight, and the very practical charity of one of the greatest of the Popes, whose name is usually associated with ambitious schemes for making the Papacy a great political power in Europe, rather than as the prime mover in what was probably the most far-reaching good work of supreme social significance that was ever accomplished.

At the beginning of the thirteenth century, mainly as the result of those much abused sources of many benefits to mankind in the Middle Ages, the Crusades, the people of Europe had begun to dwell together in towns much more than before. It is closeness of population that gives rise to the social needs. While people were scattered throughout the country diseases were not so prevalent, epidemics were not likely to spread, and the charitable spirit of the rural people themselves was quite sufficient to enable them to care for the few ailing persons to be found. With the advent of even small city life, however, came the demand for hospitals in the true sense of the word, and this need did not long escape the watchful eye of Pope Innocent III. He recognized the necessity for a city hospital in Rome, and in accordance with his very practical character and wonderful activity, at once set about its foundation. As was to be expected from his wise foresight, he did not do so without due consideration. He consulted many visitors to Rome and many distinguished medical authorities as to what they considered to be the best conducted and most ably-managed institution for the care of the sick in Europe at that time.

Almost by common consent he was assured that the most successful hospital management was to be found at Montpelier. This French town near the shores of the Mediterranean had succeeded to the medical prestige formerly held by Salerno, and was now the favourite place of pilgrimage for the nobility and reigning sovereigns of Europe, whenever they became so ill that their ordinary medical attendants seemed to be able to do nothing for them. Pope Innocent was further told that the institution at Montpelier which was best conducted was undoubtedly the Hospital of the Holy Spirit.

The greatest of all Innocent's services to the citizens of Rome was the foundation of the hospital of the Holy Spirit.[23] The old hostel for English pilgrims, the *Schola Anglorum*, had been founded by King Ina around 728, as a hostel for English pilgrims. By the end of the twelfth century this hostel had fallen somewhat into disuse. Conditions in Rome were not favourable to pilgrimages.

The time had come for the house to be dissolved. On its site, partly with the balance of its funds, partly from his own re-sources, Innocent erected the hospital that became the first of any size in Europe and for centuries was the largest. The hospital is that of Santo Spirito, originally called Santa Maria in Sassia. Many times rebuilt, it still stands on the Vatican side of the Tiber by the Vittorio Emanuele bridge.

The Santo Spirito was not the first hospital to be opened in Europe. About the middle of the twelfth century (c. 1145), Guy de Montpellier had opened in that French city a hospital in honour of the Holy Spirit and prescribed the Rule of St Augustine for the brothers in charge. Approved 23 April 1198 by Pope Innocent III, this institute spread rapidly throughout France. In 1204 the same pontiff built a hospital in Rome named Santa Maria in Sassia. By the pope's command, Guy de Montpellier came to Rome and took charge of this hospital, which was thenceforward Santo Spirito in Sassia. Guy de Montpellier, with his confraternity of the Holy Spirit for the care of the sick, was at work in Montpellier twenty years before Innocent founded his hospital in Rome.[24] Pope Innocent had looked to Montpellier for a model. He entrusted the new hospital to Brother Guy's confraternity and from this confraternity it took its name. Inspired by the charity of God, the brethren of the confraternity brought into the hospital all sick persons whom they found in the streets of Rome, sought out all who needed the nursing and medical aid that was impossible to be given in overcrowded and insanitary houses, encouraged friends and relatives to bring all persons suffering from wounds, accidental injuries, and common afflictions to the care of the hospital. Pope Innocent desired that the hospital in Rome be a centre of healing, where, as at Montpellier, the hungry might be fed, the naked clothed, the sick supplied with every necessary help and those in greatest need receive the greatest help.

This hospital of the Holy Spirit soon attained a world-wide reputation for careful nursing and medical attendance and for the discretion with which its surgical cases were treated. It was understood that all the ailing picked up on the streets should be brought to the hospital, and that all the wounded and injured would be welcomed there. Besides, certain of the attendants of the hospital went out every day to look for any patients who might be neglected or be without sufficient care, especially in the poorer quarters of the city, and these were also transported to the hospital. This old Santo Spirito hospital then was exactly the model of the modern city hospitals.

Funds were needed of course. Therefore Innocent contributed to the hospital from his private purse. Furthermore, he authorised the confraternity of the Holy Spirit to collect for its support throughout Italy and Sicily and in England and Hungary. Not content with opening this hospital in Rome, Innocent next urged that similar hospitals should be established throughout Europe. He lived to see this done in Germany. It has been asserted that Innocent was the founder of the modern city hospital and there is truth in the assertion. He was certainly the pioneer of the general hospital in Europe, for a number of German hospitals trace their foundation to the reign of Pope Innocent. Statesman of Europe that he was, Innocent saw the misery and disease at his own door and from the duty to his neighbour his eyes were never turned away.

Pope Innocent's idea, however, was not to establish a hospital at Rome alone, but his fatherly solicitude went out to every city in Christendom. In accordance with this pre-determined plan, by personal persuasion, by the display of an interest in hospital work, and by official Papal encouragement he succeeded in having, during his own pontificate, a number of hospitals established in all parts of the then civilized world on the model of this hospital of the Holy Spirit at Rome. The initiative thus given proved lasting, and even after the Pontiff's death hospitals of the Holy Spirit continued to multiply in various parts of Europe, until scarcely a city of any importance was without one.

That the influence of the movement initiated by Innocent III. was felt even in distant England is very clear, from the fact that practically all of the famous old British hospitals date their existence as institutions for the care of the ailing from the thirteenth century.

During the first quarter of the twelfth century (c.1123), St Bartholomew's hospital was founded on the site of a priory by Rahere, who had been jester of Henry I, but had joined a religious community and secured from the king a grant of land in Smoothfield near London. This continued to be the most prominent hospital of London until its confiscation by Henry VIII.

The Holy Cross hospital at Winchester was founded in 1132 by Henry of Blois, half-brother to King Stephen; St Mary's Spital, in 1197 by Walter Brune, citizen of London, and his wife Roesia. The latter, at the Dissolution, had 180 beds for sick persons and travellers. St Thomas's Hospital, was named after St Thomas Becket—which suggests it may have been founded after 1173 when Becket was canonised. St Thomas' was founded in 1213 by Richard, Prior of Bermondsey, as an Almonry, or house of alms. It was destroyed by a terrible fire it was founded again more fully in 1215 for canons regular, by Peter de Rupibus, Bishop of Winchester. This bishop had written: "Behold at Southwark an ancient spital, built of old to entertain the poor, has been entirely reduced to cinders and ashes." The hospital was confiscated by Henry VIII but was re-established by Edward VI. The hospitals were created for the benefit of the general public, originally more as places of general hospitality, from which the word is derived. At the present time St Bartholomew's and St Thomas's are still among the most important hospitals in London.

Innumerable pontifical documents attest the interest and zeal of the popes in favour of hospitals. The Holy See extends its favour and protection to the charitable undertakings of the faithful in order to ensure their success and to shield them against molestation from any source. It grants the hospital permission to have a chapel, a chaplain, and a cemetery of its own: exempts the hospital from episcopal jurisdiction, making it immediately subject to the Holy See; approves statutes, intervenes to correct abuses, defends the hospitals property rights, and compels the restitution of its holdings where these have been unjustly alienated or seized. In particular, the popes are liberal in granting indulgences, for example to the founders and patrons, to those who pray in the hospital chapel or cemetery, to all who contribute when an appeal is made for the support of the hospital, and to all who lend their services in nursing the sick.[25]

Notes

1 See H. S. Wellcome, *Medicine in Ancient Erin* (London: Burroughs Welcome & Co., 1909), p. 17.

2 C. Bryan, *Ancient Egyptian Medicine: The Papyrus Ebers* (Chicago, IL: Ares Publishers, 1930), p. 1.

3 *Ibid.*, p. 15.

4 *Ibid.*, p. 73.

5 See S. I. McMillen and D. Stern, *None of These Diseases* (Grand Rapids, MI: Revell, 2000), p. 10.

6 Bryan, *Ancient Egyptian Medicine*, p. 92.

7 *Ibid.*, pp. 98, 115, 131.

8 *Ibid.*, p. 102.

9 McMillen and D. Stern, *None of These Diseases*, p. 10.

10 See K. Butt, "Scientific Foreknowledge and Medical Acumen of the Bible" on www.apologeticspress.org.

11 See McMillen and D. Stern, *None of These Diseases*.

12 D. I. Macht, "An Experimental Pharmacological Appreciation of Leviticus XI and Deuteronomy XIV" in *Bulletin of the History of Medicine*, 27/5 (September–October 1953), p. 450.

13 Eusebius, *Ecclesiastical History*, V, I, 49–51.

14 *Ibid.*, VIII, XIII, 4.

15 *Ibid.*, VII, XXXIII, 23.

16 See H. van der Loos, *The Miracles Of Jesus* (Leiden: Brill Academic Publishers, 1968), p. 86.

17 The *gens Fabia* was one of the most ancient patrician families at Rome. The gens played a prominent part in history soon after the establishment of the Republic, and three brothers are said to have been invested with seven successive consulships, from BC 485 to 479.

18 St Jerome, *Letter 77*, 6.

19 See *Liber Pontificalis*, I, n. 63, p. 263.

20 See *ibid*, I, c 296.

21 *Penitential of Theodore*, VI, 15: "in potestate et libertate est monasterii susceptio infirmorum in monasterium".

22 Hildegard von Bingen, *Causae et Curae*, trans. by M. Pawlik and P. Madigan, ed. by M. Palmquist and J. Kulas (Collegeville, MN: Liturgical Press, 1994); Hildegard von Bingen, *Physica*, trans. P. Throop (Rochester, Vermont: Healing Arts Press, 1998).

23 J. J. Walsh, *The Popes and Science: The history of papal relations to science during the middle ages down to our own time* (New York: Fordham University Press, 1915), pp. 249–251.

24 The Order of the Holy Ghost was a Roman Catholic religious order, founded by Guy de Montpellier in Provence for the care of the sick by groups of lay people. The order was officially established by Pope Innocent III (c. 1161–June 16, 1216) in Santo Spirito in Sassia in Rome.

25 See L. Lallemand, *Histoire de la charité* III (Picard: Paris, 1906), pp. 92–100.

4

Pope Gregory XIII and his Calendar

We have arranged a gathering in the Holy City, to reform the calendar, of the very qualified men on the matter whom we had chosen from the principal countries of the Christian world a long time before. Those, after having devoted much time and attention to this work and having discussed between them cycles which they had collected from everywhere, old ones as well as modern ones, and as they had carefully studied the reflections and the opinions of erudite men who wrote on this subject, chose and preferred this cycle of epacts, adding to it elements which, after thorough examination, appeared essential to the realization of a perfect calendar.

Pope Gregory XIII, Bull *Inter Gravissimas*

Pope Gregory XIII succeeded Pope St Pius V, and he was born at Bologna in 1502 as Ugo Buoncompagni. He sprang from a Bolognese family, which, according to tradition, hailed from Umbria, and which belonged to the middle classes. His father, Cristoforo, who was born in 1470, and died in 1546, had been a merchant, and by his skill had raised his family to a certain level of affluence; nevertheless, the beautiful palace which he built near the Duomo was finer than his means warranted. Cristoforo was distinguished for his piety and his generosity towards the poor. By his marriage to Angela Marescalchi, Cristoforo Buoncompagni took his place among the aristocracy of Bologna. Of his four sons, Ugo, who was born on 1 January 1502, devoted himself with distinction to the study of law in the university of his birthplace. He obtained various academic degrees, and, at twenty-eight he graduated as a doctor with sufficient distinction to become a professor of law in the University of Bologna between the years 1531–1537, and 1538–1539. Among his pupils he numbered, together with Ippolito Riminaldi, who became celebrated in the study of law, five other students who later on became cardinals, and rendered great services to the Catholic Church: Otto Truchsess, Reginald Pole, Cristoforo Madruzzo, Francesco Alciati and Alessandro Farnese.[1]

His career illustrates very well the reality of the Catholic "reformation" in the sixteenth century. As a young man, and a young professor in minor orders, Ugo's conduct was not unblemished. Since his education had been to all intents and purposes of a worldly character, he had not, though he was in himself of a religious turn of mind, altogether escaped the profane influence of the dying Renaissance. It was therefore of decisive importance for him that he should have completed his period of development and maturity in close contact with St Charles Borromeo.[2] By 1538 he changed his ways and was ordained, after which his life was exemplary and notably austere. He attracted the attention of Pope Paul III who used his talents as a canon lawyer. Under Pope Paul IV he was unfortunately associated with Cardinal Carlo Carafa, and Pius IV continued to encourage him, making him a cardinal, and sending him to the Council of Trent.

He was elected pope on 13 May 1572 after a conclave lasting three days. The Romans welcomed the elevation of Cardinal Buoncompagni, principally because neither a religious nor an austere Theatine had been elected, as most people had feared.[3] The good nature of the new Pope confirmed the court in the opinion that he would prove himself, as it was put in an expressive saying of the time, a "*buon compagno*". The ambassadors built happy auguries on the fact that Pope Gregory XIII had lived so long in the Curia as to have passed through all the ranks of office, and had thus acquired a deep knowledge of practical jurisprudence.

Gregory had high hopes of the reconciliation of Sweden. John III of Sweden had married a Polish princess who was a Catholic. Under her influence King John submitted to Rome. He was not prepared to allow the resumption of communion between the Swedish Church and Rome to cause political trouble. The pope, in a most statesmanlike way, abandoned all claims to the confiscated Church property although this would have impoverished the Swedish Church. Unfortunately John Ill's conversion was not very deep and he reverted to Lutheranism. His son was, however, brought up a sincere Catholic but was later driven from Sweden because of his faith.

In political matters Gregory's pontificate was not distinguished but in other spheres he was a true leader of the Catholic reform. Perhaps most important was the enormously enhanced prestige the Holy See was gaining under a series of popes of respectable life. In 1572 the Venetian ambassador remarked that nothing had done more for the good of the Church than this succession of popes of irreproachable life. Gregory also worked tirelessly for the completion of the work of the Council of Trent. He put all his energy behind the creation of diocesan seminaries for the proper education of the clergy. He himself founded or substantially contributed to twenty-three of them. He gave generously to the Roman College —he was reckoned its second founder—the nucleus of the present Gregorian University. He also founded the German and English Colleges. Gregory began the work of reconciling the dissident Orthodox Churches. While insisting on the correctness of the Latin version of the Creed and the Latin custom of using unleavened bread in the Mass, he permitted the use of leavened bread where it had been customary. He founded a Greek college in Rome. Much was sown in his time that bore fruit later on, and he set important precedents.

The religious orders were not forgotten. The Jesuits and Theatines, the two representative orders of the Catholic Reformation, were supported. In 1575 the modern Oratory was founded by St Philip Neri whose influence in Rome was rapidly growing. Gregory carried on his predecessor's work of improving the quality of the episcopate. He began the practice of keeping lists of suitable priests from each country, who might be made bishops with advantage to the Church. He also reformed papal ceremonials and protocol. He had been a distinguished canon lawyer. It had already been noticed that the Church needed an up-to-date and authoritative collection of the established laws of the Church. Pius V had started a commission for this purpose on which Gregory, as cardinal, had been the leading light. In 1582 the work was completed and the edition of the *Corpus Iuris Canonici* was completed. It remained substantially the law book of the Church until the present century.

The most spectacular event of the pontificate for contemporaries, and the achievement Gregory was most proud of, was the reform of the calendar. The calendar in use went back to the Romans and the time of Julius Caesar. The Romans had not been able to calculate the length of the solar year with complete accuracy and by the sixteenth century the calendar year was ten days "slow". That is it was ten days behind the sun. The Council of Trent had required some reform of the liturgical calendar, and this was seen to need some correction of Julius Caesar's calculations. Under Gregory's orders an extremely accurate calendar was constructed and proposals for replacing the Julian calendar were put to all the Catholic courts of Europe. The princes consented; the fourth of October, 1582 was followed by the fifteenth of October and the Gregorian calendar was in force. It was a most impressive piece of international co-operation. The non-Catholic countries continued to resist this necessary reform out of hostility toward the pope. The English adopted it in 1751. The Russians held out until the Revolution with the odd result that the famous "October Revolution" actually took place in November. Gregory also invented leap years in their present form. The "day" of the changeover in 1582 was notable also as the day of the death of St Teresa of Avila.

The Reform of the Calendar

The Council of Trent approved a plan in 1563 for correcting the errors in the calendar. Since the First Council of Nicaea in 325, Easter has been celebrated on the first Sunday after the first full moon after the spring equinox (that is, 21 March, when day and night are exactly the same length). In the thirteenth century Joannes Campanus and the Franciscan, Roger Bacon, had laid their suggestions before the Holy See for a reform. In the thirteenth century the chancellor of Oxford University and bishop of Lincoln Robert Grosseteste noticed that the true vernal equinox had drifted with respect to the calendar prediction, by more than a week towards earlier dates.[4] In 1344 Pope Clement VI had the question examined by a body of scientists. Pierre d'Ailly and Nicholas of Cusa brought the issue before the Councils of Constance and Basle, but the matter did not then seem to be ripe for decision. The plans of Sixtus IV, who summoned to Rome the celebrated Johannes Müller von Königsberg (6 June 1436–6 July 1476) (Regiomontanus) for the reform of the calendar, unfortunately came to nothing owing to the premature death of that scholar. Again, during the pontificate of Pope Leo X, who energetically reopened the question, no decision was reached. The Fathers of the Council of Trent, who had to deal with more important questions, left the matter to the Holy See at their last session. Neither Pius IV, in spite of requests which came from many quarters, nor St Pius V, arrived at any solution of this difficult question. With all the greater energy, therefore, did Gregory XIII take up the matter of a reform which was daily becoming more necessary.

At the height of the Counter Reformation, one of many reaffirmations made during the Council of Trent was the necessity of celebrating Easter on the correct date. Following the instructions of the Council of Trent, Pope Gregory XIII assembled a commission of scholars around 1572 to help determine how to correct the roughly one-day-per-century shortfall of the ancient Roman calendar, and how to determine the date of Easter in a way that would be practical for a Christendom that was now spreading from East Asia to the Americas.

In 1577, a Compendium was sent to expert mathematicians outside the reform commission for comments.[5] Some of these experts, including Giambattista Benedetti and Giuseppe Moleto, believed Easter should be computed from the true motions of the sun and moon, rather than using mean motions, but these recommendations were not adopted.[6] The reform adopted was a modification of a proposal made by the Calabrian doctor Aloysius Lilius (or Luigi Giglio in Italian).[7] Lilius's proposal included reducing the number of leap years in four centuries from 100 to 97, by making 3 out of 4 centurial years common instead of leap years: this part of the proposal had been suggested before by Pietro Pitati among others. Lilius also produced an original and practical scheme for adjusting the epacts of the moon when calculating the annual date of Easter, solving a long-standing obstacle to calendar reform.

Lilius's proposals consisted of two components. First, he proposed a correction to the length of the year. The mean tropical year is 365.24219 days long, while the mean vernal equinox year is 365.2424 days.[8] As the average length of a Julian year is 365.25 days, the Julian year is almost 11 minutes longer than the mean year. The discrepancy results in a drift of about three days every 400 years. Lilius' proposal resulted in an average year of 365.2425 days.[9] The discrepancy between the tropical year and the calendar year in Lilius' plan was just a little more than 24 seconds.[10] At the time of Gregory's reform there had already been a drift of 10 days since the Council of Nicaea, resulting in the vernal equinox falling on 11 March instead of the ecclesiastically fixed date of 21 March, and if unreformed it would have drifted further. Lilius proposed that the 10-day drift should be corrected by deleting the Julian leap day on each of its ten occurrences over a period of 40 years, thereby providing for a gradual return of the equinox to 21 March. Lilius' work was expanded upon by Christopher Clavius in a closely-argued, 800-page volume.[11] He would later defend his work and that of Lilius against detractors. Clavius' opinion was that the correction should take place in one move, and it was this advice which prevailed with Gregory.

The second component consisted of an approximation which would provide an accurate yet simple, rule-based calendar. Lilius' formula was a 10-day correction to revert the drift since the Council of Nicaea, and the imposition of a leap day in only 97 years in 400 rather than in 1 year in 4. The proposed rule was that years divisible by 100 would be leap years only if they were divisible by 400 as well.

Because the spring equinox was tied to the date of Easter, the Catholic Church considered the seasonal drift in the date of Easter undesirable. The Church of Alexandria celebrated Easter on the Sunday after the 14th day of the moon (computed using the Metonic cycle) that falls on or after the vernal equinox, which they placed on 21 March. However, the Church of Rome still regarded 25 March as the equinox (until 342) and used a different cycle to compute the 14th day of the moon.[12] In the Alexandrian system, since the 14th day of the Easter moon could fall at earliest on 21 March its first day could fall no earlier than 8 March and no later than 5 April. This meant that Easter varied between 22 March and 25 April. In Rome, Easter was not allowed to fall later than 21 April, that being the day of the *Parilia* or birthday of Rome and a pagan festival. The first day of the Easter moon could fall no earlier than 5 March and no later than 2 April.

Easter was the Sunday after the 15th day of this moon, whose 14th day was allowed to precede the equinox. Where the two systems produced different dates there was generally a compromise so that both churches were able to celebrate on the same day. By the 10th century all the churches (except some on the eastern border of the Byzantine Empire) had adopted the Alexandrian Easter, which still placed the vernal equinox on 21 March, although Bede had already noted its drift in 725—it had drifted even further by the sixteenth century.[13]

Furthermore, the reckoned Moon that was used to compute Easter was fixed to the Julian year by a 19-year cycle. That approximation built up an error of one day every 310 years, so by the sixteenth century the lunar calendar was out of phase with the real Moon by four days. The 19-year cycle used for the lunar calendar was also to be corrected by one day every 300 or 400 years (8 times in 2500 years) along with corrections for the years that are no longer leap years (namely 1700, 1800, 1900, 2100, and so forth). In fact, a new method for computing the date of Easter was introduced.

On 24 February 1582, Pope Gregory XIII published his Bull *Inter gravissimas* reforming the calendar. The Bull identified what was necessary for the correct determination of the date of Easter: correct placement of the northern vernal equinox; correct identification of the 14th day of the moon (effectively full moon) that happens on or next after the vernal equinox, and the first Sunday that follows that full moon. Easter was to be computed with reference not only to the new March 21, but also by the use of new Paschal tables.

Pope Gregory dropped 10 days to bring the calendar back into synchronisation with the seasons. Accordingly, when the new calendar was put in use, the error accumulated in the 13 centuries since the Council of Nicaea was corrected by a deletion of ten days. The Julian calendar day Thursday, 4 October 1582 was followed by the first day of the Gregorian calendar, Friday, 15 October 1582 (the cycle of weekdays was not affected). These 10 missing days were not to be counted in calculating end days of loans, taxes and the like. The Bull also achieved a reduction of the number of leap years. Centennial years, such as 1700, 1800, and 1900 ceased to be leap years, but years that can be divided by 400, such as 1600 and 2000 continued to be such.

On the occasion of the fourth centenary of the promulgation of the Gregorian Calendar, Pope St John Paul II highlighted the importance of research in the area where we seek to blend the rhythms of human life in society with the fundamental rhythms of the universe in which we live. This study helps to stress the unity between man and creation which testifies to the existence of the one Creator.[14] The Church has had a profound personal interest and continues to have such an interest, concerning calendar revisions, since such work influences the occurrence of religious feasts which constitute, as it were, the rhythm of the Church's daily life. Pope John Paul II added that "examination of how the Gregorian Calendar was received by various societies and by various Churches will surely be of great help to all of us in these days when we sincerely seek a strengthening of that unity which Christ desired for his Church."[15]

Pontifical Gregorian University

Background and History

On 18 February 1551, St Ignatius of Loyola, founder of the Society of Jesus, set up the first school of the Jesuit fathers with its first library in a Roman palace (no longer existent) located at the foot of the Capitol, in the Via Capitolina (today Piazza d'Aracoeli), and this was called the Roman College. It was known as a school of Grammar, Humanity, and Christian Doctrine and St Francis Borgia, the viceking of Catalonia who became a Jesuit, provided financial patronage. Within a year, the site was transferred to a larger facility behind the church of San Stefano del Cacco due to the large number of students seeking enrolment. After only two years of existence, the Roman College already counted 250 alumni. In January 1556, Pope Paul IV authorized the College to confer academic degrees in theology and philosophy, thereby raising the school to the rank of university. During the following two decades, due once again to an increased number of students, the university changed its location twice. During this period, a chair in moral philosophy was added, as well as a chair in Arabic, alongside the already-existing chairs in Latin, Greek, and Hebrew.

The university enjoyed enormous success, and counted more than a thousand pupils in its ranks at the start of the pontificate of Pope Gregory XIII, who wished to assign it more suitable premises. Two blocks near the Via del Corso were expropriated, and the architect Bartolomeo Ammannati was commissioned to design a fine new edifice for the institute. The new building was inaugurated in 1584, in what became known as the *Piazza del Collegio Romano*, across from the Palazzo Doria Pamphilj. For his sponsorship of the Roman College, Gregory XIII became known as its founder and protector, and from that point the school acquired the title of the Gregorian University.

The university in its new space was able to increase the number of disciplines that were taught. New chairs of Church history and liturgy were added. At this time, the university also attained great prestige in the fields of mathematics, physics, and astronomy. The Gregorian calendar as has been seen, established by Gregory XIII, was developed by the Jesuit Christopher Clavius, a professor of the university at the time. The illustrious Jesuit mathematician, physicist, and inventor Athanasius Kircher also taught at the university during this period. Not long after the new buildings were opened, the student body increased to over two thousand. The university chapel, too small for so many students, was rebuilt as the Church of Sant'Ignazio between 1626 and 1650, becoming one of the major Baroque churches of the area.

In 1773, following the suppression of the Society of Jesus, the College was committed to the care of the Roman secular clergy. The College was then returned to the re-established Company of Jesus on 17 May 1824 by Pope Leo XII. Following the takeover of Rome by the revolutionary army of the new Kingdom of Italy in 1870, the new Italian government confiscated the property of the university and its buildings, which then became the Liceo Ginnasio Ennio Quirino Visconti. This forced the university to move once again in 1873, this time to the Palazzo Gabrielli-Borromeo on the Via del Seminario, now home to the Bellarmine College. In that same year, after the University of Rome *La Sapienza* became the Roman university of the Italian state, Pope Blessed Pius IX, with the Rescript of 4 December 1873, bestowed upon the Roman College the name of Pontifical University of the Roman College. Furthermore, he also gave the Rector of the College the right to sign himself as the Rector of the Pontifical Gregorian University.

During this difficult period, the academic endeavours of the university were dramatically affected. Due to a lack of space, the university had to reduce its faculties to theology and philosophy. The number of students also dropped substantially, so that in 1875 no more than 250 students were registered. However, the university was gradually able to recover again. In 1876, the Faculty of Canon Law was transferred from the University of Rome *La Sapienza* to the Gregorian, and the latter was gradually able to resume the teaching of many disciplines.

By the early twentieth century, the Gregorian had grown so much that, in 1919, Pope Benedict XIV bought a plot of land at Piazza della Pilotta in the heart of Rome on the edge of the Quirinal Hill, near the Trevi Fountain. It was a magnificent location in one of the more suggestively quiet and more characteristically papal squares in the centre of Rome, at the foot of the Quirinal Palace, facing the monumental Villa Colonna. Then Pope Pius XI repeatedly expressed the firm desire that the construction of the new building for the Gregorian University should be delayed no longer. The laying of the foundation stone with the customary rite was celebrated by His Eminence Cardinal Bisleti on 27 December 1924, the feast day of St John the Evangelist, the beloved apostle of the Heart of Jesus: to His divine Heart this noble and arduous enterprise was entrusted in a special way. The new building constructed there was inaugurated in 1930.

From the very beginning the Roman College has played a key role in scientific questions. An early example is the reform of the calendar, which became known as the Gregorian Calendar, which we have just discussed. Among its famed scientists was Christopher Clavius, one of the most influential seventeenth-century mathematicians and friend of Galileo, who also was indebted to the Roman College for his own scientific formation.

Today the Gregorian University has 6 faculties (Theology, Philosophy, Canon Law, History and the Cultural Patrimony of the Church, Missiology, Social Sciences), 4 institutes (Spirituality, Psychology, Religious Sciences, Religion and Culture), various centres, schools, and special programs of study. It numbers approximately 3000 students who represent 122 countries, 800 dioceses and 90 religious congregations from every continent. About 20% of the bishops and 40% of the cardinals in the Church studied at the Gregorian and 17 popes studied there as well. There are around 380 professors–140 Jesuits, 95 lay and 125 priests or members of religious communities–who make up the faculty.

Pope Benedict XVI at the Pontifical Gregorian University

On 3 November 2006, Pope Benedict XVI visited the Pontifical Gregorian University. He addressed the students and professors in the following terms:

> Since its origins as the *Collegium Romanum*, the Gregorian University has been distinguished for the study of philosophy and theology. (...) Today, one must take into account the confrontation with secular culture in many parts of the world, which not only tends to deny every sign of God's presence in the life of society and of the individual, but, with various means that bewilder and cloud the upright human conscience, is seeking to corrode the human being's capacity and readiness to listen to God. Moreover, it is impossible to ignore relations with other religions, which will only prove constructive if we avoid all forms of ambiguity, which in a certain way undermine the essential content of Christian faith in Christ, the one Savior of all mankind, and in the Church, the necessary sacrament of salvation for all humanity.[16]

Pope Benedict XVI recalled the other human sciences which are encouraged at this famous University in the wake of the glorious academic tradition of the Roman College. He mentioned how the Gregorian Calendar, enabled by his predecessor, Gregory XIII, was compiled in 1582 by Fr Christopher Clavius, a Lecturer at the Roman College. Today, the natural sciences are no longer taught at the Gregorian University, but have been replaced by other human sciences such as psychology, the social sciences and social communications. Thus, man desires to be more deeply understood, both in his profound personal dimension and his external dimension as a builder of society in justice and peace, and as a communicator of the truth. For the very reason that these sciences concern the human being, they cannot set aside reference to God. In fact, man, both in his interiority and in his exteriority, cannot be fully understood unless he recognizes that he is open to transcendence.

Deprived of his reference to God, man cannot respond to the fundamental questions that trouble and will always trouble his heart concerning the end of his life, hence, also its meaning. As a result, it is no longer possible to introduce into society those ethical values that alone can guarantee a co-existence worthy of man. Human destiny without reference to God cannot but be the desolation of anguish, which leads to desperation. Only in reference to God's Love which is revealed in Jesus Christ can man find the meaning of his existence and live in hope, even if he must face evils that injure his personal existence and the society in which he lives. Hope ensures that man does not withdraw into a paralyzing and sterile nihilism but opens himself instead to generous commitment within the society where he lives in order to improve it. This is the task that God entrusted to man when he created him in his own image and likeness, a task that fills every human being with the greatest possible dignity, but also with an immense responsibility.[17]

Notes

1 L. von Pastor, *History of the Popes* 19 (London: Kegan Paul, 1930), p. 17.

2 *Ibid.*, p. 20.

3 "Questo popolo di Roma sta molto allegro poiche non hanno fatto papa ne frate ne chietino come si dubitava." Report of Cusano, Rome, May 13 1572, State Archives, Vienna.

4 See J. D. North, "The Western Calendar—'Intolerabilis, Horribilis, et Derisibilis'; Four Centuries of Discontent" in G. V. Coyne, M. A. Hoskin, & O. Pedersen, *Gregorian Reform of the Calendar: Proceedings of the Vatican Conference to Commemorate its 400th Anniversary 1582-1982* (Vatican City: Pontificia Academia Scientiarum, 1983), pp. 75–113.

5 The term Compendium is short for *Compendium novae rationis restituendi kalendarium* (Romae: apud haeredes Antonij Bladij, 1577). In English this is the *Compendium of the New Plan for*

Restoring the Calendar.

6 See A. Ziggelaar, "The Papal Bull of 1582 promulgating a Reform of the Calendar" in Coyne, Hoskin, Pedersen, *Gregorian Reform of the Calendar*, pp. 214–215.

7 See G. Moyer, "Aloisius Lilius and the Compendium Novae Rationis Restituendi Kalendarium" in Coyne, Hoskin, Pedersen, *Gregorian Reform of the Calendar*, pp. 171–188.

8 J. Meeus & D. Savoie, "The history of the tropical year" in *Journal of the British Astronomical Association* 102/1 (1992), pp. 40–42.

9 This is 365;14,33 days in sexagesimal notation—the length of the tropical year, rounded to two sexagesimal positions; this was the value used in the major astronomical tables of the day.

10 See Moyer, "Aloisius Lilius and the Compendium Novae Rationis Restituendi Kalendarium", p. 181.

11 See U. Baldini, "Christoph Clavius and the Scientific Scene in Rome" in Coyne, Hoskin, Pedersen, *Gregorian Reform of the Calendar*, pp. 137–169.

12 See O Pedersen, "The Ecclesiastical Calendar and the Life of the Church" in Coyne, Hoskin, Pedersen, *Gregorian Reform of the Calendar*, pp. 42–44.

13 See *ibid.*, pp. 54–59.

14 Pope St John Paul II, *Address on the occasion of the 400th Anniversary of the Gregorian Calendar* (31 August 1982), 2.

15 *Ibid.*, 2.

16 Pope Benedict XVI, Discourse at the Pontifical Gregorian University (3 November 2006).

17 See *ibid.*

5

THE PONTIFICAL ACADEMY OF SCIENCES

Our gatherings have also enabled me to clarify important aspects of the Church's doctrine and life relating to scientific research. We are united in our common desire to correct misunderstandings and even more to allow ourselves to be enlightened by the one Truth which governs the world and guides the lives of all men and women. I am more and more convinced that scientific truth, which is itself a participation in divine Truth, can help philosophy and theology to understand ever more fully the human person and God's Revelation about man, a Revelation that is completed and perfected in Jesus Christ. For this important mutual enrichment in the search for the truth and the benefit of mankind, I am, with the whole Church, profoundly grateful.

Pope St John Paul II, *Address on the Fourth Centenary of the Pontifical Academy of Sciences* (10 November 2003)

THE ROOTS OF the Pontifical Academy of Sciences can be traced back to the post-Renaissance epoch. Its origins lie in the ancient *Accademia dei Lincei,* (the Academy of Lynxes) established on 17 August 1603 by Prince Federico Cesi (1585–1630) when he had just reached the age of eighteen.[1] Cesi was a botanist and naturalist, the son of the Duke of Acquasparta, and a member of a noble Roman family. Three other young men took part in this initiative: Giovanni Heck, a Dutch physician aged twenty-seven; Francesco Stelluti di Fabriano, a mathematician; and the polymath Anastasio de Filiis de Terni.

Early history

The four men chose the name *Lincei* (lynxes) from Giambattista della Porta's book *Magia Naturalis*, which had an illustration of this fabled cat on the cover and the words "… with lynx-like eyes, examining those things which manifest themselves, so that having observed them, he may zealously use them".[2] Their emblem was a lynx battling with Cerberus, the guardian of the underworld, invoking the lynx's reputation for seeing through falsehood and discovering the truth.[3] The sharp vision of the lynx symbolizes the observational prowess that scientists require, in order to penetrate the secrets of nature, observing it at both microscopic and macroscopic levels. Cesi bestowed his own motto on the Academy, which was: "Take care of small things if you want to obtain the greatest results."[4]

The first headquarters of the fledgling Academy was the Palazzo Cesi situated in the Via Maschera d'Oro in Rome. The members lived communally and almost monastically in this house, where Cesi provided them with books and laboratory equipment. The new ideals of science and faith that animated this Academy can be expressed succinctly by the spirit of linceality.[5] This concept is often found in the letters of Federico Cesi and corresponds to an ideal of the religious lay person devoted to study, celibacy and scientific research, the basic source for acquiring knowledge of the wonderful work of God the Creator. Interestingly the Palazzo Cesi is not far from St Philip Neri's church of Santa Maria in Vallicella, and there is evidence that this church was linked with the Cesi family.[6]

Thus it was that the first Academy of its kind dedicated to the sciences came into being, and it took its place alongside the other Academies—of literature, history, philosophy and art—which had arisen in the humanistic climate of the Renaissance. The example of Cesi and of the group of scholars led by him was followed some years later in other countries—the Royal Society was created in London in 1662 and the Académie des Sciences was established in France in 1666.

Galileo was inducted to the exclusive Academy on 25 December 1611, and became its intellectual centre. Galileo clearly felt honoured by his association with the Academy for he adopted *Galileo Galilei Linceo* as his signature. The Academy published his works and supported him throughout his disputes with the Roman Inquisition. Federico Cesi engaged in an important activity of mediation between the Roman theological world and Galileo, eventually advising the latter to not insist in his polemics about the interpretation of Holy Scripture, so that he could dedicate himself in a more effective way to scientific research.[7] Among the Academy's early publications in the fields of astronomy, physics and botany were the study of sunspots and the famous *Saggiatore* of Galileo.

From the records of the meetings they held in Cesi's house, we know that the members of the *Accademia dei Lincei* discussed and shared ideas on a wide range of subjects. They examined the contents of Plato's works, the constitution of the universe and the structure of matter. One of the most important topics they broached was the origin of plant life: the reproduction, generation and classification of plants.[8] Both in Rome and in Acquasparta, Cesi had organized a chemical laboratory, in which the Linceans could repeatedly perform experiments using distillation in their search for the hidden nature of vegetables.[9] Cesi carried out numerous experiments of this kind by liquefying the solid part of the plants. His purpose was to discover the corpuscular components that made up plants and all types of vegetable life.[10]

Interestingly, Cesi's scientific method differed from those used by herbalists and alchemists of his time, as it was both practical and theoretical. In Cesi's view, research had to be supported by philosophical ideas and connected to a broad concept of nature, wherein all beings were closely bound and joined together in a continuous chain. The Roman prince had a vivid imagination and was able to develop many techniques belonging to the use of memory. These techniques enabled him to conceive a kind of scientific method different from Aristotelian and Scholastic tenets. In some ways, Cesi regarded nature as a great living entity which had a propensity to conciliate all its quantitative and qualitative substances.[11] The Linceans immediately attempted to get in touch with the most prominent naturalists in Europe: they wrote to Jean Robin in Paris,[12] Johannes Kepler in Prague,[13] Charles l'Écluse in Leiden,[14] Kaspar Bahuin in Basel,[15] Matthias de l'Obel in London,[16] and Thomas Mermann in Cologne.[17]

By the middle of the sixteenth century, the European naturalists already had a vast knowledge of American plants and animals. Medicinal herbs and spices had been traded for a long time, and this evoked the need for more and more well-documented catalogues and lists of American natural resources. The American medicinal plants were the main interest of European naturalists. This interest greatly increased when, in 1526, Gonzalo Fernández de Oviedo published his *Historia general y natural de las Indias occidentales*, consisting of a documentary catalogue of Central American medicinal plants.[18]

In 1570, Francisco Hernández departed from Spain in order to classify and catalogue for King Philip II the naturalistic riches of the overseas colonies; Philip II's chief desire was to possess a full and systematic catalogue of the resources that could be exploited and marketed. During his stay in Mexico, Hernández made use of numerous Native American physicians and painters, whom he ordered to gather as many natural specimens as possible and reproduce exact images. Concerned about finding a suitable system of classification, he asked for particular care in reproducing the colours of plants and animals. To denote the specimens he maintained the original native Náhuatl names.[19]

In 1576, Hernández forwarded sixteen manuscripts to Madrid which contained texts and pictures, and Philip II ordered their conservation in the Royal Library at the Escorial, awaiting their publication. Two years later, the King decided to assign this task to his new personal physician, the Neapolitan Leonardo Antonio Recchi, who was ordered to prepare a selection from the Hernández work to be printed. Recchi, who finished his work in 1582, drafted a naturalist treatise which focused on the most important medicinal plants gathered by his predecessor in Mexico, and made exact copies of their images. Recchi's selection was printed for the first time without pictures in Mexico, edited by the Dominican Francisco Ximénez in 1615.[20]

Cesi bought Petilio Recchi's text in Rome and also made a copy of all the appended pictures. After coming into possession of these papers, Cesi scheduled their publication. At the beginning, he deemed it useful to print only Recchi's text with pictures and a short commentary, but later he decided to add two large commentaries. He entrusted the task of the edition of the first part to Johannes Schreck, an interesting Lincean figure of German origin. Schreck became a member of the Academy but soon left when he decided to become a Jesuit.[21]

Cesi copied and printed all the pictures of the American plants edited by Schreck and, in 1613, a great assortment of the engravings were bound in a book which was presented to the bishop of Bamberg, Johannes Gottfried Ashhaunsen, the extraordinary imperial ambassador to Pope Paul V.[22] When Cesi started printing the Recchi manuscript, he decided to change its original arrangement, and divided its four books into ten, the first one concerning the methodology of natural history, the following seven devoted to Mexican plants, and the last two respectively dedicated to the animals and minerals of the New World.

Cesi added a wide commentary on Mexican animals arranged by Johannes Faber, whose title was *Aliorum Novae Hispaniae Animalium* [...] *imagines et nomina* to the first section of his Mexican Treasury. This commentary was printed separately and with its own title page in 1628. Cesi also added the *Annotationes et Additiones* of the Neapolitan Fabio Colonna, which provided a considerable amount of information lacking in Schreck's notes. All these sections were bound together with extensive onomastic and analytical indexes, arranged by Francesco Stelluti. Cesi enlisted the talents of the German artist, Matthias Greuter who was then active in Rome, to design an imposing and allegorical title page, including a map of the Mexican territories and cities. Shortly before publication, Cesi resolved to add his *Tabulae phytosophicae* to the book. It was a laborious text, arranged in tabular form and intended as a large botanical encyclopaedia. However, in 1628 only thirteen *Tabulae* out of twenty were finished. Meanwhile, two years before, Cassiano dal Pozzo and Cardinal Francesco Barberini had found the original manuscripts of Hernández, and they asked the librarian of the Escorial, Andrés de los Reyes, to compile a large summary of what was contained in the zoological and mineralogical books, as well as an index of their botanical elements. Cassiano and Barberini took these documents to Rome and Cesi planned to publish the summary in the Mexican Treasury as the second book of the whole work.[23]

Finally, in 1628, the *Rerum medicarum thesaurus novae Hispaniae* later known as the *Tesoro Messicano* (Mexican Treasury) describing the flora, fauna and geography of the New World, was published in Rome. With this publication, the first, most famous phase of the Lincei was concluded. The Mexican Treasury is important historically for at least two general reasons. The Linceans were the first in Europe to conceive an encyclopedic group project, joining texts and pictures systematically. Until that time, nobody had scheduled such a large and annotated naturalistic encyclopaedia concerning the New World, carefully cross-referencing pictures of plants, animals, and minerals with morphological, classificatory, and medical information, as well as suggesting parallels between European and American specimens.[24] The second general reason lies in its large use of original materials, made up in Central America by skilful Native Americans, with special knowledge in botany and medicine. The Linceans did not lack respect for the Náhuatl language nor for the medical and naturalistic customs of the Native Americans.[25]

The new usage of microscopy, with "references to magnification tools can be found in the works of Galileo and several Lincei, Harvey, Gassendi, Marco Aurelio Severino—who was probably also in contact with the Lincei—and Nathanial Highmore".[26] Microscopes were not used by the Lincei just for astronomical and mathematical work, but also for new experimentations in anatomy, as this was the era of the rise of mechanistic anatomy, and the theories of atomism.

The religious dimension of the Academy is evident; it was placed under the protection of St John the Evangelist who was often portrayed in the miniatures of its publications with an eagle and a lynx, both of which were symbols of sight and reason. It was therefore conceived as an assembly of scholars whose goal—as one can read in its Rules—was knowledge and wisdom of things to be obtained not only through living together with honesty and piety, but with the further goal of communicating them peacefully to men without causing any harm.[27] Nature was envisaged not only as a subject of study but also of contemplation. Amongst the suggestions of the Rules, is to pray before study and work: "the Lynxes, before doing anything at all, must first raise their minds to God, and humbly pray to Him and invoke the intercession of the saints."[28] Amongst the practices of the spiritual piety of the members featured the celebration of the liturgical Office of the Blessed Virgin Mary and the Psalter. For this reason, the religious inspiration of the *Accademia dei Lincei* cannot be overlooked, nor can it be reduced to an "almost mystical glow of the school of Pythagoras". The high moral figure of Cesi acted to guarantee the sincere and loyal profession of its religious faith.[29]

Cesi's intense activity was cut short by his sudden death in 1630 at only forty-five years old. Galileo was about to finish his work, the *Dialogo sui Massimi Sistemi,* the manuscript of which Galileo wanted to send to Cesi himself so that the latter could organise its publication. After Cesi's death the activities of the Academy diminished and this eventually brought about its closure.

Refounding the Academy

The first attempts to bring the *Lincei* back to life took place in 1745 in Rimini thanks to the efforts of a group of scientists belonging to the circle made up of Giovanni Paolo Simone Bianchi (known as Janus Plancus), Stefano Galli and Giuseppe Garampi. However, this new Academy sadly enjoyed a very short life. The attempt at refoundation made by Padre Feliciano Scarpellini (1762–1840) in Rome at the beginning of the nineteenth century met with greater success. He gave the name of *Lincei* to a private academy that he had established in 1795. Despite a lack of funds and many other difficulties, Scarpellini managed to keep the name of the *Lincei* alive, and he gathered together into a single academic body the various scientists working in the Papal States such as the mathematician Domenico Chelini, the naturalist Carlo Bonaparte, the anatomist Alessandro Flajani, the chemists Domenico Morichini and Pietro Peretti, Prince Baldassarre Odescalchi, the physicists Gioacchino Pessuti and Paolo Volpicelli, and the physician Benedetto Viale.[30]

The authorities of the Papal States took new practical initiatives to refound the Academy during the first half of the nineteenth century in response to the wishes of Popes Pius VII (1800–1823) and Leo XII (1823–1829), allocating the second floor of Palazzo Senatorio in Campidoglio to the Academy as its headquarters. In 1847 Blessed Pius IX officially renewed the Academy with the name (already suggested by Gregory XVI in 1838) of the *Accademia Pontificia dei Nuovi Lincei* (the Pontifical Academy of the New Lynxes). New statutes were drawn up, which envisaged, amongst other things, the presence of thirty resident members and forty correspondent members. During this period of activity famous astronomers and priests were present within its ranks, such as Francesco de Vico and

Angelo Secchi. During the violent revolutionary upheavals of 1848, the Roman Republic sought to expel the Academy from the Campidoglio. However, the institution managed to hold on to its headquarters by using various bureaucratic manoeuvres. In 1870, following the fall of the independent Papal States and the unification of the Kingdom of Italy, the Academy divided into two different institutions: the *Reale Accademia dei Lincei,* which later became the present *Accademia Nazionale dei Lincei* with its headquarters in Palazzo Corsini alla Lungara, and the *Accademia Pontificia dei Nuovi Lincei,* which was transferred from the Campidoglio to the Casina Pio IV villa in the Vatican Gardens.[31]

Pope Pius XI

The real renewal of the Academy only took place in 1936, in response to the insistent requests of the Jesuit Father Giuseppe Gianfranceschi. This scientist was Professor of Physics at the Pontifical Gregorian University and had been the President of the Accademia Pontificia dei Nuovi Lincei since 1921. A new Pontifical Academy of Sciences was thus created on 28 October 1936 by Pope Pius XI (1922–1939) with his Motu Proprio *In Multis Solaciis.*

The goals and the hopes of the Academy, within the context of the dialogue between science and faith, were expressed by Pius XI in the following way in the Motu Proprio which brought about its refoundation:

> Amongst the many consolations with which divine Goodness has wished to make happy the years of our Pontificate, I am happy to place that of our having being able to see not a few of those who dedicate themselves to the studies of the sciences mature their attitude and their intellectual approach towards religion. Science, as a real cognition of

> things, is never in contrast with the truths of the Christian faith. Indeed, as is well known to those who study the history of science, it must be recognised on the one hand that the Roman Pontiffs and the Catholic Church have always fostered the research of the learned in the experimental field as well, and on the other hand that such research has opened up the way to the defence of the deposit of supernatural truths entrusted to the Church.[32]

Over forty years later, on 10 November 1979, Pope St John Paul II once again emphasized the role and goals of the Academy, commemorating, at the same time, the centenary of the birth of Albert Einstein:

> The existence of this Pontifical Academy of Sciences, with which Galileo was associated in a certain way through the old institution which preceded the present one, to which eminent scientists belong today, is a visible sign which manifests, without any form of racial or religious discrimination, the deep harmony that can exist between the truths of science and the truths of faith ... The Church of Rome united with all those in the world, attaches great importance to the function of the Pontifical Academy of Sciences. The title "Pontifical" attributed to this Academy signifies, as you know, the interest and support of the Church. These are manifested in very different forms, of course, from those of ancient patronage, but they are no less deep and effective. As the distinguished President of your Academy, the late Mgr Lemaître, wrote: "Does the Church need science? Certainly not, the cross and the gospel are sufficient for her. But nothing human is alien to the Christian. How could the Church have failed to take an interest in the most noble of the strictly human occupations: the search for truth?"

> In this Academy which is yours and mine, believing and non-believing scientists collaborate, concurring in the search for scientific truth and in respect for the beliefs of others. Allow me to quote here again an enlightening passage by Mgr Lemaître: "Both of them, (the believing scientist and the non-believing scientist) endeavour to decipher the palimpsest of nature, in which the traces of the various stages of the long evolution of the world are overlaid on one another and confused. The believer has perhaps the advantage of knowing that the enigma has a solution, that the underlying writing is, when all is said and done, the work of an intelligent being, therefore that the problem raised by nature has been raised in order to be solved, and that its difficulty is doubtless proportionate to the present or future capacity of mankind. That will not give him, perhaps, new resources in his investigation, but it will contribute to maintaining in him a healthy optimism without which a sustained effort cannot be kept up for long."
>
> May the science that you profess, Members of the Academy and scientists, in the field of pure research as in that of applied research, help mankind, with the support of religion and in agreement with it, to find again the way to hope and to reach the ultimate aim of peace and faith.[33]

The Presidency of the newly re-founded Pontifical Academy of Sciences was entrusted to the Rector of the Catholic University, Father Agostino Gemelli, who was flanked by the Chancellor, Pietro Salviucci, and by a Council composed of four Academicians. Annual (and later two-yearly) plenary sessions were proposed for all the Academicians. The accounts of the activities and the contributions of the members were published in the *Acta*

Pontificiae Academiae Scientiarum and later on in the *Commentationes.*

The first assembly was inaugurated on 1 June 1937 by the then Cardinal Secretary of State, Eugenio Pacelli, the future Pope Pius XII. During this period of the Academy many distinguished members graced its halls, such as Ugo Armaldi, Giuseppe Armellini, Niels Bohr, Lucien Cuenot, Georges Lemaître, Tullio Levi-Civita, Guglielmo Marconi, Robert Millikan, Umberto Nobile, Max Planck, Ernest Rutherford, Erwin Schrödinger, Francesco Severi, Edmund Whittaker, and Pieter Zeeman.

The Academy today

The statutes of the Pontifical Academy of Sciences were subsequently updated by Paul VI in 1976 and by St John Paul II in 1986. Since 1936 the Pontifical Academy of Sciences has grown increasingly international in character. While continuing to further the work of the separate sciences, it stresses the growing importance of interdisciplinary cooperation. Today the Academy's activities range from a traditional interest in pure research to a concern with the ethical and environmental responsibility of the scientific community.

The premises of the Academy are in the exquisite Casina Pio IV which was completed in 1561 as a summer residence for Pope Pius IV. Surrounded by the trees and lawns of the Vatican gardens, the Casina is a well-preserved treasury of sixteenth-century frescoes, stucco reliefs, mosaics and fountains. The first floor plan of the Casina and the first part of the building, designed by Pirro Ligorio, began under Pope Paul IV. This one-storey building featured a courtyard and a fountain. Pirro Ligorio was probably chosen by Paul IV because he was a keen scholar of antiquities who had already worked on Tivoli's

Villa d'Este under Pope Julius III, and because he shared the same Neapolitan origins. Surviving documents tell us that when Paul IV died, on 18 August 1559, the Casina comprised only the ground floor without the corner tower. It appears to have been Pius IV who commissioned the extension consisting in a loggia, galleria, chapel, three more rooms and a second storey and the addition of the stucco, mosaic and fresco decoration throughout the whole complex.

The Pontifical Academy of Sciences is an independent entity within the Holy See. Its rebirth was the result of papal initiative, and it is placed under the direct protection of the reigning Supreme Pontiff, and defines its own goals with regard to its mission: "to promote the progress of the mathematical, physical and natural sciences and the study of epistemological problems relating thereto".[34] Pius XII stressed scientific freedom of inquiry in his address of 1939 to the Academicians: "To you noble champions of human arts and disciplines the Church acknowledges complete freedom in method and research."[35] Since the deliberations and studies which it undertakes are not influenced by any one national, political or religious point of view, the Academy constitutes an invaluable source of objective information upon which the Holy See and its various bodies can draw.

The Academy is governed by a President who is nominated from among the Academicians by the Supreme Pontiff. The President is assisted by the Council and by the Chancellor. The Academy maintains relationships and publication exchanges with other academies and with institutions of scientific research. It is a member of the International Council of Scientific Unions (ICSU). The operating costs of the Academy are defrayed mainly by the Holy See. In addition, gifts from foundations, firms, membership organizations and individuals have assisted the Academy's efficacy and outreach.

The Pontifical Academicians are eighty women and men from many countries who have made outstanding contributions in their fields of scientific endeavour. They are nominated by the Holy Father after being elected by the body of the Academicians. The work of the Academy comprises six major areas: Fundamental science; Science and technology of global problems; Science for the problems of the developing world; Scientific policy; Bioethics; Epistemology. The Pontifical Academicians participate in study groups and meetings organized by the Academy to examine specific issues. Their deliberations and scientific papers are published by the Academy. They assemble in the Vatican in the Casina Pio IV for Plenary Sessions.

Every two years, the Academy awards the Pius XI Medal, a prize which was established in 1961 by John XXIII. This medal is given to a young scientist who has distinguished himself or herself at an international level in his or her scientific achievements. Amongst the publications of the Academy there are three series: *Scripta Varia*, *Documenta*, and *Commentarii*. The most important works, such as for example the papers produced by the study-weeks and the conferences, are published in the *Scripta Varia*. In a smaller format, the *Documenta* series publishes the short texts produced by various activities, as well as the speeches by the Popes or the declarations of the Academicians on subjects of special contemporary relevance. The *Commentarii* series contains articles, observations and comments of a largely monographic character on specific scientific subjects.

During its various decades of activity, the Academy has had a number of Nobel Prize winners amongst its members, many of whom were appointed Academicians before they received this prestigious international award. Amongst these should be listed: Pieter Zeeman (Physics, 1902), Lord Ernest Rutherford (Physics, 1908), Guglielmo Marconi (Physics, 1909), Alexis Carrel (Physiology, 1912), Max von Laue (Physics, 1914), Max Planck (Physics, 1918), Niels Bohr (Physics, 1922), Werner Heisenberg (Physics, 1932), Paul Dirac (Physics, 1933), Erwin Schroedinger (Physics, 1933), Sir Alexander Fleming (Physiology, 1945), Chen Ning Yang (Physics, 1957), Rudolf L. Mössbauer (Physics, 1961), Max F. Perutz (Chemistry, 1962), John Eccles (Physiology, 1963), Charles H. Townes (Physics, 1964), Manfred Eigen and George Porter (Chemistry, 1967), Har Gobind Khorana and Marshall W. Nirenberg (Physiology, 1968). Recent Nobel Prize winners who have also been or are presently Academicians may also be listed: Christian de Duve (Physiology, 1974), Werner Arber e George E. Palade (Physiology, 1974), David Baltimore (Physiology, 1975), Aage Bohr (Physics, 1975), Abdus Salam (Physics, 1979), Paul Berg (Chemistry, 1980), Kai Siegbahn (Physics, 1981), Sune Bergström (Physiology, 1982), Carlo Rubbia (Physics, 1984), Rita Levi-Montalcini (Physiology, 1986), John C. Polanyi (Chemistry, 1986), Jean-Marie Lehn (Chemistry, 1987), Joseph E. Murray (Physiology, 1990), Gary S. Becker (Economics, 1992), Paul J. Crutzen (Chemistry, 1995), Claude Cohen-Tannoudji (Physics, 1997), Ahmed H. Zewail (Chemistry, 1999), Günter Blobel (Physiology, 1999), Ryoji Noyori (Chemistry, 2001) Aaron Ciechanover (Chemistry, 2004), Gerhard Ertl (Chemistry, 2007), and Shinya Yamanaka (Physiology, 2012).

The current goals of the Pontifical Academy of Science can be summarized in these terms. The Academy aims to promote the progress of the mathematical, physical and natural sciences, and the study of related epistemological questions and issues. It recognises excellence in science, and stimulates an interdisciplinary approach to scientific knowledge. The Academy encourages international interaction and furthers sharing in the benefits of science and technology by the greatest number of people and peoples. It promotes education and the public understanding of science, ensuring that science works to advance of the human and moral dimension of man. The Academy seeks to achieve a role for science which involves the promotion of justice, development, solidarity, peace, and the resolution of conflict. It fosters interaction between faith and reason and encourages dialogue between science and spiritual, cultural, philosophical and religious values. It provides the Pope and the Church with authoritative advice on scientific and technological matters, cooperating with the members of other Academies in a friendly spirit to promote such objectives.[36]

In some ways Pope Benedict XVI summarized this task of the Academy when he stated:

> Such an interdisciplinary approach to complexity also shows that the sciences are not intellectual worlds disconnected from one another and from reality but rather that they are interconnected and directed to the study of nature as a unified, intelligible and harmonious reality in its undoubted complexity. Such a vision has fruitful points of contact with the view of the universe taken by Christian philosophy and theology, with its notion of participated being, in which each individual creature, possessed of its proper perfection, also shares in a specific nature and this within an ordered cosmos originating in God's creative Word.[37]

Notes

1 Cesi was hereditary Marquis of Monticello and Duke of Acquasparta, and later made a prince by Pope Paul V.

2 L. G. Clubb, *Giambattista Della Porta Dramatist* (Princeton, New Jersey, Princeton University Press 1965).

3 H. Hallam, *Introduction to the Literature of Europe: in the Fifteenth, Sixteenth and Seventeenth Centuries*, Volume 3 (London: J. Murray, 1847), p. 235.

4 In Latin: "minima cura si maxima vis".

5 This neologism corresponds to the Italian expression *lincealità*. See R. Morghen, *L'Accademia nazionale dei Lincei nel CCCLXVIII anno della sua fondazione, nella vita e nella cultura dell'Italia unita* (Roma: Accademia Nazionale dei Lincei, 1972), p. 16.

6 *Ibid.*

7 See M. Sánchez Sorondo, *The Pontifical Academy of Sciences: A Historical Profile* (Vatican City: Pontifical Academy of Sciences, 2003), p. 11.

8 L. Guerrini, *The "Accademie dei Lincei" and the New World. Preprint/Max-Planck-Institut für Wissenschaftsgeschichte: Vol. 348* (Berlin: Max-Planck-Inst. für Wissenschaftsgeschichte, 2008).

9 A. Clericuzio & S. De Renzi, "Medicine, Alchemy and Natural Philosophy in the Early Accademia dei Lincei" in *Italian Academies of the Sixteenth Century*, edited by D. S. Chambers and F. Quiviger (London: The Warburg Institute, 1995), pp. 175–194.

10 G. Gabrieli, *Contributi alla storia della Accademia dei Lincei* (Roma: Accademia Nazionale dei Lincei, 1989), vol. I, p. 510.

11 For an idea of Cesi's naturalism see L. Guerrini, *I trattati naturalistici di Federico Cesi* (Roma: Accademia Nazionale dei Lincei, 2006); A. Graniti (ed.), *Federico Cesi. Un principe naturalista* (Roma: Bardi, 2006); A. Battistini–G. De Angelis–G. Olmi (eds.), *All'origine della scienza moderna: Federico Cesi e l'Accademia dei Lincei* (Bologna: Il Mulino, 2007).

12 G. Gabrieli, *Il carteggio Linceo* (Roma: Accademia Nazionale dei Lincei, 1996), p. 100.

13 *Ibid.*, p. 99.

14 *Ibid.*, pp. 29, 32, 97 and 101.

15 *Ibid.*, pp. 27–28.

16 *Ibid.*, pp. 29–30.

17 *Ibid.*, pp. 30–31.

18 G. Fernández de Oviedo, *Sumario de la natural y general historia de las Indias* (Toledo, 1526).
19 Guerrini, *The "Accademie dei Lincei" and the New World*, p. 6.
20 *Ibid.*
21 *Ibid.*, p. 7.
22 *Ibid.*
23 *Ibid.*, p. 8.
24 *Ibid.*, pp. 8–9.
25 D. Freedberg, *The Eye of the Lynx. Galileo, his friends, and the beginnings of Modern Natural History* (Chicago and London: Chicago University Press, 2002), pp. 254–255 and 263–264.
26 D. Bertoloni Meli, *Mechanism, Experiment, Disease: Marcello Malpighi and Seventeenth-Century Anatomy* (Baltimore, MD: John Hopkins University Press, 2011), p. 41.
27 See Sánchez Sorondo, *The Pontifical Academy of Sciences: A Historical Profile*, p. 9. The Rules were described as the *Linceografo*.
28 Cf. E. di Rovasenda and G. B. Marini-Bettòlo, *Federico Cesi nel quarto centenario della nascita* (Vatican City: Pontificiae Academiae Scientiarum Scripta Varia, 63, 1986), p. 18.
29 *Ibid.*, p. 19.
30 Cf. G. B. Marini-Bettòlo, *Historical Aspects of the Pontifical Academy of Sciences* (Vatican City: Pontificae Academiae Scientiarum Documenta, 21, 1986), p. 10.
31 See Sánchez Sorondo, *The Pontifical Academy of Sciences: A Historical Profile*, p. 12.
32 Pope Pius XI, Motu Proprio *In Multis Solaciis* in *AAS* 28, 1936, p. 427. The original Latin text reads: "In multis solaciis, quibus Dei benignitas Pontificatus Nostri cursum prosecuta est, illud etiam adnumerare libet, Nos videlicet eorurn cernere potuisse non paucos, qui naturae secreta experiundo rimantur, mentium habitum propensionemque, ad religionem quod attinet, ita immutasse, ut animos alio iam intendisse videantur. Scientia, quae vera rerum cognitio sit, numquam christianae fidei veritatibus repugnat; immo etiam—ut qui scientiarum annales pervolutaverit, non fateri non poterit—quemadmodum Romani Pontifices unaque simul Ecclesia nullo non tempore doctorum hominum vestigationes, iis etiam in rebus quae experimentis cognoscuntur, provehendas curarunt, ita vicissim eiusmodi disciplinae ad tutandum caelestis veritatis thesaurum, eidem Ecclesiae creditum, viam munierunt."
33 Pope John Paul II, *Address to the Pontifical Academy of Sciences* (10

November 1979). See also O. Godart and M. Heller, *Les relations entre la science et la foi chez Georges Lemaître* (Vatican City: Pontificae Academiae Scientiarum Commentarii, vol. III, 21, 1978), pp. 7, 11.

34 Pontifical Academy of Sciences, *Statutes* 1:2.

35 Pope Pius XII, *Address to the Pontifical Academy of Sciences* (3 December 1939).

36 See the website of the Pontifical Academy of Sciences at the page: http://www.casinapioiv.va/content/accademia/en/about/goals.html.

37 Pope Benedict XVI, *Discourse to the Pontifical Academy of Sciences* (8 November 2012).

6

THE VATICAN OBSERVATORY

We are very happy and very grateful to God that we can be present among you, my beloved sons and daughters, to rejoice in the inauguration of this new, and might we say improved, Specola Vaticana *in this our residence at Castel Gandolfo, which has also been renovated. What we are doing today, and your presence my beloved sons and daughters makes it all the more beautiful and solemn, adds some lines to the truly golden and most glorious pages which have already been written about the history of the Roman Pontificate. It carries us, like winged Pegasus, through the centuries in an immense and magnificent world of things, of ideas, of events.*

Pope Pius XI, *Discourse for the Inauguration of the New Specola* (29 September 1935)

IN ITS HISTORICAL roots and traditions the Vatican Observatory is one of the oldest astronomical institutions in the world. The Vatican is a sovereign state, with its own national astronomical observatory, the *Specola Vaticana* (Vatican Observatory). Astronomy has been supported at the Vatican since the 1582 reform of the calendar; the present-day Observatory has been in operation since 1891. The work of the Observatory is divided between two sites, one in the papal summer gardens south of Rome, Italy, and the other affiliated with the Steward Observatory at the University of Arizona, in Tucson, Arizona, USA.[1]

To the Catholic Church, the study of creation has long been viewed as an act of reverence to God the Creator. Astronomy was one of the seven subjects that made up the curriculum of the medieval universities, which were themselves founded by the Church. Understanding the motions of objects seen in the sky had philosophical and theological implications in the cosmology of those times: the physical universe was thought to parallel the metaphysical universe.[2]

Historical roots

In fact, three early observatories were founded by the Papacy: the Observatory of the Roman College (1774-1878), the Observatory of the Capitol (1827-1870), and the *Specula Vaticana* (1789-1821) in the Tower of the Winds within the Vatican. These early traditions of the Observatory reached their climax in the mid-nineteenth century with the researches at the Roman College of the famous Jesuit, Father Angelo Secchi, the first to classify stars according to their spectra. From that time and with some degree of continuity the Holy See has manifested an interest in and support for astronomical research.

Specific papal interest in astronomy can be traced to Pope Gregory XIII who had the Tower of the Winds built in the Vatican between 1578 and 1580.[3] The Tower of the Winds takes its name from the anemoscope it possesses, an instrument that gauges the direction of the wind, designed by the Dominican Father Ignazio Danti (1537–1586), the papal cosmographer. The Vatican anemoscope consisted in a weathervane on the roof which, through a mechanism of iron rods and gears, pointed an arrow to the corresponding wind direction on the ceiling of the main room of the tower.[4]

On the lower of the two levels of the tower, the windowless Meridian Room, there was a floor meridian, also the work of Danti, to correctly identify the spring equinox. A hole is located in the south wall at a height of about 5 meters and the artist placed it right in the mouth of a genie blowing wind. A ray of sunlight passing through this hole falls on the floor across which there is a long marble strip, placed north-south, whose centre opens up into a circle. The meridian line is inserted along this marble strip and the signs of the zodiac are cut into it at those positions where the ray of sunlight coming through the hole falls at noon on the day when the sun enters the respective constellation. One of these positions coincides with the vernal and autumnal equinoxes. At noon on the spring equinox, the ray should fall on a specific line. When it was tested for the first time, in 1582, it occurred on 11 March instead of 21 March; the calendar was ten days off. Thus Pope Gregory XIII was able to verify that his reform already in progress was necessary.[5]

Now the meridian had not been placed in the Tower of the Winds until 1582, when the reform of the Calendar had already taken place, so it was not actual used for the preparation of this reform.[6] Nevertheless it is possibly true that Fr Ignazio Danti desired to reproduce in Rome the meridian he had developed in Florence and in Bologna, with "the explicit intention of measuring the length of the tropical year and determining the equinox", as a contribution to the reordering of the calendar.[7] Since the Meridian Room is also known as the Room of the Calendar, it is likely, as an inscription of the year 1797 recalls, that some of the discussions of the calendar commission also took place there.[8]

The Jesuit priest Christopher Clavius (1537–1612) was one of the mathematicians involved in the reform. At the

Pope's request, he wrote a lengthy explanation of the reasons for the reform, published in 1602; but even after that work was completed he and other Jesuits at the Roman College continued to do astronomical research. They were among the first to confirm Galileo's telescopic observations, though they remained sceptical about the Copernican system. Galileo aroused the anger of many of the Jesuits by claiming priority over the German Jesuit Christof Scheiner (1575–1650) on the discovery of sunspots, and belittling the (essentially accurate) observations of comets by the Roman Jesuit Orazio Grassi (1583–1654).

Ten years later, Galileo was brought to his infamous trial; historians still argue over the reasons for that trial, which may have had as much to do with politics as with philosophical differences (the trial occurred at the height of the Thirty Years War), but it is clear that this enmity with the Jesuits cost him their friendship when it would have been most helpful.[9]

This period of the Vatican Observatory is particularly connected with Mgr Filippo Luigi Gilii. Gilii was born in Corneto in 1756, and died in Rome, in 1821, a beneficed cleric of St Peter's Basilica. He was effectively Director of the Vatican Observatory from 1800–1821, and during these twenty-one years, Gilii made twice-daily meteorological readings at the Observatory. He was a universal genius, well versed in physics and in biology, in archaeology and in the Hebrew language. The Tower of the Winds was then held by the Vatican librarian; Cardinal Zelada had been appointed to this office in 1780. Zelada wished to honour the traditions of the tower by using its upper part as an observatory. In 1797 he obtained the permission of Pope Pius VI, and placed over the entrance to the tower the Latin inscription *Specula Vaticana*. The upper floor was equipped with meteorological and magnetic instruments, with a seismograph, a Dolland telescope, a small transit and pendulum clock, and the observatory was given into the charge of Mgr Gilii. From 1800 to 1821 Gilii made an uninterrupted series of meteorological observations, reading the instruments twice a day (around 6 am and 2 pm), according to the programme of the Mannheim Meteorological Society. The observations of about seven years of the long series are published, while the rest are in great part preserved as manuscripts in the Vatican Library. There are also deposited astronomical observations of eclipses, comets, Jupiter's satellites, and of a transit of Mercury.

Gilii's scientific activity extended beyond the Vatican Observatory and beyond Rome. The meridian line in front of St Peter's, with the obelisk as gnomon and the readings of the seasons cast by the length of the shadow, was organized by him; so are also the signs on the floor of St Peter's Basilica, indicating the lengths of the largest churches of the world, likewise the two old clocks of French and Italian style, in the front of the basilica, and finally the first lightning rod protecting St Peter's cupola. Similar memories of him exist in various churches and cities of Italy.

At the death of Gilii the Vatican Observatory was discontinued, there was no successor to take up his work. The instruments drifted away and the Specola Vaticana went into hibernation for seventy years, until finally Pope Leo XIII would awaken it to modern productive research.[10]

Since the first days of its foundation by Gregory XIII the Roman College fostered scholarly work even in the fields of mathematics, physics, and astronomy. Notwithstanding the the Galileo trial, astronomy remained a rich field of study for the Jesuits at the Roman College, even during and after this trial. In 1616, Nicholas Zucchi (1586–1670) built what was perhaps the first reflecting telescope; Gilles-Franois de Gottignies (1630–1689) observed the comets of 1664, 1665, and 1668; and Athanasius Kircher (1601–1680) made detailed telescopic drawings of Jupiter and Saturn.[11] In the following century, Roger Boscovich (1711–1787) convinced the Vatican to lift its formal opposition to the Copernican system; in addition, he studied transits, cometary orbits, and the optics of telescopes. In fact, it was only towards the end of the eighteenth century that astronomical instruments were actually installed in the Tower of the Winds.

In 1787 the observatory at the Roman College had been founded, under Giuseppe Calandrelli (1749–1827), and was declared preferable to the Vatican, as more accessible to students in the city, and not obstructed by the great cupola of St. Peter's. On the advice of the Jesuit Father Roger Boscovich (1711–1787), the instruments were then transferred from the Gregorian Tower of the Winds to the Roman College.

At the Roman College, Giuseppe Calandrelli, Andrea Conti (1777–1840), and Giacomo Ricchebach (1776–1841) produced eight volumes of *Opuscoli Astronomici* (Astronomical Tracts), detailing their research on the sun, planets, comets, and stellar occultations.[12] Meanwhile, from the towers of the Vatican itself, Feliciano Scarpellini (1762–1840), Ignazio Calandrelli (1792–1866; nephew of Giuseppe Caladrelli), and Lorenzo Respighi (1824–1889) observed the solar chromosphere and made astrometric observations.

After the suppression of the Society of Jesus, sanctioned by Pope Clement XIV in 1773, instruction at the Collegio Romano was entrusted to the secular clergy. Already in the following year, on 14 July 1774, Clement XIV , with a Motu Proprio, ordered the Pontifical Foundation of the Observatory of the Roman College. Pope Pius VII expressed his personal interest in the Observatory: on 11

February 1804 he went to the Roman College to admire a total solar eclipse. Influenced by this extraordinary event, he promised appropriate equipment and adequate funding for the Observatory. True to his word, that same year when he went to Paris to crown Napoleon, he took the opportunity to acquire for his observatory an achromatic telescope and a good pendulum clock of Ponce. Later on he acquired a good transit telescope of Reichenbach (Munich) and a compensated pendulum clock of Breguet.[13]

In 1824 the Roman College (also known from that time as the Gregorian University) and the adjoining Church of St Ignatius were returned to the Society of Jesus, which had been restored. By the Apostolic Letter, *Quod Divina Sapientia*, Pope Leo XII set up that year an ordinance for scientific studies in the state universities of the Church. Norms were also established for observatory directors: they should observe the heavens continuously, they should compile and publish bulletins. Furthermore, they were to maintain correspondence with the most renowned astronomers of the day so that they would be up to date on new discoveries, which they were to evaluate and use for the good of the students, so as to benefit not only the natural but also the sacred sciences.

Although he reassigned the College to the Jesuits, the Pope wanted Calandrelli, who certainly merited it, to remain as director of the observatory. Calandrelli, however, together with his associates, preferred to leave and he carried off his instruments to the College of St Apollinarius. His scientific programs terminated with his sudden death in 1827.[14]

Father Etienne Dumouchel (1773–1840), who had received his scientific training at the Paris Polytechnic, was appointed as new director of the Observatory of the Roman College. He found the Observatory in great difficulty. The tower erected in 1787 was so unstable that not even a portable transit instrument could be set up there, much less any kind of fixed telescope. The new director was insistent in reminding his superiors of the need for a new building and of equipment necessary to carry on research. In 1825 Father Fortis, the General of the Society of Jesus, donated to the Observatory a telescope of Cauchoix on an altazimuth mounting, which was for those times an optical masterpiece. In 1842 Father General Roothaan acquired a meridian circle of Ertel. However the unstable tower continued to be used until 1850. Dumouchel is known in the annals of the history of astronomy for having rediscovered Halley's Comet on its return in 1835, a discovery which he communicated on 6 August to the editor of the *Astronomische Nachrichten*, the mostly widely circulated journal at that time for reporting such announcements. The real merit goes to his young assistant, Father Francesco de Vico (1805–1848) who, from orbital determinations based on previous apparitions, calculated the probable position and prepared a finding chart. It was only because of this assistance and the tireless collaboration of a team of researchers, that it was possible to observe the comet with the large refractor of Cauchoix.[15]

Towards the end of his life Dumouchel had already left a good part of the direction of the Observatory to his competent collaborator, De Vico, who was officially appointed director in 1839. Between 1844 and 1847 there were a prolific number of comets, and eight of them were discovered at the Roman College. One of these with a 6.5 year period was named for De Vico. The discovery of the first seven was recognized officially and a prize was given by the King of Denmark. A great deal of merit for these discoveries must go to Brother Bernardino Gambara, assistant to De Vico for the observatory's physical plant and for weather reports.[16] De Vico also observed the Saturnian satellites Mimas and Enceladus, determining their orbits.

However, by far the most notable astronomer in Rome during this century was Angelo Secchi (1818–1878), a Jesuit at the Roman College. His reputation went far beyond Italy; he was honoured by both the Emperor of Brazil and Napoleon III of France (who named him an Officer of the Legion of Honour). He published more than 700 scientific papers on topics as diverse as terrestrial magnetism and solar physics, and established the connection between sunspots and solar flares. He was also a pioneer in spectroscopy, the first to systematically classify stars by their spectral features. His spectral work included the first identification of carbon in stars, comets, meteors, and nebulae. His work on solar physics was so fundamental that even today it has been honoured in the naming of the Sun Earth Connection Coronal and Heleospheric Investigation (SECCHI) instrument package on NASA's Stereo spacecraft. So great was his reputation that when the anti-clerical Italian government confiscated the Roman College following the capture of Rome from the Holy See in 1870, Secchi was still allowed to continue his work even though he refused to take an oath to the new government. Secchi died in 1878, however, leading to a hiatus in Vatican-sponsored astronomy until Pope Leo XIII formally re-established an observatory in 1891. The present day Vatican Observatory is dated itself from this moment.

There was also a third observatory of Papal foundation which may also been seen as a precursor of the present Specola Vaticana. The founding of the Observatory on the Capitoline Hill, which up until 1870 had been the papal observatory of the Archiginnasio Romano (today's University of Rome), goes back to Pope Leo XII. In 1827 this pontiff had a small round building erected on the terrace of the Capitoline tower so that the Abbé Feliciano Scarpellini could set up his collection of instruments for physics and astronomy. Scarpellini owned a good repeater circle of Reichenbach, but he did not have a dome. So he had a small pillar built on the terrace where he would set up and standardize his instrument each time that the weather would permit observations. When the observations were finished he would put the instrument back in the little building. In this way he carried out observations up until the time of his death in 1840.

In 1848 his successor, Fr Ignazio Calandrelli, took up in a definitive way the direction of the observatory on the Capitoline. He had taught optics and astronomy at the University of Rome, *La Sapienza*. For three years he directed the observatory of Bologna. On the Capitoline he found that the instruments were antiquated and that the *Specola* was in a pitiful state. He asked the Pope to reconstruct the observatory and to provide it with a meridian circle. Pope Blessed Pius IX became convinced of the need for a truly modern observatory for the University of Rome and in 1848 he completely reestablished it. Drawing upon his own private funds he acquired a high quality meridian instrument of Ertel. The Holy See had a new building with a rotating dome constructed and in it was placed a 12.6 cm Merz equatorial telescope, a gift of the Marchese Ferraioli.

Upon Calandrelli's death a world-renowned successor was named in the person of Lorenzo Respighi (1824–1889), who years before had succeeded to Calandrelli at Bologna.[17] Respighi was well known for his pioneering studies in astronomical spectroscopy; on 15 February 1869 he was the first to attach an objective prism to a telescope, a technique which has proved to be indispensable to research in astrophysics. He was the first to produce a design of the complete solar chromosphere with details of the prominences along the entire edge of the sun. He also discovered that the chromosphere is higher at the poles than at the equator. He was also the first to propose that stellar scintillation was related to the earth's rotation.[18] To him is due the beginning of a star catalogue which, upon its completion by his successors, was one of the most important in Italy.

However, due to the events of 1870 this observatory also ceased to be papal and it took the name of *Regio Osservatorio di Roma sul Campidoglio* (The Rome Royal Observatory on the Capitoline). It exists today, after having in 1923 taken in the observatory of the Roman College and having been transferred in 1938 to Villa Mellini, as the *Osservatorio Astronomico di Roma su Monte Mario* (The Rome Astronomical Observatory on Monte Mario). It now has a second location at Monte Porzio Catone and an observing site in the mountains at Campo Imperatore (L'Aquila).[19]

Thus three early observatories were founded by the Papacy: the Observatory of the Roman College (1774–1878), the Observatory of the Capitol (1827–1870), and the Specula Vaticana (1789–1821) in the Tower of the Winds within the Vatican. These three observatories continued to operate in parallel into the nineteenth century.

The expropriation of the Observatory of the Roman College by the Italian State in 1879 deprived the Holy See of the last place to carry out astronomical research. However, only ten years later the Barnabite Father Francesco Denza, director of the Meteorological Observatory of the Barnabites at Moncalieri, wisely profited from a propitious occasion to recall the attention of Pope Leo XIII to the re-founding of the Specola Vaticana. This would involve restoring the old and respected Gregorian Observatory of the Tower of the Winds.

As the jubilee of the priesthood of Leo XIII approached, 1 January 1888, the whole Catholic world was preparing to celebrate it in a solemn way and they vied with one another in sending gifts and in organizing an exhibition. Father Denza called together the scholars of the Italian clergy so that they might offer to the Pope the fruits of their talents by preparing a selection of apparatus used for meteorology and seismology. The initiative had a clear apologetic purpose: the display was meant to show that the Italian clergy were not as backward in science as, at least in certain quarters, one was led to believe. The collection of instruments made up one of the most interesting sections of the great fair and it met with approval of the Pope who was known for his interest in the development of science. When the exposition ended, the gifts of artistic value found a home in the various parts of the Pontifical rooms. It was then that Denza suggested to the Holy Father that the instruments be arranged in Gregory XIII's Tower of the Winds which had been abandoned for some time. There, where there had been the Vatican Observatory up until the death of Gilii in 1821, observations would once more be made which would bring new glory to this ancient place of study and research.

In agreement with the plans proposed, the Pope appointed Fr Denza as director of the new institute and appointed to the staff those who had helped him in preparing the exhibition. Denza was able almost immediately to enrich the existing array of instruments with others coming from the estate of Marquis of Montecuccoli, who had operated a private observatory at Modena. Among these instruments there were two valuable Merz refractors, one of aperture 10.2 cm on an equatorial mounting and the second of 10.6 cm aperture on an altazimuth mounting; there was a Stark coude meridian telescope and four precision pendulum clocks for the measurement of sidereal time plus another clock donated by Riefler of Munich for the jubilee of the Holy Father. A rotating dome of 3.5 meters with a slit opening of 58 cm was immediately installed on the Tower of the Winds and it housed the small Merz equatorial. This was the first of four domes which would be erected within the next few years in the Vatican. New instruments for meteorological observations and for measures of terrestrial magnetism were also acquired. Thus the observatory began to operate soon after its founding in 1888.[20]

Foundation of the Specola

On 14 March 1891, Pope Leo XIII solemnly confirmed, with his Motu Proprio, *Ut Mysticam*, the foundation of what would officially be called from then on, as it had been in the past, the *Specola Vaticana* and with a financial contribution he assured its operation.[21] He clearly indicated the apologetic intent of this project:

> With the intention of showing disrespect and hatred of the mystical spouse of Christ, the true light, the children of darkness have grown accustomed to open calumniation of the Church by twisting the essential meaning of words and reality as they accuse her of being a friend of obscurantism, one who spreads ignorance, and an enemy of science and progress... In undertaking this project, we have not only been concerned to contribute to the progress of a most noble science, one which more than other pursuits raises the human spirit to the contemplation of heavenly realities, but we have first of all put before ourselves a task which we have constantly and energetically pursued right

> from the beginning of our Pontificate through discourses, writings, and actions whenever the opportunity presented itself, the task, namely, that everyone would clearly see that the Church and her Pastors, far from being opposed to true and solid science, whether human or divine, embrace, encourage and promote it with all the zeal that they can muster.[22]

In this document the Pope also described how the Observatory was built on the preceding interest of the Church in astronomy:

> Gregory XIII ordered a tower to be erected in a convenient part of the Vatican buildings, and to be fitted out with the greatest and best instruments of the time. There he held the meetings of the learned men to whom the reform of the calendar had been entrusted. The tower stands to this day, a witness to the munificence of its author. It contains a meridian line by Ignazio Danti of Perugia, with a round marble plate in the centre adorned with scientific designs. When touched by the rays of the sun that are allowed to enter from above, the designs demonstrate the error of the old reckoning and the correctness of the reform.[23]

When, in 1906, through the generosity of Pius X the Specola received the Villa of Leo XIII with the adjacent tower, the circumstances under many aspects were ideal. Placed at the far western edge of the Eternal City, the nightime darkness of the Vatican Gardens suffered very little disturbance from the electrical lights towards the east, since they were in great part protected by St Peter's dome and by the Vatican Palace.

The renewed Specola Vaticana had a number of directors before the arrival of Johann Hagen (1847–1930) in 1906. He was the first Jesuit in the reformed observatory, which included at that time a combination of clerical and lay staff. Hagen made the decision to concentrate the work of the observatory purely on astronomy; his own research centred on cataloguing nebulae, especially dark nebulae (which he correctly deduced were masses of interstellar matter), and variable stars.[24]

Hagen carried out an interesting project with a series of experiments to demonstrate the rotation of the Earth. Though no one doubted by this time that the Earth was spinning, its actual motion had only been shown by Foucault's Pendulum in 1851. Hagen devised a series of ingenious experiments to demonstrate the action of the Coriolis force arising from motions on the Earth's spinning surface. These including the very careful observation of a falling weight (via an Atwood machine) in a stairwell at the Vatican;[25] the mapping of the apsidal rotation of a pendulum; and the motion of a long suspended beam on which heavy weights travelled in a north-south direction. Thus arose the irony that the Vatican, infamous for having opposed Galileo and his championing of the Copernican system, three centuries later supported some of the first laboratory experiments that actually confirmed the Copernican hypothesis of the Earth's spin.[26]

However, the most important work of the observatory during this period was its participation in the *Carte du Ciel* photographic map of the sky. The stimulus for the Vatican to take part in this international project came from the Specola's first director, the Barnabite priest Francesco Denza (1834–1894); but following his early death, the work proceeded under the direction of the Oratorian priest Giuseppe Lais (1845–1921). This project met the desire of the Vatican to participate in work that was both scientifically important and internationally recognized. Though never stated in so many words, one can infer that the Specola played an important political role for the Vatican at this time: by being accepted as a full participant in this program, the astronomical world was in effect recognizing the Holy See itself as a sovereign nation, the equal to the other nations participating in this project—including Italy, which at that time still claimed jurisdiction over the Vatican.

In the following years Rome continued to grow toward the North and Southeast of the Specola and, in the new urban areas nearby, the myriad electric lights continued to glow. Increasingly the sky brightness increased from the east and even passed the zenith and began to obscure the pallid glow of the Milky Way. In fact, during the period 1920–1930 the observations of the cosmic clouds with their very weak half-shadowings, which are a real challenge for the eyesight, could only be done to the west.

In 1929, Italy and the Holy See came to an agreement which acknowledged the independence of the Vatican and restored territories to the Popes that had been confiscated in 1870. Among these territories were the gardens and palace in Castel Gandolfo that had previously served as the papal summer residence. Thus it was that Pope Pius XI provided a new location for the Observatory at the Papal Summer Residence at Castel Gandolfo in the Alban Hills some 25 kilometers southeast of Rome. It is here that the modern observatory, entrusted to the Jesuits, was refounded in the 1930s with the construction of two new telescopes, the installation of an astrophysical laboratory for spectro-chemical analysis, and the expansion of several important research programs on variable stars.

After the construction work had been completed and most of the instruments were set up and functioning, Pius XI wished to have a solemn inauguration of the new Specola on 29 September 1935 with the presence of his

Secretary of State, Cardinal Pacelli, and of a large number of ecclesiastical and lay dignitaries, and scientists. In his discourse the Holy Father lauded astronomy, a science which more than any other brings one to religions considerations.

> What we are doing today, and your presence my beloved sons and daughters makes it all the more beautiful and solemn, adds some lines to the truly golden and most glorious pages which have already been written about the history of the Roman Pontificate. It carries us, like winged Pegasus, through the centuries in an immense and magnificent world of things, of ideas, of events.
>
> And one might say that the Creator himself, He who at the end of his work of creation was pleased and proclaimed that all was good, is in a special way pleased with the magnificence of the heavens and the stars.
>
> In fact, the divinely inspired Text emphatically and repeatedly calls upon the heavens and the stars to praise and bless the Lord (Psalm 148:3; Daniel 3:63 and elsewhere) and the Creator himself gives it the name "Beautiful Star" (Apocalypse 22:16). That same sacred text finds one of the happiest expressions of divine wisdom when, in the presence of those infinite multitudes of heavenly bodies, which the new modem instrumentation magnifies and multiplies, it sees God numbering the multitude of stars and listens to him calling each by name, a prerogative which God reserves to himself (Genesis 15:5; Psalm 146:4). Again it is the divinely inspired Text which sees the uncreated Wisdom (Wisdom 7:29) shining sovereign among the stars: even more, in the beauty of the heavens and in the glory of the stars it sees God himself who illuminates the world from on high (Ecclesiastes 43:4). It is always the

> divine word which puts in the mouth of the disciple of Wisdom a special thanks for the knowledge that has been acquired of the stars (Wisdom 7:19).[27]

Inspired by the words of the Three Wise Men, "We have seen his star and have come to adore him", he gave the following motto to the Specola: *Deum Creatorem, Venite Adoremus* (Come, let us adore God the Creator). This invitation, inscribed in the bright marble which stands out on the south wall of the dome of the double astrograph, has been an incentive to the astronomers who for years have gone there to their night's work and it is still an inspiration to the visitors who come to admire the grandiose work of a Pope who was an enthusiastic champion of the sciences.[28]

At the death of Hagen in 1930, Pope Pius XI had entrusted the Observatory and its staffing to the Jesuit order; with this move to new quarters, the Jesuits provided a number of young scientists, notably specialists in laboratory spectroscopy Josef Junkes (1900–1984) and Ernst Salpeter (1912–1976) under the direction of Alois Gatterer (1886–1953). Over the next forty years this laboratory would draw up a number of atlases of the spectra of metals of interest to astronomers, and it was instrumental in the founding of the journal *Spectrochimica Acta*.

At the same time, the observation of stellar spectra was promoted with two telescopes provided by the Vatican: a 60 cm/40 cm Zeiss Double Astrograph installed in 1934 on the roof of the Papal Palace itself, and a 65/98 cm Schmidt telescope placed in the adjacent gardens in 1957. Among the projects performed on these telescopes were the completion of Hagen's Atlas of Variable Stars and the final cataloguing of the Carte du Ciel plates.

Another project which was begun, but not particularly developed at this time, was the study of meteorites. In

1905, the French meteorite collector Adrien-Charles, the Marquis de Mauroy (1848–1927) had donated a small selection of his samples to the Vatican; in 1935 his widow donated the bulk of his collection, amounting to more than one thousand meteorite samples. However, early plans to take spectra of these samples did not proceed beyond the measurement of two meteorites, as it was found that the metal from these samples produced spectra far too complex to be interpreted at that time.

The onset of World War II did not bring scientific work at the Specola to a halt. The observatory grounds, on Papal territory, were neutral and the Jesuit staff continued to live and work together even though they had come from countries on both sides of the conflict (many of the staff were Germans, but Gatterer was Belgian and the director of the Specola, Johan Stein, was Dutch). The Papal territory in which the telescopes and summer palace were located became the home to thousands of refugees during the invasion of nearby Anzio in the winter of 1944, and the Jesuits in residence dealt on a daily basis with the trials of living in a war zone.

Recent developments

With the continuously increasing population of Rome the skies above the Observatory again became too bright. For this reason in 1981, for the first time in its history, the Observatory founded a second research centre, the Vatican Observatory Research Group (VORG), in Tucson, Arizona in the United States, one of the world's largest and most modern centres for observational astronomy. The Observatory staff have offices at Steward Observatory of the University of Arizona. From here they have access to all of the modern telescopes located in the Tucson area.

In 1985, which marked the fiftieth anniversary of scientific research at the renewed Specola, Pope John Paul II remarked:

> Through the natural sciences, and cosmology in particular, we have become much more aware of *our true physical position within the universe,* within physical reality—in space and in time. We are struck very forcibly by our smallness and apparent insignificance, and even more by our vulnerability in such a vast and seemingly hostile environment. Yet this universe of ours, this galaxy in which our sun is situated and this planet on which we live, is our home. And all of it in some way or other serves to support us, nourish us, fascinate us, inspire us, taking us out of ourselves and forcing us to look far beyond the limits of our unaided vision. What we discover through our study of nature and of the universe in all its immensity and rich variety serves on the one hand to emphasize our fragile condition and our littleness, and on the other hand to manifest clearly our greatness and superiority in the midst of all creation—the profoundly exalted position we enjoy in being able to search, to imagine and to discover so much.[29]

The Pope highlighted the importance of a realist perspective in approaching scientific work:

> *We are made in the image and likeness of God.* Thus, we are capable of knowing and understanding more and more about the universe and all that it contains. We can reach out and grasp its inner workings and designs, plumbing its depths with questioning reverence and with awestruck imagination.[30]

This realist perspective is a springboard for appreciating the work of God the Creator:

> The more we know about physical reality, about the history and structure of the universe, about the fundamental make-up of matter and the processes and patterns which at the roots of the material world, the more we can appreciate the immensity of *the mystery of God*, the more we are in a position to grasp *the mystery of ourselves*—our origin and our destiny. For creation, as we have come to know it, speaks to us in fragmentary yet very true reflections of the God who created it and maintains it in existence.[31]

In 1993 the Vatican Observatory, in collaboration with Steward Observatory, completed the construction of the Vatican Advanced Technology Telescope (VATT) on Mount Graham, Arizona, probably the best astronomical site in the Continental United States. This is the first optical-infrared telescope of the Mount Graham International Observatory (MGIO), a project which in the coming years will see the construction of some of the world's most sophisticated and largest telescopes. The VATT has pioneered the new technology of creating large, light-weight, stable mirrors in a rotating furnace (see picture to right). With the VATT the Specola are pursuing long-term research programs which, although they were the hall-mark of research at Castel Gandolfo, have never been able to be carried out before in Tucson. Thus from its two centres, located at Castel Gandolfo and at Tucson, the Observatory is continuing various current studies and international collaborations. The dedication plaque of the VATT reads:

> This new tower for studying the stars has been erected during the XV year of the reign of John Paul II on this peaceful site so fit for such studies, and it has been equipped with a new large mirror for detecting the faintest glimmers of light from distant objects. May whoever searches here night

> and day the far reaches of space use it joyfully with the help of God.

The Specola Vaticana today thus consists of two sites. The headquarters is located in the gardens of the Papal Summer Residence, an extraterritorial Vatican property in Castel Gandolfo, 30 km south of Rome; and the Vatican Observatory Research Group is associated with the University of Arizona in Tucson, Arizona.

On 16 September 2009, Pope Benedict XVI inaugurated the new premises of the Vatican Observatory now physically located at the southern end of the Papal summer gardens, adjacent to Piazza Pia in the Italian city of Albano. Besides containing the offices and the living quarters of the Jesuit community, this building (originally a convent dating from the eighteenth century, completely rebuilt in 2009) houses the Specola's library, plate vault, and meteorite collection and laboratory, along with a classroom for the biennial Vatican Observatory summer schools. The library contains more than 22,000 items, mostly twentieth-century astronomical journals and nineteenth and twentieth century observatory reports, but also including many astronomy and physics journals and rare antique books dating back to the sixteenth century, including original copies of works of Copernicus, Galileo, Newton, Kepler, Brahe, Clavius, and Secchi. The plate vault contains roughly 10,000 items, including plates from the Specola telescopes described below, dating to 1891. The meteorite collection holds more than 1,000 samples of more than 500 different falls; the laboratory includes stereo and petrographic microscopes and instruments to measure meteorite physical properties such as density, porosity, and magnetic susceptibility.

Additional facilities in the papal gardens include a building erected in 1942 to house the Carte du Ciel telescope with a second dome added in 1957 for the Schmidt telescope. Neither telescope is presently operational, though there is a proposal to convert this structure into a museum of astronomical photography.

On the roof of the Papal Palace itself the two telescopes set up in 1934 still remain operational. In a dome over the central staircase is a Zeiss (Jena) 40cm refractor with a 6m focal length; attached to it is a Coronado solar telescope. A second dome on the roof houses a Zeiss Double Astrograph, consisting of two telescopes on a common German mount: a 60cm reflector which can be set up either as a Newtonian or a Cassegrain, and a 40cm refractor camera designed to be used with photographic plates. The latter has an 8° field of view onto 30 cm × 30 cm plates, for a 1.42 arcminute/mm image scale. The reflector is usually set up in Cassegrain mode; it has a 15cm convex secondary mirror and an equivalent focal length of 1.82m. The reflector is still functional, but the camera is no longer used.

Several religious orders contributed personnel and directors to the Observatory. These included Barnabites, Oratorians, Augustinians, and Jesuits. Since 1930 the staffing of the Specola Vaticana has been entrusted by the Vatican to the Society of Jesus, whose typical work has been in higher education, and whose charism and spirituality are particularly suited for scientific work.

Pope Benedict XVI encapsulated the mission of the Specola as follows:

> Since its establishment in 1891, the Vatican Observatory has sought to demonstrate the Church's desire to embrace, encourage and promote scientific study, on the basis of her conviction that "faith and reason are like two wings on which the human spirit rises to the contemplation of truth".[32]

Notes

1. G. Consolmagno & C. Corbally, "The Specola Vaticana: Astronomy at the Vatican" in *Organizations, People and Strategies in Astronomy* 2 (OPSA 2013), p. 217.
2. *Ibid.*
3. The 73-metre-high tower was so named because it was decorated with depictions of the four winds on its walls, and contained an elaborate mechanical wind vane.
4. J. Casanovas, "The Vatican Tower of the Winds and the Calendar Reform" in G. V. Coyne, M. A. Hoskin, & O. Pedersen, *Gregorian Reform of the Calendar: Proceedings of the Vatican Conference to Commemorate its 400th Anniversary 1582-1982* (Vatican City: Pontificia Academia Scientiarum, 1983), p. 190.
5. See S. Maffeo, *The Vatican Observatory: In the service of nine popes* (Vatican City State: Vatican Observatory Publications, 2001), p. 4.
6. See Casanovas, "The Vatican Tower of the Winds and the Calendar Reform", pp. 191–192.
7. *Ibid.*, p. 192.
8. Maffeo, *The Vatican Observatory*, p. 5.
9. See Consolmagno & Corbally, "The Specola Vaticana: Astronomy at the Vatican", p. 218.
10. Maffeo, *The Vatican Observatory*, pp. 7–8.
11. For a description of the use of cathedrals as astronomical observatories during this time see J. L. Heilbron, *The Sun in the Church: Cathedrals as Solar Observatories* (Cambridge, MA: Harvard University Press, 2001); see also, regarding the work of the Jesuits Riccioli and Grimaldi during this era, C. M. Graney, "Science rather than God: Riccioli's review of the case for and against the Copernicus hypothesis" in *Journal for the History of Astronomy* 43 (2012), pp. 215–226.
12. A stellar occultation occurs when the light from a star is blocked by an intervening body (such as a planet, moon, ring, or asteroid) from reaching an observer.
13. Maffeo, *The Vatican Observatory*, p. 10.
14. *Ibid.*, p. 11.
15. *Ibid.*, p. 12.
16. *Ibid.*, p. 13.
17. Lorenzo Respighi was professor at the University of Bologna, first of mechanics and hydraulics and later of optics and astronomy.

He was director of the observatory there from 1855 until 1865 when, upon refusing to take an oath of fidelity to the new Italian regime, he was fired. He was invited by the Vatican to direct the observatory on the Capitoline and he held that post until his death.

18 Respighi discovered that in the spectra of stars near the horizon, scintillation produces a succession of dark bands which move across the spectrum, going from violet to red for stars that are setting and from red to violet for stars that are rising. It was precisely the study of this phenomenon which led Respighi to connect scintillation with the earth's rotation. This was one of his finest achievements and it correctly and inseparably linked the theory of scintillation with the name of this illustrious Director of the Observatory of the Capitoline. After Respighi had published his observations, the famous Lord Rayleigh judged it to be "the most important work on this subject" (*Philosophical Magazine*, XXXVI, 129).

19 See Maffeo, *The Vatican Observatory*, p. 19.

20 See Maffeo, *The Vatican Observatory*, pp. 33–34.

21 *Specola* is an antique Italian word meaning observatory.

22 Pope Leo XIII, Motu Proprio *Ut Mysticam*.

23 *Ibid.*

24 See Consolmagno & Corbally, "The Specola Vaticana: Astronomy at the Vatican", p. 220.

25 The Atwood machine was invented in 1784 by Rev. George Atwood as a laboratory experiment to verify the mechanical laws of motion with constant acceleration. The ideal Atwood Machine consists of two objects of mass m_1 and m_2, connected by an inextensible massless string over an ideal massless pulley.

26 See Consolmagno & Corbally, "The Specola Vaticana: Astronomy at the Vatican", pp. 220–221.

27 Pope Pius XI, *Discourse at Castel Gandolfo for the Inauguration of the New Specola* (29 September 1935).

28 See Maffeo, *The Vatican Observatory*, pp. 139–140.

29 Pope John Paul II, *Discourse to the Participants in the Vatican Conference on Cosmology* (6 July 1985), 2.

30 *Ibid.*

31 *Ibid.*, 4.

32 Pope Benedict XVI, Discourse *to the Faculty and Students of the Eleventh Vatican Observatory Summer School* (11 June 2007). See also Pope John Paul II, *Fides et Ratio*, Proemium.

7

POPE PIUS XII AND PROOFS FOR THE EXISTENCE OF GOD

Yet we, who are borne on one dark grain of dust
Around one indistinguishable spark
Of star-mist, lost in one lost feather of light,
Can by the strength of our own thought, ascend
Through universe after universe; trace their growth
Through boundless time, their glory, their decay;
And, on the invisible road of law, more firm
Than granite, range through all their length and breadth,
Their height and depth, past, present and to come.
So, those who follow the great Workmaster's law
From small things up to great, may one day learn
The structure of the heavens, discern the whole
Within the part, as men through Love see God.

Alfred Noyes, *The Torch-Bearers*

IN ORDER TO understand more fully the importance of the discourse of Pope Pius XII concerning a renewed approach to the proofs for the existence of God, we need to take a look at the history and background of these proofs.

In the eighteenth century the famous mathematician Leonard Euler reputedly was capable of solving any problem which was set before him. At the court of Catherine the Great of Russia he was faced with the French philosopher Denis Diderot, who was an atheist. Catherine the Great did not want Diderot to turn the Russians into atheists, and so asked Euler to help her. The mathematician thought about this and came up with an algebraic proof of the existence of God. Euler and Diderot were convened to the palace of the Empress Catherine, where Euler stood before the assembly and simply stated:

"Sir, $\frac{a+b^n}{n} = x$, hence God exists; reply!"

Diderot had no special understanding of algebra and so was unable to discuss the point with Euler. Diderot left St Petersburg and returned to France apparently defeated.[1] Clearly this is not the type of proof we are proposing in support of God's existence, because it confuses mathematical proof with philosophical proof. It reduces philosophical demonstration to a mathematical formula.

In everyday life, three types of proof are commonly encountered. First, scientific proof, where the tools used are measurement, controlled testing environments, repeatability of observations, statistical methods, and various others. However, scientific endeavour makes a set of hidden assumptions which *may* be valid, but which we cannot prove. For example, we assume that an experiment which has the same result five thousand times will always have the same result. We assume that the laws of nature that we observe will be the same tomorrow. We assume that these laws are uniform across the universe. None of these assumptions can be proven. The second kind of proof is mathematical proof, where every step in reasoning must be cautious and precise and justified according to rules that are specific and fixed. Many consider this to be probably the best and purest form of human reasoning. A drawback to this kind of proof is that it works "on paper," in a highly abstract world of manipulated symbols. Its principles spill over into science and even into everyday life, and they are useful; but their usefulness in "real life" is limited because of the extreme complexity of the universe in which we live. The third major kind of proof is termed legal and historical proof. This is the kind of reasoning used, for example, by detectives, lawyers, judges, and historians. It is frequently confused with scientific proof, because the methods and tools of science are sometimes used as forensic aids. Legal proof is concerned with the gathering and analysis of physical evidence, but it is also concerned with eyewitness testimony and the reliability of those witnesses, with alibis, with circumstantial evidence, and the analysis of motives and human psychology. It is the most useful in everyday life, but by the same token, it is also fallible and inexact. These three types of proof should be distinguished from and related to philosophical proof, which involves a greater degree of abstraction.

Actually, centuries before Euler, the Fathers of the Church had come up with rational ways of demonstrating God's existence, based on the fact that in creating the cosmos and the human person God has left a seal, an imprint or a trade mark upon His creation. Saint Augustine, in a Platonic key, opened a new way in the West for a rational demonstration of the existence of God, based on the value of truth. According to this great Doctor of the Church, nothing within man is superior to reason. However, truth, which is eternal, necessary and immutable, forms the basis upon which reason makes its judgement; this truth is above reason and transcends it. Therefore God, who is in Himself absolute Truth, exists. "God exists, and on a supreme and absolute level: this truth is not only the object of our unshakeable faith, but is also received by us through a process of rational knowing."[2] In the East, St Basil explained that God "has left a clear and evident mark of His immense wisdom" even in a little creature like the sea-urchin, which seamen use as an indication of fine or stormy weather.[3] St John Damascene, another Greek Father paved the way for the medieval proofs for the existence of God, this time in an Aristotelian framework. He furnished three demonstrations of God's existence, the first based on the mutability and contingence of the cosmos, the second upon the conservation and government of the universe, and the third from the ordered arrangement of beings, which cannot be the result of chance.[4]

While the demonstrations of the Church Fathers often sustained a apologetic rôle in order to convince pagans and non-believers, the thinkers of the Middle Ages developed proofs of God's existence not so much to confute atheistic ideas, but rather to illustrate the marvellous harmony between faith and reason.[5] The medieval Scholastics proposed two essential ways to prove the existence of God. These two ways are classified according to the distinction between an *a priori,* or deductive process, and an *a posteriori,* or inductive process. While all admit the validity and sufficiency of the latter method, opinion is divided in regard to the former. Some maintain that a valid *a priori* proof (usually called the ontological argument) is possible; others deny this completely; while some others maintain an attitude of compromise or neutrality. This difference of opinion applies only to the question of proving God's actual existence; since, once His self-existence has been affirmed, it is necessary to employ *a priori* or deductive inference in order to arrive at a knowledge of His nature and attributes, and as it is impossible to develop the arguments for His existence without some working notion of His nature, it is necessary to some extent to anticipate the deductive stage and combine the *a priori* with the *a posteriori* method. The *a posteriori* approach of demonstrating God's existence from his creation, can be subdivided according to a twofold point of departure: the physical world, and the human person.

The Ontological Argument

This argument starts from a reflection upon God as being "thought" in order to arrive at His reality as an "existing" being. This approach, which has its origin in Platonic and Augustinian thought, was principally expounded by St Anselm of Canterbury (1033–1109), and later accepted by Alexander of Hales (died 1245) and St Bonaventure (1217–1274). As propounded by St Anselm, the ontological argument runs as follows. The idea of God as the Infinite means the greatest Being that can be thought of. However, unless actual existence outside the mind is included in this idea, God would not be the greatest conceivable Being since a Being that exists both in the mind as an object of thought, and outside the mind or objectively, would be greater than a Being that exists in the mind only. This presupposes that existence in reality is greater than mere existence in the understanding. Therefore, God must exist in reality, not just in the understanding.[6] Further, Anselm pointed out that it is impossible to imagine that God does not exist. If a mind could imagine a being greater than God, "the creature would rise above the Creator; and this is most absurd."[7] So, then, no one who truly understands what God is can conceive that God does not exist. For God is that than which nothing greater can be imagined.[8] Gaunilo, a contemporary monk of Anselm, wrote an attack on Anselm's argument in which he offered several criticisms. The most well-known of these is a parody on Anselm's argument in which he proves the existence of the greatest possible island. If instead of using the expression "something than which nothing greater can be conceived" one used "an island than which none greater can be conceived" then we would prove the existence of that island.[9] Gaunilo's point was that we could prove the existence of almost anything using Anselm's style of argument. St Anselm replied to Gaunilo's critique, and stated that it is not possible to infer the real existence of a lost island from the fact of its being conceived. For the real existence of a being which is said to be *greater than all other beings* cannot be demonstrated in the same way with the real existence of one that is said to be *a being than which a greater cannot be conceived.*[10] Gaunilo overlooked the fact that the argument was not intended to apply to finite ideals but only to the strictly infinite; and if it is admitted that we possess a true idea of the infinite, and that this idea is not self-contradictory, it does not seem possible to find any flaw in the argument.

Later, Descartes proposed the ontological argument in a slightly different form as follows. Whatever is contained in a clear and distinct idea of a thing must be predicated of that thing; but a clear and distinct idea of an absolutely perfect Being contains the notion of actual existence; therefore since we have the idea of an absolutely perfect Being, such a Being must really exist. In a third form of the ontological demonstration of the existence of God, Leibniz affirmed: God is at least possible since the concept of Him as the Infinite implies no contradiction; but if He is possible He must exist because the concept of Him involves existence. Actual existence is certainly included in any true concept of the Infinite, and the person who admits that he has a concept of an Infinite Being cannot deny that he conceives it as actually existing. However, the difficulty is with regard to this preliminary proposition of conceiving an actually existing Infinite Being, which requires to be justified by recurring to the *a posteriori* argument, namely to an inference by way of causality from contingency to necessarily existing Being and thence by way of deduction to infinity. Hence the great majority of philosophers have rejected the ontological argument as propounded by St Anselm, Descartes and Leibniz.

In particular, when St Thomas Aquinas indicated that the existence of God is not self-evident, he illustrated the weakness of the ontological argument. He argued that even if everyone understands the word "God" to signify something than which nothing greater can be thought, nevertheless, it does not therefore follow that he understands that what the word signifies exists actually, but only that it exists mentally. Nor can it be argued that it actually exists, unless it be admitted that there actually exists something than which nothing greater can be thought; and precisely this is not admitted by those who hold that God does not exist.[11] St Thomas preferred the *a posteriori* approach to the demonstration of God's existence, preceding from the effects to the Cause, because the effects are better known to us than the Cause.[12] Although God transcends sense and the objects of sense, nevertheless sensible effects are the basis of rational demonstration of the existence of God.[13]

The Five Ways

St Thomas advanced the five following arguments to prove the existence of God. The first is the argument from motion, by which he meant passing from potency to act. When this takes place in the universe implies a first unmoved Mover (*primum movens immobile*), who is God; otherwise it would be necessary to postulate an infinite series of movers, which is inconceivable.[14] The second way proposed by the Angelic Doctor involves the idea of efficient causality. Efficient causes, as they are seen to operate in the universe, imply the existence of a First Cause that is uncaused, a Cause that possesses in itself the sufficient reason for its existence; and this is God.[15] The third way is based on contingency, whereby the fact that contingent beings exist (namely beings whose non-existence is recognised as possible) implies the existence of a necessary being, who is God.[16] The fourth way of St Thomas involves the consideration that the gradated perfections of being actually existing in the universe can be understood only by comparison with an absolute standard that is also actual, namely the infinitely perfect Being who is God.[17] In the fifth way, St Thomas suggested that the marvellous order in the cosmos is evidence of intelligent design within the universe. This design implies the existence of a Designer beyond the cosmos, who is God Himself.[18]

Blessed John Duns Scotus adopted both of the two processes in his proofs of God's existence. The first process is an entirely *a posteriori* approach, which resembled the first three ways of St Thomas. The objects of our experience are changing realities, or are beings in the course of "becoming." Now that which changes possesses in itself neither the sufficient reason for its existence nor for its activity. Hence we are led to admit the existence of a Being, namely God, that is outside the chain of succession and change, and that justifies the existence and action of beings in various stages of becoming. Scotus' second process consists in a development of the argument of St Anselm. To supply validity to this *a priori* argument, Scotus inserts *a posteriori* elements, namely the analysis of the possibility (contingency) that is affirmed by our experience. For Scotus, to say that God is "a being than which a greater cannot be conceived" is to say that God is infinite. Now, according to Scotus, the weakness of St Anselm's argument does not rest with the transition from possibility to real existence, but in this: that St Anselm did not prove that the concept of the infinite is possible. Scotus proves this possibility negatively by showing that the concept of an infinite being involves no contradiction. If it did involve a contradiction, our mind, which has for its object "being as being", would notice it. Positively, Scotus begins with the data of experience, which tells us that many things are possible. However, all possible series of beings are related to the Uncaused Being, which, since it is uncaused, is infinite Perfection. Hence an infinite being not only is possible, but actually exists. "Thus, absolutely speaking, the primary efficient cause can exist in its own right; hence it exists by itself."[19]

The Cosmological Argument

The first of St Thomas' ways can be developed into the Cosmological Argument for God's existence, also known as the argument from general causality. It is so called because it assumes as a starting point objective validity of the principle of causality, an assumption upon which the procedure of the physical sciences in particular and of human knowledge in general is based.[20] To question its objective certainty, as did Kant, and represent it as a mere mental *a priori*, or possessing only subjective validity, would open the door to subjectivism and universal scepticism. It is impossible to prove the principle of causality, just as it is impossible to prove the principle of contradiction; but it is not difficult to see that if the former is denied the latter may also be denied and the whole edifice of human reasoning crumbles. In the universe, certain things are observed to be effects, as they depend for their existence on other things, and these again on others; but, however far back this series of effects and dependent causes be extended, we must, if human reason is to be taken seriously, come ultimately to a cause that is not itself an effect, in other words to an uncaused cause or self-existent being which is the ground and cause of all being. Thus there cannot be an infinite number of regressions of causes to things that exist, but a final uncaused Cause of all things. This uncaused Cause is asserted to be God. The Cosmological Argument takes several forms but is basically represented as follows. Things exist, but it is possible for those things to not exist. Whatever has the possibility of non existence, yet exists, has been caused to exist. Something cannot bring itself into existence since it must exist to bring itself into existence which is illogical. There cannot be an infinite number of causes to bring something into existence, because an infinite regression of causes ultimately has no initial cause which means there is no cause of existence. Since the universe exists, it must have a cause. Therefore, there must be an uncaused Cause of all things, who is God.

Pantheism is the view that God is identical with the world or is completely immanent within it.[21] The pantheist critique of the cosmological argument is fallacious, namely that the world, whether of matter or of mind or of both, contains within itself the sufficient reason of its own existence. A self-existing world would exist of absolute necessity and would be infinite in every kind of perfection; but we certain from experience than that the universe as we know it, in its totality as well as in its parts, actualises only finite degrees of perfection. It is simply a contradiction in terms, however much one may try to conceal the contradiction by an ambiguous use of language, to predicate infinity of matter or of the human mind, and the pantheist holds one or the other or both to be infinite. In other words the distinction between the finite and the infinite must be abolished and the principle of contradiction denied. While theism safeguards certain primary truths like the reality of human personality, freedom, and moral responsibility, pantheism tends to sacrifice all these, to deny the existence of evil, whether physical or moral, to destroy the rational basis of religion, and, under pretence of making man his own God, to rob him of nearly all his plain, common sense convictions and of all his highest incentives to good conduct. The philosophy which leads to such results must be radically flawed.

The Argument from Contingency

The second and third ways of St Thomas have been developed into the *argument from contingency.* For Avery Dulles, contingency means that the whole of reality is made up of dependent beings, things that exist not by their own intrinsic powers. "If A depends on B, and B is also dependent, there must be a C to account for the existence of B." Dulles points out that the chain of dependency cannot extend endlessly, or else "there would be no sufficient reason why anything exists."[22] He illustrates the impossibility of an infinite regress with an amusing example: "A student can get a good mark by copying a paper from another student who got the right answers. That student, in turn, could have copied from a third. But it is absurd to argue that all the students were copying from other students, even in an infinite series. There must be at least one student who got the right answers by personal knowledge. A chain of dependent causes, even if infinitely long, does not explain the effect."[23] Thus we are led to the one Necessary Being, who must be the absolute fullness of reality and power, and be endowed with every positive perfection, that does not of itself bespeak limitation. The Necessary Being is life, intelligence, and freedom, and is therefore personal.[24]

Stanley Jaki defines the meaning of the word "contingent" as follows: "'Contingent', that is, dependent on a factor outside the set of parameters that determine the scientific handling of the problem or configuration. In the case of the universe as a whole, the factor in question can only be a metaphysical factor. Such a meaning of "contingent" is essentially different from its being taken equivalent to "accidental"."[25] Jaki states that a "contingent universe and a created universe are two sides of the same philosophical coin."[26] For Jaki, the concept of contingency is related to the notion of boundary conditions which make the whole of the universe coherent. They are given, are not derivable from laws, and all exist in relation to the overall boundary conditions which make nature a totality of beings. The "explanation of a given set of boundary conditions can only be done in terms of a more general set", but in such a procedure, there can be no regress to infinity. The overall boundary condition of the universe cannot therefore be self-explaining: it depends upon an explanation outside the universe which is therefore contingent. This link between contingency and createdness implies that, for Jaki, Aquinas' five ways are essentially one way, "the way from contingency."[27]

The description of the physical universe is highly mathematical. Every mathematical structure is constructed from a series of axioms. The theorems within that structure are then derived from those axioms. Within that given mathematical structure it can be shown how the theorems are derived logically from the axioms. However, the original choice of axioms cannot be justified from within the system. This kind of justification has to be provided from outside of the system. This relates to what Kurt Gödel demonstrated in 1931, namely that it is impossible to prove from within mathematical methods that the axioms are consistent. By consistent is meant that the conclusions drawn from such axioms are always contradiction free. Even if it were possible to prove the consistency of a given system, that system would never be complete within itself. In other words, from within a given system it is impossible to prove the truth of all the true statements contained within it.[28] Thus within mathematical descriptions of reality there lies an inherent incompleteness. So within the universe each system depends on a broader system to demonstrate its validity. For the universe as a whole, the proof of its consistency must lie outside of it, in its Creator. The cosmos, imbued with intelligibility, is then penultimate, the ultimate in intelligibility being God the Creator, who alone is above all things.[29]

The Teleological Argument

St Thomas Aquinas' fifth way has been developed by many thinkers under the name of the Teleological Argument, also known as the argument from design. In its basic form, it states that a Designer must exist since the universe and living things exhibit marks of design in their order, consistency, unity, and pattern. One form of this argument was the image of the Watchmaker offered by William Paley (1743–1805). The argument runs as follows:

> In crossing a heath, suppose I pitched my foot against a stone, and were asked how the stone came to be there; I might possibly answer, that, for anything I knew to the contrary, it had lain there forever: nor would it perhaps be very easy to show the absurdity of this answer. But suppose I had found a watch upon the ground, and it should be

> inquired how the watch happened to be in that place; I should hardly think of the answer which I had before given, that, for anything I knew, the watch might have always been there. Yet why should not this answer serve for the watch as well as the stone?[30]

Paley then states that a simple examination of the watch leads the mind inexorably forward to affirm that the watch must have had a maker; that there must have existed, at sometime, and at some place or other, an artificer or artificers, who formed it for the purpose which we find it actually to answer; who understood its construction, and designed its use.[31] The logical conclusion is that it was designed and not the product of random formation.

Paley extends his argument to all the works of nature, every organised natural body whether plant or animal, simple or complex, which also must have a Maker. Paley argues not only as a theologian but also as a scientist, where he compares the human eye and the telescope. Both manifest similar principles of design and construction; both are modelled according to the same laws of optics; the eye differs only in being more versatile and more subtle in its operations. As the telescope is inconceivable apart from its designers, so too is the eye. The eye is an amazing organ, for in order for it to work there must be many different convergent parts that individually have no function but have value only in a designed whole. Only in the organic whole does each part carry out its function for the whole, indicating design and purpose.

Paley's work is open to the criticism that he espoused a rather mechanical view of the cosmos, in vogue during his time. Paley also mistakenly proposed that God has sacrificed omnipotence, allowing the creative process to proceed according to clearly discernible laws of nature; in and through the very laws of nature God has accomplished the creation of life. "It is this," concludes Paley, "which constitutes the order and beauty of the universe. God, therefore, has been pleased to prescribe limits to his own power, and to work his ends within those limits. The general laws of matter have perhaps the nature of these limits."[32] At the same time, Paley's natural theology was a stimulus for science, for his natural theology was imbued with a really concrete interaction between the phenomena of nature and its Creator: "The world thenceforth becomes a temple, and life itself one continued act of adoration."[33]

The evolutionary perspective, far from diminishing the value of design and purpose in the cosmos as pointers to its Creator, only serves to strengthen the argument. The evidence for design which the universe manifests are even more impressive when viewed from the evolutionary standpoint. The eye, for example, as an organ of sight is a clear embodiment of intelligent purpose, even more so when viewed as the product of God's providence in an evolutionary process rather than the immediate handiwork of the Creator. The eye is only one of the countless examples of adaptation to particular ends discernible in every part of the universe, inorganic as well as organic; for the atom as well as the cell contributes to the evidence in favour of design. Another example lies in the incredible complexity of the human genetic code. The word "code" itself implies an Intelligence who designed it; human intelligence has then deciphered the human genome. The only alternative to an intelligence is "chance", however the chances of the genome coming together by accident are nil, even less than the probability of throwing all the parts of a computer together and hoping that, one day, all these parts will come together in the right order to make the computer. Nor is the argument weakened by our inability in many cases to explain the particular purpose of certain structures or organisms. Furthermore, in the search for particular instances of design, evidence supplied by the harmonious unity of nature as a whole must not be overlooked. The universe as we know it is a cosmos.[34] This is a vastly complex system of correlated and interdependent parts, each subject to particular laws, and all together subject to a common law or a combination of laws, as the result of which the pursuit of particular ends is made to contribute in a marvellous way to the attainment of a common purpose. It is simply unimaginable that this cosmic unity should be the product of chance or accident.

If it be objected that there is another side to the picture, that the universe abounds in imperfections, such as disfunctionality, failures, seemingly purposeless waste, at least reply is possible. The existing world is not the best of all possible ones, and it is only on the supposition of its being so that the imperfections referred to would be excluded. Admitting the existence of physical evil, but without exaggerating its reality, there still remains a large balance on the side of order and harmony, and to account for this there is required not only an intelligent mind but one that is good and benevolent. The full sweep of cosmic design cannot be comprehended, for it is not a static universe in question, but a universe that is progressively developing and moving towards the fulfilment of an ultimate purpose under the guidance of a master Mind. The imperfect as well as the perfect, apparent evil and discord as well as obvious good order, may contribute towards that purpose in ways which can only be dimly discerned. The humble and balanced investigator of nature is aware of his or her own limitations in the presence of the Designer of the universe, not claiming that every detail of that Designer's purpose should at present be plain, but rather is happy to await the final solution of enigmas which the hereafter promises to furnish.

The Esthetical Argument

Related to the argument from design is the argument from beauty in the cosmos, also termed the *Esthetical Argument* for the existence of God. St Augustine was perhaps one of the first exponents of this approach: "Question the beauty of the earth, question the beauty of the sea, question the beauty of the air distending and diffusing itself, question the beauty of the sky ... question all these realities. All respond: 'See, we are beautiful.' Their beauty is a profession. These beauties are subject to change. Who made them if not the Beautiful One who is not subject to change?"[35] St Thomas Aquinas defined beauty in the clearest terms: "Beauty includes three conditions, integrity or perfection; due proportion or harmony; and lastly, brightness, or clarity."[36] Man is capable of seeing that creation is good, notwithstanding Original Sin. He can also perceive that there is a unity within creation. Noting the different forms of truth, goodness, and unity of the cosmos, man appreciates beauty within the universe in the various wonders of nature. Man does not create all this beauty but rather he receives and unveils it and thus co-operates in its revelation. However, more than this, man can arrive, via a reflection upon creation, at the fact that beauty is not able to explain its own existence, it is not here by chance, it is not chaotic, but rather it is created. Furthermore, the human person enjoys the capacity to appreciate beauty which also cannot be a chance link with the cosmos, but this connatural connection between the harmony of the universe and man the perceiver must be the result of a supreme design. Kant made beauty a subjective quality (purely in the eye of the beholder) once he made it non-conceptual: "The beautiful is that which pleases universally without a concept."[37] Clearly this is false, there must be objective criteria for beauty. Otherwise how could one explain that the beauty of St Peter's Square attracts many non-Christians, that beauty spots in the countryside get very crowded at the weekend, that famous fashion models, actresses and actors can make a good living. We realise that there is always something more beautiful than what we have experienced or uncovered, and so we are led by degrees to Uncreated Beauty. It is as if God has left a kind of metaphysical trade-mark upon creation which can thus be traced back to its Creator. Hence, man fully discovers and admires beauty only when he refers it back to its source, the transcendent beauty of God.

St John of the Cross offered a stark reminder of the inadequacy of the beauty of creatures as a road to God, a sharp *via negativa* in proceeding to God:

> All the being of creation, then, compared with the infinite Being of God, is nothing. And therefore the soul that sets its affection upon the being of creation is likewise nothing in the eyes of God, and less than nothing; for, as we have said, love makes equality and similitude, and even sets the lover below the object of his love ... And, coming down in detail to some examples, all the beauty of the creatures, compared with the infinite beauty of God, is the height of deformity. even as Solomon says in the Proverbs: "Favour is deceitful and beauty is vain." And thus the soul that is affectioned to the beauty of any creature is the height of deformity in the eyes of God. And therefore this soul that is deformed will be unable to become transformed in beauty, which is God, since deformity cannot attain to beauty; and all the grace and beauty of the

> creatures, compared with the grace of God, is the height of misery and of uncomeliness.[38]

At the same time this great saint and mystic nuances his position elsewhere by referring to the grove from the Song of Songs:

> The grove, because it contains many plants and animals, signifies God as the Creator and Giver of life to all creatures, which have their being and origin from Him, reveal Him and make Him known as the Creator. The beauty of the grove, which the soul prays for, is not only the grace, wisdom, and loveliness which flow from God over all created things, whether in heaven or on earth, but also the beauty of the mutual harmony and wise arrangement of the inferior creation, and the higher also, and of the mutual relations of both. The knowledge of this gives the soul great joy and delight.[39]

Anthropological arguments

Many of the arguments above dealt with demonstrations of God's existence based upon a reflection upon the physical world. It is also possible to adopt arguments drawn from the nature and dignity of the human person, which can be termed anthropological arguments for God's existence. Many of these arguments run in the following manner. The human being is open to truth and beauty, possesses a sense of moral goodness, has freedom and possess the voice of his or her conscience. Man and woman bear longings for the infinite and for happiness, and ask questions about God's existence. In all this man and woman discern signs of their spiritual soul. The soul, the "seed of eternity we bear in ourselves, irreducible to the merely material"[40] can have its origin only in God.[41]

Some of these arguments can now be examined in more detail.

The argument from conscience

The moral argument for the existence of God was developed by the eighteenth-century German philosopher Immanuel Kant, who maintained that the highest good includes moral virtue, with happiness as its appropriate reward. He held that it is the duty of humanity to seek this highest good and that it must therefore be possible to realise it. Furthermore, Kant claimed that this highest good cannot be realised unless there is "a supreme cause of nature," one that has the power to bring about harmony between happiness and virtue. Such a cause could only be God. Critics of the moral argument counter that it is by no means clear that the highest good is what Kant supposed. To Newman and others, the argument from conscience, or the sense of moral responsibility, has seemed the most deeply persuasive of all the arguments for God's existence. Newman stated that while some people think that there is a moral obligation because God exists, rather the contrary is true, namely that God exists because we can perceive a moral law.[42] The existence within of a sense which is termed conscience indicates the concept of a Father or Judge, of One who sees my heart.

For Newman, the conscience enables man to make the right choices. In a sense it transcends the human person; man did not make it, nor can he destroy it.. Because conscience is an authoritative voice, there necessarily arises in our mind the idea of a Being who completely transcends us as the source of moral obligation. The voice of conscience impels us to avoid evil and do good. Now the absolute quality of doing good is not founded only within man, but rather outside of him upon the absolute

Good, who is the End of man.[43] It is not that conscience, as such, contains a direct revelation or intuition of God as the author of the moral law, but that, taking man's sense of moral responsibility as a phenomenon to be explained, no ultimate explanation can be given except by supposing the existence of a Superior and Lawgiver whom man is bound to obey. And just as the argument from design evokes prominently the attribute of intelligence, so the argument from conscience brings out the attribute of holiness in the First Cause and self-existent Personal Being with whom we must ultimately identify the Designer and the Lawgiver. "Thus conscience is a connecting principle between the creature and his Creator."[44]

The argument from universal consent

An example of this argument was provided by William Rees-Mogg:

> I would endeavour to show that religious experience is very widely distributed, virtually universal in terms of history, region, faith and culture. I would argue that a majority of people report some type of religious experience, but that this ranges up to a group of higher mystics who have known something close to the direct perception of God. They now constitute for us what St Paul called "a cloud of witnesses".
>
> I would go on to argue that these witnesses could not be dismissed as weak-minded or mentally disturbed; on the contrary, they include many of the wisest, most self-sacrificing and most admired of human beings. In a world which often seems to be crazy, they seem exceptionally sane. Such figures have been recorded in all periods, and have not ceased to exist. To mention only a few, we have lived in the time of Yehudi Menuhin, Mother

> Teresa and Basil Hume, people almost universally admired.[45]

The confirmatory argument based on the consent of mankind may be stated briefly as follows: mankind as a whole has at all times and everywhere believed and continues to believe in the existence of some superior being or beings on whom the material world and man himself are dependent, and this fact cannot be accounted for except by admitting that this belief is true or at least contains a germ of truth. It is admitted of course that polytheism, dualism, pantheism, and other forms of error and superstition have mingled with and disfigured this universal belief of mankind, but this does not destroy the force of the argument under consideration. For at least the seminal truth which consists in the recognition of some kind of deity is common to every form of religion and can therefore claim in its support the universal consent of mankind. This consent seems best explained as a result of people's perception of the evidence for the existence of deity.

Discussion of the various theories that have been proposed to account in some other way for the origin and universality of religion is beyond the scope of this work. This consent of mankind speaks ultimately in favour of theism. It is clear from history that religion is liable to degenerate, and has in many instances degenerated instead of progressing; nevertheless, there is a good deal of positive evidence supporting the idea that monotheism was the primitive historical religion. If this be the true reading of history, it is correct to interpret the universality of religion as witnessing implicitly to an original truth which could never be entirely extinguished. Even if the history of religion is to be read as a record of progressive development one ought in all fairness, to seek its true meaning and significance not at the lowest but at the highest point of development; and it cannot be denied that theism in the strict sense is the ultimate form which religion naturally tends to assume.

The argument from human restlessness

St Augustine provided the foundation for this approach when he wrote: "Despite everything, man, though but a small a part of your creation, wants to praise you. You yourself encourage him to delight in your praise, for you have made us for yourself, and our heart is restless until it rests in you."[46] According to Avery Dulles, within the human person is a great capacity to love, to worship, and to serve. The nature of the human spirit is such that it starts from the double experience of knowing and willing. On the one hand, we experience a deep desire for happiness and fulfilment; on the other hand we know that no finite reality can satisfy this desire. From this contrast, the aspiration towards the Infinite is born. The basis for this aspiration lies in the fact that the human intelligence and the will cannot be fulfilled in finite being, so that they are launched towards the Infinite. Actually, human intelligence is never satisfied with what it knows but always wants to go further, and the human will is never really gratified by a partial good, but tends towards the Infinite Good. This dynamism of the human intellect and will is an indication of the existence of God in Whom alone are found the total Truth and the total Good. Man and woman are constantly on the lookout for some reality, some Person, to whom they can dedicate their full energies and who commands their full devotion. Unless we find God, we are likely to idolise creatures and eventually be disillusioned. Either we must live with a void of meaning, which leaves us spiritually famished, or we must turn to God as the supreme object of our love.[47]

Pascal's Wager

In the seventeenth century, Blaise Pascal affirmed that it was essentially by faith that we know of God's existence.[48] Thus he developed an argument not so much for the *existence* of God but for the *value* of believing in God. He claimed that even if there was no satisfactory evidence for believing God existed it is still better for us to believe in God rather than not. Pascal's argument was proposed in the form of a bet or wager. People have more to lose by not believing in God than believing. If we 'wager' on God existing (theism), yet when we die there is no God, we have lost nothing, except maybe a few hours a week at church and other religious activities. If we 'bet' on God not existing (atheism), yet when we die there is a God, we will have lost everything.[49] Thus according to Pascal it is better to be a theist rather than an atheist. Apart from the philosophical difficulties of assigning probabilities to such a weighty matter as God's existence, the argument smacks of a pragmatist or utilitarian approach. It would be more praiseworthy to carefully weigh up the evidence and make an honest and open-hearted search for God.

It would be quite mistaken therefore to maintain that faith ultimately rests on an accumulation of probabilities.[50] Newman adopted the expression "an *accumulation* of various probabilities"[51] and pointed out that from probabilities we may construct legitimate proof. Here, Newman refers solely to the proof of faith afforded by the motives of credibility, and he rightly concluded that, since these are not demonstrative, this line of proof may be termed "an accumulation of probabilities." Therefore, Newman did not base the final assent of faith on this accumulation, for here he was not examining the act of faith, but only the grounds for faith. His analysis of the accumulation of probabilities does not undermine authority.

Pius XII and proofs for the existence of God

Pope Pius XII in certain of his addresses to the Pontifical Academy of Sciences was a major influence on renewed approaches to proofs for the existence of God and this is especially true of the Pope's discourse of 22 November 1951 dealing with the proofs of the existence of God in the light of modern scientific discovery.[52] Pope Pius XII examined the science of his time to point to an initial moment of creation; the Pope's conclusion was:

> Indeed, it seems that the science of today, by going back in one leap millions of centuries, has succeeded in being a witness to that primordial Fiat Lux, when, out of nothing, there burst forth with matter a sea of light and radiation, while the particles of chemical elements split and reunited in millions of galaxies.[53]

Pius XII cited in his address a passage from Whittaker's Donnellan Lectures which ran as follows:

> different estimates converge to the conclusion that there was an epoch about 10^9 or 10^{10} years ago, on the further side of which the cosmos, if it existed at all, existed in some form totally different from anything known to us: so that it represents the ultimate limit of science. We may perhaps without impropriety refer to it as the Creation.[54]

Whittaker's position seems to employ scientific arguments to arrive at the beginning of time of the cosmos. There are scientific uncertainties present in this kind of argument since "the determination of the age of the earth and that of the universe stood in serious disagreement." Also, it cannot be proven that the rate of expansion was constant in the distant past, nor that an oscillatory universe was impossible; moreover, there could have existed a state of matter before the expansion started and this earlier state may not be accessible to scientific investigation. The observation that science cannot measure the beginning of time is wholly consistent with the nature of science as incomplete in all its phases. Thus it is "dangerous to consider the actual state of scientific research as the ultimate word," for "scientific explanations are by no means exhaustive, nor can one take it for granted that all the physical forces are known to science today."

Pope Pius XII also expressed a certain caution in his discourse: "The pope's speech stressed that the data reviewed still needed further research, that they were in need of further development before they could provide a sure foundation for philosophical arguments, that the scientific answer in question was neither explicit nor complete."[55] Indeed, the Pope was clear that from science there could be no absolute proof of creation in time; such arguments would need to be drawn from "metaphysics and revelation, in so far as they concern creation in its widest sense, and from revelation alone in so far as they concern creation in time." In this way Pius XII held (along with St Thomas Aquinas) that creation with time lies outside the reach of reason alone. Pius XII noted further that the whole line of reasoning from science to creation of itself "lies outside the sphere of the natural sciences."[56]

Concerning the import of this discourse by Pius XII, Hawking remarked: "The Catholic Church ... seized on the big bang model and in 1951 officially pronounced it to be in accord with the Bible."[57] It is true that the Pope was enthusiastic about the compatibility of a big bang scientific conception with the creation of the universe. It is also true that Pius XII rejected the steady-state cosmology which is opposed to creation with time and is lacking in logical and scientific basis.[58] However, it is certainly an exaggeration to say that the Church "seized on" the big-bang model;[59] the Pope merely regarded it as compatible with the vision of the Church based on Scripture and Tradition.

Further developments are also to be seen in the approach of subsequent incumbents in the Chair of St Peter. For example Pope St John Paul II has been most cautious concerning the use of the big-bang theory in arriving at a notion of creation with time: "Any scientific hypothesis on the origin of the world, such as the hypothesis of a primitive atom from which derived the whole of the physical universe, leaves open the problem concerning the universe's beginning. Science cannot of itself solve this question: there is needed that human knowledge that rises above physics and astrophysics and which is called metaphysics; there is needed above all the knowledge that comes from God's revelation."[60] John Paul II observed that metaphysics and revelation are needed in any discussion of the origin of the cosmos. Generally science, metaphysics and revelation are required to furnish a full picture concerning the beginning of the cosmos.

Finally, the convergence of all of the demonstrations of the existence of God is in itself a further proof. All the individual proofs are as many pointers conspiring to demonstrate God's existence, Who is the Ultimate Truth able to explain the otherwise unexplainable. The various proofs of God's existence can encourage a predisposition to faith and help people to see that faith is not opposed to reason.[61]

Notes

1 See S. Singh, *Fermat's Last Theorem* (London: Fourth Estate, 1998), p. 82.

2 St Augustine, *De libero arbitrio*, Book 2, chapter 15, n. 39 in *PL* 32, 1262.

3 St Basil, *Sermon 7 on the Hexaemeron*, chapter 5 in *PG* 29, 159–160.

4 See St John Damascene, *De fide orthodoxa*, Book 1, chapter 3 in *PG* 94, 795–798.

5 See Editorial, "Prove dell'esistenza di Dio" in *La Civiltà Cattolica* 147/II (1996) p.7.

6 See St Anselm, *Proslogion*, chapter 2 in *PL* 158, 227–228: "For, it is one thing for an object to be in the understanding, and another to understand that the object exists. When a painter first conceives of what he will afterwards perform, he has it in his understanding, but be does not yet understand it to be, because he has not yet performed it. But after he has made the painting, he both has it in his understanding, and he understands that it exists, because he has made it....Therefore, if that, than which nothing greater can be conceived, exists in the understanding alone, the very being, than which nothing greater can be conceived, is one, than which a greater can be conceived. But obviously this is impossible. Hence, there is no doubt that there exists a being, than which nothing greater can be conceived, and it exists both in the understanding and in reality."

7 *Ibid.*, chapter 3 in *PL* 158, 228.

8 See *Ibid.*, chapter 4 in *PL* 158, 229.

9 See Gaunilo, *On behalf of the fool*, n.6 in *PL* 158, 246–247: "For example: it is said that somewhere in the ocean is an island, which, because of the difficulty, or rather the impossibility, of discovering what does not exist, is called the lost island. And they say that this island has an inestimable wealth of all manner of riches and delicacies in greater abundance than is told of the Islands of the Blest; and that having no owner or inhabitant, it is more excellent than all other countries, which are inhabited by mankind, in the abundance with which it is endowed. Now if some one should tell me that there is such an island, I should easily understand his words, in which there is no difficulty. But suppose that he went on to say, as if by a logical inference: 'You can no longer doubt that this island which is more excellent than all lands exists somewhere, since you have no doubt that it is in your understanding. And since it is more excellent not to be in the understanding alone, but to exist both in the understanding and in reality, for this reason it must exist. For if it does not exist, any land which really exists will be more excellent than it; and so the island already understood by you to be more excellent will not be more excellent.' If a man should try to prove to me by such reasoning that this island truly

exists, and that its existence should no longer be doubted, either I should believe that he was jesting, or I know not which I ought to regard as the greater fool: myself, supposing that I should allow this proof; or him, if he should suppose that he had established with any certainty the existence of this island. For he ought to show first that the hypothetical excellence of this island exists as a real and indubitable fact, and in no wise as any unreal object, or one whose existence is uncertain, in my understanding."

10 See St Anselm, *In reply to Gaunilo's answer in behalf of the fool,* chapters 3 and 5 in *PL* 158, 252 and 255–256.

11 See St Thomas Aquinas, *Summa Theologiae* I, q. 2, a. 1.

12 See St Thomas Aquinas, *Summa Theologiae* I, q. 2, a. 2.

13 See St Thomas Aquinas, *Summa Contra Gentiles* Book 1, chapter 12. Here, St Thomas also remarked that "our knowledge, even of things which transcend the senses, originates from the senses."

14 See St Thomas Aquinas, *Summa Theologiae* I, q. 2, a. 3: "The first and more manifest way is the argument from motion. It is certain, and evident to our senses, that in the world some things are in motion. Now whatever is in motion is put in motion by another, for nothing can be in motion except it is in potentiality to that towards which it is in motion; whereas a thing moves inasmuch as it is in act. For motion is nothing else than the reduction of something from potentiality to actuality. But nothing can be reduced from potentiality to actuality, except by something in a state of actuality. Thus that which is actually hot, as fire, makes wood, which is potentially hot, to be actually hot, and thereby moves and changes it. Now it is not possible that the same thing should be at once in actuality and potentiality in the same respect, but only in different respects. For what is actually hot cannot simultaneously be potentially hot; but it is simultaneously potentially cold. It is therefore impossible that in the same respect and in the same way a thing should be both mover and moved, i.e. that it should move itself. Therefore, whatever is in motion must be put in motion by another. If that by which it is put in motion be itself put in motion, then this also must needs be put in motion by another, and that by another again. But this cannot go on to infinity, because then there would be no first mover, and, consequently, no other mover; seeing that subsequent movers move only inasmuch as they are put in motion by the first mover; as the staff moves only because it is put in motion by the hand. Therefore it is necessary to arrive at a first mover, put in motion by no other;

and this everyone understands to be God."See also Idem, *Summa Contra Gentiles* Book 1, chapter 13: "Whatever is in motion is moved by another: and it is clear to the sense that something, the sun for instance, is in motion. Therefore it is set in motion by something else moving it. Now that which moves it is itself either moved or not. If it be not moved, then the point is proved that we must needs postulate an immovable mover: and this we call God. If, however, it be moved, it is moved by another mover. Either, therefore, we must proceed to infinity, or we must come to an immovable mover. But it is not possible to proceed to infinity. Therefore it is necessary to postulate an immovable mover."

15 See St Thomas Aquinas, *Summa Theologiae* I, q. 2, a. 3: "The second way is from the nature of the efficient cause. In the world of sense we find there is an order of efficient causes. There is no case known (neither is it, indeed, possible) in which a thing is found to be the efficient cause of itself; for so it would be prior to itself, which is impossible. Now in efficient causes it is not possible to go on to infinity, because in all efficient causes following in order, the first is the cause of the intermediate cause, and the intermediate is the cause of the ultimate cause, whether the intermediate cause be several, or only one. Now to take away the cause is to take away the effect. Therefore, if there be no first cause among efficient causes, there will be no ultimate, nor any intermediate cause. But if in efficient causes it is possible to go on to infinity, there will be no first efficient cause, neither will there be an ultimate effect, nor any intermediate efficient causes; all of which is plainly false. Therefore it is necessary to admit a first efficient cause, to which everyone gives the name of God."

16 See St Thomas Aquinas, *Summa Theologiae* I, q. 2, a. 3: "The third way is taken from possibility and necessity, and runs thus. We find in nature things that are possible to be and not to be, since they are found to be generated, and to corrupt, and consequently, they are possible to be and not to be. But it is impossible for these always to exist, for that which is possible not to be at some time is not. Therefore, if everything is possible not to be, then at one time there could have been nothing in existence. Now if this were true, even now there would be nothing in existence, because that which does not exist only begins to exist by something already existing. Therefore, if at one time nothing was in existence, it would have been impossible for anything to have begun to exist; and thus even now nothing would be in existence—which is absurd. Therefore,

not all beings are merely possible, but there must exist something the existence of which is necessary. But every necessary thing either has its necessity caused by another, or not. Now it is impossible to go on to infinity in necessary things which have their necessity caused by another, as has been already proved in regard to efficient causes. Therefore we cannot but postulate the existence of some being having of itself its own necessity, and not receiving it from another, but rather causing in others their necessity. This all men speak of as God."

17 See St Thomas Aquinas, *Summa Theologiae* I, q. 2, a. 3: "The fourth way is taken from the gradation to be found in things. Among beings there are some more and some less good, true, noble and the like. But "more" and "less" are predicated of different things, according as they resemble in their different ways something which is the maximum, as a thing is said to be hotter according as it more nearly resembles that which is hottest; so that there is something which is truest, something best, something noblest and, consequently, something which is uttermost being; for those things that are greatest in truth are greatest in being... Now the maximum in any genus is the cause of all in that genus; as fire, which is the maximum heat, is the cause of all hot things. Therefore there must also be something which is to all beings the cause of their being, goodness, and every other perfection; and this we call God."

18 See St Thomas Aquinas, *Summa Theologiae* I, q. 2, a. 3: "The fifth way is taken from the governance of the world. We see that things which lack intelligence, such as natural bodies, act for an end, and this is evident from their acting always, or nearly always, in the same way, so as to obtain the best result. Hence it is plain that not fortuitously, but designedly, do they achieve their end. Now whatever lacks intelligence cannot move towards an end, unless it be directed by some being endowed with knowledge and intelligence; as the arrow is shot to its mark by the archer. Therefore some intelligent being exists by whom all natural things are directed to their end; and this being we call God."

19 J. Duns Scotus, *Opus Oxoniense*, n. 16.

20 See chapter 1, pp. above for an explanation of the principle of causality.

21 For more on pantheism, see my *Mystery of Creation* (Leominster: Gracewing, 2010^{2}), pp. 8–10, 65 , 70–72, 136–137, 149, 208, 290, 294, 298.

22 A. Dulles, *The New World of Faith* (Huntington, IN: Our Sunday

Visitor, 2000), p. 31.

23 *Ibid.*, p. 32. For a further amusing illustration of the impossibility of an infinite regress see the exposition of Hilbert's Hotel in W. L. Craig, "The Existence of God and the Beginning of the Universe" in *Truth: A Journal of Modern Thought* 3 (1991), pp. 85–96: "Let us imagine a hotel with a finite number of rooms. Suppose, furthermore, that *all the rooms are full.* When a new guest arrives asking for a room, the proprietor apologizes, 'Sorry, all the rooms are full.' But now let us imagine a hotel with an infinite number of rooms and suppose once more that all the rooms are full. There is not a single vacant room throughout the entire infinite hotel. Now suppose a new guest shows up, asking for a room. 'But of course!' says the proprietor, and he immediately shifts the person in room #1 into room #2, the person in room #2 into room #3, the person in room #3 into room #4 and so on, out to infinity. As a result of these room changes, room #1 now becomes vacant and the new guest gratefully checks in. But remember, before he arrived, all the rooms were full! Equally curious, according to the mathematicians, there are now no more persons in the hotel than there were before: the number is just infinite. But how can this be? The proprietor just added the new guest's name to the register and gave him his keys—how can there not be one more person in the hotel than before? But the situation becomes even stranger. For suppose an infinity of new guests show up the desk, asking for a room. 'Of course, of course!' says the proprietor, and he proceeds to shift the person in room #1 into room #2, the person in room #2 into room #4, the person in room #3 into room #6, and so on out to infinity, always putting each former occupant into the room number twice his own. As a result, all the odd numbered rooms become vacant, and the infinity of new guests is easily accommodated. And yet, before they came, all the rooms were full! And again, strangely enough, the number of guests in the hotel is the same after the infinity of new guests check in as before, even though there were as many new guests as old guests. In fact, the proprietor could repeat this process *infinitely many times* and yet there would never be one single person more in the hotel than before. But Hilbert's Hotel is even stranger than the German mathematician gave it out to be. For suppose some of the guests start to check out. Suppose the guest in room #1 departs. Is there not now one less person in the hotel? Not according to the mathematicians–but just ask the woman who makes the beds!

Suppose the guests in room numbers 1, 3, 5, ... check out. In this case an infinite number of people have left the hotel, but according to the mathematicians there are no less people in the hotel—but don't talk to that laundry woman! In fact, we could have every other guest check out of the hotel and repeat this process infinitely many times, and yet there would never be any less people in the hotel. But suppose instead the persons in room number 4, 5, 6, ... checked out. At a single stroke the hotel would be virtually emptied, the guest register reduced to three names, and the infinite converted to finitude. And yet it would remain true that the *same number* of guests checked out this time as when the guests in room numbers 1, 3, 5, ... checked out. Can anyone sincerely believe that such a hotel could exist in reality? These sorts of absurdities illustrate the impossibility of the existence of an actually infinite number of things. If the universe never began to exist, then prior to the present event there have existed an actually infinite number of previous events. Hence, a beginningless series of events in time entails the existence of an actually infinite number of things, namely, past events."

24 Dulles, *The New World of Faith*, p. 32.

25 S. L. Jaki, "The History of Science and the Idea of an Oscillating Universe" in *The Center Journal* 4 (1984), p. 164, footnote 50.

26 *Ibid.*, p. 159.

27 S. L. Jaki, *The Road of Science and the Ways to God* (Edinburgh: Scottish Academic Press, 1978), p. 292.

28 See R. Stannard, "God's Purpose in and Beyond Time" in J. M. Templeton (ed.) *Evidence of Purpose* (New York: Continuum, 1994), p. 43.

29 S. L. Jaki was the first to offer the extension of Gödel's theorem to cosmology in his seminal work *The Relevance of Physics* (Edinburgh: Scottish Academic Press, 1992^2), pp. 127–130; this treatment has been articulated in greater detail in his *Cosmos and Creator* (Edinburgh: Scottish Academic Press, 1980), pp. 49–51, 54, 108; *The Savior of Science* (Washington, DC: Regnery Gateway, 1988), pp. 108–109, 198; "From Scientific Cosmology to a Created Universe" in *Irish Astronomical Journal* 15 (1982), pp. 257–258; *God and the Cosmologists* (Washington, D.C./Edinburgh: Gateway Editions/Scottish Academic Press, 1989), pp. 103–109. For the explanation of the universe as penultimate and God as the Ultimate in intelligibility, see S. L. Jaki, "Physics and the Ultimate" in *Ultimate Reality and Meaning* 11/1 (March 1988), pp. 68–72.

[30] W. Paley, *Natural Theology: or, Evidences of the Existence and Attributes and of the Deity, Collected from the Appearances of Nature* (Boston: Gould, Kendall and Lincoln, 1849), p. 6.

[31] Cf. *Ibid.*, p. 6.

[32] *Ibid.*, p. 26.

[33] *Ibid.*, pp. 293–94.

[34] Stanley Jaki defines the cosmos as the totality of consistently and most specifically interacting contingent but rationally coherent and ordered beings. This composite definition has been put together from S. L. Jaki, *The Road of Science and the Ways to God*, pp. 38, 122; Idem, *Chesterton: A Seer of Science* (Urbana/Chicago: University of Illinois Press, 1986), p. 112. It appears in a large number of Jaki's books and articles in some shape or form. See St Thomas Aquinas, *Summa Theologiae* I, q. 47 art. 3.

[35] St Augustine, *Sermon 241*, chapter 2, 2 in *PL* 38, 1134.

[36] St Thomas Aquinas, *Summa Theologiae* I, q. 39, a. 8.

[37] I. Kant, *Critique of Judgment* §9, trans. J. H. Bernard (New York: Hafner Publications, 1966), p. 54.

[38] St John of the Cross, *Ascent of Mount Carmel*, Book I, Chapter 4, 4.

[39] St John of the Cross, *A Spiritual Canticle of the Soul*, Stanza XXXIX, 14.

[40] Vatican II, *Gaudium et spes*, 18.1; cf. 14.2.

[41] See *CCC* 33.

[42] See J. H. Newman, *The Grammar of Assent* (London: Burns, Oates and Company, 1870) p. 101: "As from a multitude of instinctive perceptions, acting in particular instances, of something beyond the senses, we generalize the notion of an external world, and then picture that world in and according to those particular phenomena from which we started, so from the perceptive power which identifies the intimations of conscience with the reverberations or echoes (so to say) of an external admonition, we proceed on to the notion of a Supreme Ruler and Judge, and then again we image Him and His attributes in those recurring intimations, out of which, as mental phenomena, our recognition of His existence was originally gained. And, if the impressions which His creatures make on us through our senses oblige us to regard those creatures as *sui generis* respectively, it is not wonderful that the notices, which He indirectly gives us through our conscience, of His own nature are such as to make us understand that He is like Himself

and like nothing else."

43 See Newman, *The Grammar of Assent* pp. 110–111.

44 Newman, *The Grammar of Assent* pp. 113.

45 W. Rees-Mogg, "Opinion" in *The Times* (28 August 2000).

46 St Augustine, *Confessions* Book 1, Chapter 1, n. 1 in *PL* 32, 661.

47 Dulles, *The New World of Faith* p. 34.

48 See B. Pascal, *Pensées* translated by W. F. Trotter (New York: E. P. Dutton, 1958), # 233.

49 See *ibid.*. The proof runs as follows: " 'God is, or He is not.' But to which side shall we incline? Reason can decide nothing here. There is an infinite chaos which separated us. A game is being played at the extremity of this infinite distance where heads or tails will turn up... Which will you choose then? Let us see. Since you must choose, let us see which interests you least. You have two things to lose, the true and the good; and two things to stake, your reason and your will, you knowledge and your happiness; and your nature has two things to shun, error and misery. Your reason is no more shocked in choosing one rather than the other, since you must of necessity choose... But your happiness? Let us weigh the gain and the loss in wagering that God is... If you gain, you gain all; if you lose, you lose nothing. Wager, then, without hesitation that He is ... Since there is an equal risk of gain and of loss, if you had only to gain two lives, instead of one, you might still wager. But if there were three lives to gain, you would have to play (since you are under the necessity of playing), and you would be imprudent, when you are forced to play, not to chance your life to gain three at a game where there is an equal risk of loss and gain. But there is an eternity of life and happiness. And this being so, if there were an infinity of chances, of which one only would be for you, you would still be right in wagering one to win two, and you would act stupidly, being obliged to play, by refusing to stake one life against three at a game in which out of an infinity of chances there is one for you, if there were an infinity of an infinitely happy life to gain. But there is here an infinity of an infinitely happy life to gain, a chance of gain against a finite number of chances of loss, and what you stake is finite. It is all divided; wherever the infinite is and there is not an infinity of chances of loss against that of gain, there is no time to hesitate, you must give all ..."

50 The proposition, "The assent of supernatural faith ... is consistent with merely probable knowledge of revelation" was a laxist error condemned by Pope Innocent XI in 1679, as noted in DS 2121.

The Holy Office Decree *Lamentabili sane* in 1907 condemned the proposition (see DS 3425): "the assent of faith rests ultimately on an accumulation of probabilities."

51 J. H. Newman, *The Grammar of Assent* (London: Burns, Oates and Company, 1870), p. 406.

52 Italian text in *AAS* 44 (1952), pp. 31–43. English translation in *DP*, pp. 73–84.

53 Pope Pius XII, *Discourse to the Pontifical Academy of Sciences* (22 November 1951), in *DP*, p. 82.

54 E. T. Whittaker, *Space and Spirit: Theories of the Universe and the Arguments for the Existence of God* (London: Thomas Nelson, 1946), p. 118. See Pius XII, *Discourse to the Pontifical Academy of Sciences* (22 November 1951), in *DP*, p. 83.

55 See Jaki, *The Relevance of Physics*, p. 449. Cf. Idem, *Cosmos and Creator*, p. 18.

56 Pope Pius XII, *Discourse to the Pontifical Academy of Sciences* (22 November 1951), in *DP*, p. 82. Stanley Jaki also notes that in a discourse of Pius XII in 1952, the Pope was quite distanced from too close a link between the physics of his time and metaphysical conclusions. There the Pope stated: "There is still a long way to go, and it seems that the quest will be endless. It is quite unlikely that even the most gifted enquirer will succeed in recognising (and much less solving) all the mysteries locked up in the cosmos." See Jaki, *The Relevance of Physics*, p. 450. See also Pope Pius XII, *Allocutio—iis qui interfuerunt Conventui universali de Astronomia, Romae habito*, in *AAS* 44 (1952), p. 738. English translation in P. J. McLaughlin, *The Church and Modern Science* (New York: Philosophical Library, 1957), p. 192.

57 S. W. Hawking, *A Brief History of Time. From the Big Bang to Black Holes* (New York: Bantam Books, 1988), pp. 46–47.

58 Cf. Pope Pius XII, *Discourse to the Pontifical Academy of Sciences* (22 November 1951), in *DP*, p. 79 where a theory (identified with that of H. Bondi, J. Gold and later F. Hoyle, see Jaki, *Cosmos and Creator*, p. 20) of "the continuous renewal of creation" was described as "too gratuitous".

59 See S. L. Jaki, "Evicting the Creator." Review of: S. W. Hawking, *A Brief History of Time. From the Big Bang to Black Holes* (New York: Bantam Books, 1988) in *Reflections* 7/2 (Spring 1988), p. 20.

60 Pope St John Paul II, *Discourse to the Pontifical Academy of Sciences* (3 October 1981), in *DP*, p. 162. It is significant that Pope John Paul II quoted Pope Pius XII's speech of 22 November 1951,

as follows: "Thirty years ago, on 22 November 1951, my predecessor Pope Pius XII, speaking about the problem of the origin of the universe ... expressed himself as follows: 'In vain would on expect a reply from the sciences of nature, which on the contrary frankly declare that they find themselves faced by an insoluble enigma. It is equally certain that the human mind versed in philosophical meditation penetrates the problem more quickly.'"

61 See *CCC* 35.

8

Pope John Paul II and Human Dignity

The Church constantly makes herself the advocate of mankind which is capable of accepting truth in its entirety. Thus she encourages research which explores all orders of truth, convinced that they all converge to the glory of the one Creator, Himself the supreme Truth and Light of all people, those of yesterday, today and tomorrow

Pope St John Paul II, *Discourse to the Pontifical Academy of Sciences* (29 October 1990).

Pope John Paul II acknowledged the importance of Christianity for the rise of science when he proclaimed, referring to St Albert the Great:

The claim to truth of a science based on rationality is recognized; in fact, it is accepted in its contents, completed, corrected and developed in its independent rationality. And precisely in this way it becomes the property of the Christian world. In this way the latter sees its own understanding of the world enormously enriched without having to give up any essential element of its tradition, far less the foundation of its faith. For there can be no fundamental conflict between a reason which, in conformity with its own nature which comes from God, is geared to truth and is qualified to know truth, and a faith, which refers to the same divine

> source of all truth. Faith confirms, in fact, the specific rights of natural reason.[1]

The limits of science

Pope John Paul II insisted on the limited nature of the scientific enterprise in relation to itself and to other disciplines:

> Science alone is not able to give a complete answer to the question of meanings, which is raised in the crisis. Scientific affirmations are always particular. They are justified only in consideration of a given starting point, they are set in a process of development, and they can be corrected and left behind in this process.
>
> Science alone is not capable of answering the question of meanings, in fact it cannot even set it in the framework of its starting point. And yet this question of meanings cannot tolerate indefinite postponement of its answer. If widespread confidence in science is disappointed, then the state of mind easily changes into hostility to science. In this space that has remained empty, ideologies suddenly break in. They sometimes behave as if they were "scientific" but they owe their power of persuasion to the urgent need for an answer to the question of meanings and to interest in social and political change. Science that is purely functional, without values and alienated from truth, can enter the service of these ideologies; a reason that is only instrumental runs the risk of losing its freedom. Finally there are new manifestations of superstition, sectarianism, and the so-called "new religions" whose appearance is closely connected with the crisis of orientation of culture ... These wrong ways can be detected and avoided by faith.[2]

Realist perception of the cosmos

The Pope affirmed the goodness of the cosmos on many occasions:

> Science in itself is good since it is knowledge of the world, which is good, created and regarded by the Creator with satisfaction, as the book of Genesis says: "And God saw everything that he had made, and behold, it was very good" (Gn 1:31) ... Original sin has not completely spoilt this original goodness. Human knowledge of the world is a way of participating in the Creator's knowledge. It is therefore a first degree of man's resemblance to God, an act of respect towards him, for everything that we discover pays tribute to basic truth.[3]

The concept of participating in the knowledge of God the Creator also reinforces a realist perception of the cosmos. John Paul II often dealt with the real affirmation of the cosmos, and cosmology as a science of the totality:

> Cosmology, a science of the totality of what exists as experimentally observable being, is therefore endowed with a special epistemological status of its own, which sets it more than any other perhaps at the borders of philosophy and religion, since the science of totality leads spontaneously to the question about totality itself, a question which does not find its answers within this totality... Is it not a question, fundamentally, of the great mystery: one that is at the root of all things, of the cosmos and its origins, as well as of man who is capable of studying it and understanding it? If the universe is, as it were, an immense word which, though with difficulty and slowly, can at last be deciphered and understood, who is it who says this word to man?[4]

On the other hand, the cosmologist Stephen Hawking

attempts to exclude God from His own cosmos. His first step is to give an ontological status to the uncertainty principle, which he says "is a fundamental, inescapable property of the world."[5] In this way, it becomes easier to make the cosmos come into being through a quantum-mechanical quirk of nature. At first, Hawking thought that there was an initial singularity of the cosmos, and then in 1981 he used quantum gravity considerations to propose the idea that time and space together form a surface of finite dimensions, but without any edge or boundary. In Hawking's words: "There would be no singularities at which the laws of science would break down and no edge of space-time at which one would have to appeal to God or some new law to set the boundary conditions for space-time. One could say: 'The boundary condition of the universe is that it has no boundary.' The universe would be completely self-contained and not affected by anything outside itself. It would be neither created or destroyed. It would just BE."[6]

Significantly, Hawking admits that "this idea that space and time could be finite without boundary is just a *proposal*: it cannot be deduced from any other principle. Like any other scientific theory, it may initially be put forward for aesthetic or metaphysical reasons, but the real test is whether it makes predictions that agree with observation. This, however, is difficult to determine in the case of quantum gravity" [7]. It would seem that Hawking departs from the sphere of competence of science saying that a theory may be put forward for aesthetic or metaphysical reasons. We would say that a hypothesis should be proposed on the basis of an already existing hypothesis and some empirical data, however remote. It seems that Hawking eliminates God with an *a priori* hypothesis, which makes his argument circular. His conclusion is: "So long as the universe had a beginning, we could suppose it had a creator. But if the universe is really self-contained, having no boundary or edge, it would have neither beginning or end: it would simply be. What place, then, for a creator?" [8]. Hawking seems to limit God's action to an initial singularity in a deistic approach, resulting in a "God of the gaps." The proposition that the universe gave birth to itself in a type of quantum fluctuation is but one example of an illegitimate extrapolation of science outside its own sphere. Physical science has to be related to real or possible experiments, and this cannot be the case in the consideration of the absolute origin of the whole universe from nothing. Science is radically incapable of measuring the boundary of the *whole* universe in space or time, because a scientist cannot get outside of the cosmos. Atheism based on scientific misinterpretation or upon ideologies constructed around scientific theories consists of an irrational leap of reason which runs against reason; it is the gravest form of intellectual suicide. Once the reference to God has been excluded, it is not surprising that the understanding of reality then becomes profoundly deformed.[9]

On many occasions the Pope insisted on the reality of the cosmos: "One must take into account the nature of each being and of its mutual connection in an ordered system, which is precisely the cosmos."[10] He specified that: "Theology, philosophy and science all speak of a harmonious universe, of a 'cosmos' endowed with its own integrity, its own internal, dynamic balance."[11] The concept of the cosmos is linked with the doctrine of Divine Providence: "It is precisely Providence as the transcendent Wisdom of the Creator that ensures that the world is not 'chaos', but 'cosmos.'"[12] On a later occasion the Pope made a similar affirmation: "Those who engage in scientific and technological research admit, as the premise of its progress, that the world is not a chaos but a 'cosmos'; that is to say, that there exist order and natural laws which can be grasped and examined, and which, for this reason, have a certain affinity with the spirit."[13]

On another occasion, speaking to Nobel Prize winners, the Pope highlighted the toilsome nature of scientific investigation of the cosmos:

> The believer holds that the world has an explanation and that, as science advances arduously and toilsomely, even if at times it hesitates and loses its way, it must reach an understanding that the universe constitutes—as the very etymology of the word "universe" indicates—a complex order in which the various elements are harmoniously related with one another.[14]

On yet another occasion, the Pope related this universe to God the Creator, implying again that the cosmos has its explanation outside itself: "The ensemble of creatures *constitutes the universe*: the visible and invisible cosmos, in the totality and the parts of which *there is reflected eternal Wisdom* and expressed the inexhaustible *Love of the Creator.*"[15]

Today part of discussion on the cosmos involves its origins in relation to the Big Bang theory. The Pope was very careful to avoid any confusion between scientific theory and the doctrine of creation *cum tempore*:

> Any scientific hypothesis on the origin of the world, such as the hypothesis of a primitive atom from which derived the whole of the physical universe, leaves open the problem concerning the universe's beginning. Science cannot of itself solve this question: there is needed that human knowledge that rises above physics and astrophysics and which is

> called metaphysics; there is needed above all the knowledge that comes from God's revelation. Thirty years ago, on 22 November 1951, my predecessor Pope Pius XII, speaking about the problem of the origin of the universe ... expressed himself as follows: "In vain would one expect a reply from the sciences of nature, which on the contrary frankly declare that they find themselves faced by an insoluble enigma. It is equally certain that the human mind versed in philosophical meditation penetrates the problem more deeply. One cannot deny that a mind which is enlightened and enriched by modern scientific knowledge and which calmly considers this problem is led to break the circle of matter which is totally independent and autonomous—as being either uncreated or having created itself—and to rise to a creating Mind. With the same clear and critical gaze with which it examines and judges the facts, it discerns and recognises there the work of creative Omnipotence, whose strength raised up by the powerful fiat uttered billions of years ago by the creating Mind, has spread through the universe, calling into existence, in a gesture of generous love, matter teeming with energy."[16]

Hawking misrepresented Pope John Paul II when he commented that the Pope was alleged to have said "it was all right to study the evolution of the universe after the Big Bang, but we should not inquire into the Big Bang itself because that was the moment of Creation and therefore the work of God".[17] Importantly, there are no quotation marks around those words and no citation is offered. Thus this is merely Hawking's impression of what the pope said.

Pope John Paul II further clarified the relation between science and proofs of the existence of God when he stated:

> In speaking of the existence of God we should underline that we are not speaking of proofs in the

> sense implied by the experimental sciences. Scientific proofs in the modern sense of the word are valid only for things perceptible to the senses, since it is only on such things that scientific instruments of investigation can be used. To desire a scientific proof of God would be equivalent to lowering God to the level of the beings of our world, and we would therefore be mistaken methodologically in regard to what God is. Science must recognize its limits and its inability to reach the existence of God. It can neither affirm nor deny his existence.[18]

Science and ideology

At the celebration of the fiftieth anniversary of the Pontifical Academy of Sciences, Pope John Paul II proclaimed what must be the first principle of the relation between faith and science:

> The existence and the activity of this Academy, which was founded by the Holy See and is in constant liaison with it, illustrate above all the fact that there is no contradiction between science and religion. The Church esteems science, and even recognises a certain connaturality with those who dedicate their endeavours to science, as with all who seek to open up the human family to the noblest values of the true, the good and the beautiful, to the understanding of the things that have universal value.[19]

The true corresponds to the study of epistemology, the good to that of ethics and the beautiful to the study of aesthetics. The Pope once again stressed the importance of the sense of the cosmos, and the importance of the human person: "It seems to me today that the scientific community, after a necessary period of extreme specialisation on the level of experimentation, is in the process of recovering interest in things as a whole, *the question of the meaning of the universe*, the marvellous mystery of nature and of the human being."[20]

The Pope indicated the dangers of the reductionism of positivism and instrumentalism, upon the concept of science. By reducing the science to everything that can be measured, analysed and reconstructed into a mathematical system of relationships, philosophy and theology especially were ousted from the sphere of scientific knowledge. The Pope also confronted idealism, saying that the goal of science should not be manipulated or reduced *a priori* to a mathematical model, but must include the totality of the real. In favour of realism the Pope proposed that the Catholic Church believes that this narrowing of the perspective of rational and scientific knowledge does not conform to the authentic vocation of human intelligence, because man is created one in his various faculties to know the real world: be they analytic or synthetic, inductive or deductive, experimental or intuitive. In this sense, the crossroads of all thought is reality. The basis for this realism is the link between creation and incarnation was mentioned. Theology is concerned primarily with the study of the Word of God as expressed in the covenant of creation and the economy of salvation. Above all , theology is based on the fact that in our time, the final days, God has spoken to us in the person of his Son, whom he appointed heir of all things and through whom he made the ages (Heb 1:2).[21]

In a letter addressed to Fr George Coyne, Director of the Vatican Specola on 1 June 1988, on the occasion of the publication of the Acts of the Congress which it has promoted the previous year for the three hundredth anniversary of the publication of Newton's *Philosophiae*

Naturalis Principia Mathematica, Pope John Paul II declared:

> What, then, does the Church encourage in this relational unity between science and religion? First and foremost that they should come to understand one another. For too long a time they have been at arm's length. Theology has been defined as an effort of faith to achieve understanding, as *fides quaerens intellectum*. As such, it must be in vital interchange today with science just as it always has been with philosophy and other forms of learning. Theology will have to call on the findings of science to one degree or another as it pursues its primary concern for the human person, the reaches of freedom, the possibilities of Christian community, the nature of belief and the intelligibility of nature and history. The vitality and significance of theology for humanity will in a profound way be reflected in its ability to incorporate these findings ... Science can purify religion from error and superstition; religion can purify science from idolatry and false absolutes. Each can draw the other into a wider world, a world in which both can flourish.[22]

In this way, Christian faith can purify science from ideological contamination. In a speech addressed to the Pontifical Academy of Sciences, the Pope described knowledge as a mosaic, and in particular, how science is not autonomous, but requires a relationship with other disciplines to complete the picture.

> At first scientific culture grows most of all by the accumulation of many scattered studies. Little by little a mosaic of knowledge in a given field is created. This mosaic needs to be interpreted and analysed in a way that responds to the new demands of rational legitimacy made by each

> discipline. Is it not a sign of a science's maturity when it questions itself and its relationship to the more general order of knowledge?[23]

The Pope added:

> Your studies bear witness to the efforts of human reason to explore reality more fully and to discover the truth in all its dimensions ... Scholars themselves must show the validity of scientific research and its ethical and social legitimacy in the face of the anti-scientific and irrational currents which threaten our present culture. Defending reason is a priority demand of every culture. Scholars will find no better ally than the Church in this struggle ... Indeed, for the Church nothing is more fundamental than knowing the truth and proclaiming it ... The Church constantly makes herself the advocate of mankind which is capable of accepting truth in its entirety. Thus she encourages research which explores all orders of truth, convinced that they all converge to the glory of the one Creator, Himself the supreme Truth and Light of all people, those of yesterday, today and tomorrow.[24]

In a speech addressed to Symposium promoted by the Pontifical Academy of Sciences and the Pontifical Council for Culture, Pope John Paul II further elaborated how the fruitful collaboration between the Church and science continues.

> We are witnessing an extraordinary scientific and technological development. The limits of knowledge seem to be endlessly receding. But, at the same time, we shudder with fear when we see the uses to which it is put. The agitated history of our century confronts us with our respective responsibilities. Today we are more aware, than in the past, of the ambivalence of science. Man can use it for

his betterment, but also for his destruction. Science has so many implications that it calls for an increased awareness on the part of conscience.[25]

Men and women of science, you feel in the depths of your being that the human person cannot, without denying himself, avoid asking the most decisive questions, which science rightly excludes from its field, because these questions belong to another sphere of knowledge.[26]

The evolution of thought and the march of history show, often by means of crises and conflicts, an unstoppable movement towards unity. People are becoming aware that they can no longer live alone and that isolation leads to certain decline. Cultures are opening up to what is universal and are mutually enriching each other. Presumptuous philosophies and ideologies, such as scientism, positivism and materialism, which wanted to be exclusive and claimed to explain everything at the cost of reductionism, have now been overcome. Reality has been discovered in its immensity and complexity, and now produces an attitude of humility in research workers. The experimental method allows one to grasp only certain partial aspects of reality, whereas philosophy, art and religion grasp it in a more or less global way in their specific approaches.[27]

In the face of anti-scientific movements and irrational impulses, which appear as the anguished cries of individuals whose lives have lost all meaning and whom technology is overwhelming, the Church defends the dignity and necessity of scientific and philosophical research, to discover the still hidden secrets of the universe and to shed light on the nature of the human being. Scientists and believers can form a great spiritual family and

> construct a culture which is genuinely searching for the Truth.[28]

The Catechism of the Catholic Church has also stressed the importance and the limits of scientific research, as an expression of the stewardship of man in the cosmos:

> Basic scientific research, as well as applied research, is a significant expression of man's dominion over creation. Science and technology are precious resources when placed at the service of man and promote his integral development for the benefit of all. By themselves however they cannot disclose the meaning of existence and of human progress. Science and technology are ordered to man, from whom they take their origin and development; hence they find in the person and in his moral values both evidence of their purpose and awareness of their limits.[29]

Science must, however, be guided by moral virtue, and serve the good of the human person:

> It is an illusion to claim moral neutrality in scientific research and its applications. On the other hand, guiding principles cannot be inferred from simple technical efficiency, or from the usefulness accruing to some at the expense of others or, even worse, from prevailing ideologies. Science and technology by their very nature require unconditional respect for fundamental moral criteria. They must be at the service of the human person, of his inalienable rights, of his true and integral good, in conformity with the plan and the will of God.[30]

The Catechism also shows how science has shed light on the nature of the cosmos:

> The question about the origins of the world and of man has been the object of many scientific studies

> which have splendidly enriched our knowledge of the age and dimensions of the cosmos, the development of life-forms and the appearance of man. These discoveries invite us to even greater admiration for the greatness of the Creator, prompting us to give him thanks for all his works and for the understanding and wisdom he gives to scholars and researchers. With Solomon they can say: "It is he who gave me unerring knowledge of what exists, to know the structure of the world and the activity of the elements. . . for wisdom, the fashioner of all things, taught me."[31]

However the question is not only the beginning of the cosmos, but deeper issues:

> The great interest accorded to these studies is strongly stimulated by a question of another order, which goes beyond the proper domain of the natural sciences. It is not only a question of knowing when and how the universe arose physically, or when man appeared, but rather of discovering the meaning of such an origin: is the universe governed by chance, blind fate, anonymous necessity, or by a transcendent, intelligent and good Being called "God"? and if the world does come from God's wisdom and goodness, why is there evil? Where does it come from? Who is responsible for it? Is there any liberation from it?[32]

The Galileo affair

No episode in the history of the Catholic Church is so misunderstood as the condemnation of Galileo. In 1979, Pope John Paul II expressed the wish that the Pontifical Academy of Sciences conduct an in-depth study of the celebrated case. The debate, so far as the Church was concerned, had been closed since at least 1741 when

Benedict XIV bid the Holy Office grant an imprimatur to the first edition of the Complete Works of Galileo. A commission of scholars was convened, and they presented their report to Pope John Paul II on 31 October 1992. The Pope was trying to heal the tragic split between faith and science which occurred in the seventeenth century and from which Western culture has not recovered. He explained that:

> From the beginning of the Age of Enlightenment down to our own day, the Galileo case has been a sort of "myth", in which the image fabricated out of the events was quite far removed from reality. In this perspective, the Galileo case was the symbol of the Church's supposed rejection of scientific progress, or of "dogmatic" obscurantism opposed to the free search for truth. This myth has played a considerable cultural role. It has helped to anchor a number of scientists of good faith in the idea that there was an incompatibility between the spirit of science and its rules of research on the one hand and the Christian faith on the other. A tragic mutual incomprehension has been interpreted as the reflection of a fundamental opposition between science and faith. The clarifications furnished by recent historical studies enable us to state that this sad misunderstanding now belongs to the past.[33]

At the heart of the Galileo debate there are two essential aspects. The first is of the epistemological order and concerns biblical hermeneutics. In this regard, two points must be raised. In the first place, like most of his adversaries, Galileo made no distinction between the scientific approach to natural phenomena and a reflection on nature, of the philosophical order, which that approach generally calls for. That is why he rejected the suggestion made to him to present the Copernican system as a hypothesis, inasmuch as it had not been confirmed by irrefutable proof. Such, however, was an exigency of the experimental method of which he was the inspired founder. Second, the geocentric representation of the world was commonly admitted in the culture of the time as fully agreeing with the teaching of the Bible, of which certain expressions taken literally, seemed to affirm geocentrism. The problem posed by the theologians of that age was, therefore, that of the compatibility between heliocentrism and Scripture.[34]

The second aspect of the problem is the pastoral dimension. By virtue of her own mission, the Church has the duty to be attentive to the pastoral consequences of her teaching. Before all else, let it be clear that this teaching must correspond to the truth. But it is a question of knowing how to judge a new scientific datum when it seems to contradict the truths of faith. The pastoral judgement which the Copernican theory required was difficult to make, in so far as geocentrism seemed to be a part of scriptural teaching itself. It would have been necessary all at once to overcome habits of thought and to devise a way of teaching capable of enlightening the people of God. Let us say, in a general way, that the pastor ought to show a genuine boldness, avoiding the double trap of a hesitant attitude and of hasty judgement, both of which can cause considerable harm.[35]

Pope John Paul II declared on this occasion:

> Has not this case long been shelved and have not the errors committed been recognized? That is certainly true. However, *the underlying problems of this case concern both the nature of science and the message of faith.* It is therefore not to be excluded that one day we shall find ourselves in a similar situation, one which will require both sides

> to have an informed awareness of the field and of the limits of their own competencies.[36]

Thus the Galileo case still has something to teach us, the Pope implied, namely that

> the different branches of knowledge call for different methods. Thanks to his intuition as a brilliant physicist and by relying on different arguments, Galileo, who practically invented the experimental method, understood why only the Sun could function as the centre of the world, as it was then known, that is to say as a planetary system. The error of the theologians of the time, when they maintained the centrality of the Earth, was to think that our understanding of the physical world's structure was, in some way, imposed by the literal sense of the Sacred Scripture. Let us recall the celebrated saying attributed to Baronius: "*Spiritui Sancto mentem fuisse nos docere quomodo ad coelum eatur non quomodo coelum gradiatur.*" In fact the Bible does not concern itself with the details of the physical world, the understanding of which is the competence of human experience and reasoning. There exist two realms of knowledge, one which has its source in Revelation and one which reason can discover by its own power. To the latter belong especially the experimental sciences and philosophy. The distinction between the two realms of knowledge ought not to be understood as opposition. The two realms are not altogether foreign to each other; they have points of contact. The methodologies proper to each make it possible to bring out different aspects of reality.[37]

Evolution and the human person

Pope John Paul dealt with the question of evolution on several occasions. At a General Audience dealing with the Book of Genesis he remarked:

> Above all, this text has a religious and theological importance. It doesn't contain significant elements from the point of view of the natural sciences. Research on the origin and development of the individual species in nature does not find in this description any definitive norm or positive contributions of substantial interest. Indeed, the theory of natural evolution, understood in a sense that does not exclude divine causality, is not in principle opposed to the truth about the creation of the visible world, as presented in the Book of Genesis.[38]

In a later audience, he pointed out:

> In modern times the theory of evolution has raised a special difficulty against the revealed doctrine about the creation of man as a being composed of soul and body. With their own methods, many natural scientists study the problem of the origin of human life on earth. Some maintain, contrary to other colleagues of theirs, not only the existence of a link between man and the ensemble of nature, but also his derivation from the higher animal species. This problem has occupied scientists since the last century and involves vast layers of public opinion.
>
> The reply of the Magisterium was offered in the encyclical *Humani Generis* of Pius XII in 1950. In it we read: “The Magisterium of the Church is not opposed to the theory of evolution being the object of investigation and discussion among experts. Here the theory of evolution is understood as an investigation of the origin of the human body from pre-existing living matter, for the Catholic faith

> obliges us to hold firmly that souls are created immediately by God." (DS 3896).
>
> It can therefore be said that, from the viewpoint of the doctrine of the faith, there are no difficulties in explaining the origin of man in regard to the body, by means of the theory of evolution. But it must be added that this hypothesis proposes only a probability, not a scientific certainty. However, the doctrine of faith invariably affirms that man's spiritual soul is created directly by God. According to the hypothesis mentioned, it is possible that the human body, following the order impressed by the Creator on the energies of life, could have been gradually prepared in the forms of antecedent living beings. However, the human soul, on which man's humanity definitively depends, cannot emerge from matter, since the soul is of a spiritual nature.[39]

The chief document of Pope John Paul II regarding this issue is the statement on evolution presented to the Pontifical Academy of Sciences on 22 October 1996. Since "truth cannot contradict truth",[40] the pope reasoned, the findings of the biological sciences cannot conflict with the truth revealed in the gospel. The pope acknowledged that contemporary scientific research from a variety of disciplines shows that evolution is more than a "hypothesis",[41] and he insisted that the Church not maintain any wall between science and theology or suggest that faith is opposed to scientific knowledge.

John Paul made it clear that the main concern of the Church is not with the scientifically examined details of theory of evolution but rather with the religious and moral implications that are drawn from it and the epistemological contexts within which it has been interpreted. The pope in fact recognized that there are approaches to evolution, some of which are deeply influenced by ideological assumptions that need to be examined. Deeply concerned by the ideological misuses of Darwinism in the nineteenth and twentieth centuries, the pope warned against interpreting evolution through the lens of epistemological and ontological reductionism that inevitably eliminate the dignity of the human.

The moral imperative to support the dignity of the person is supported by the religious doctrine that God directly creates each human soul. Each person as a social being is called into community and is responsible for the common good; we are not simply atomistic individuals driven by "selfish genes" in an endless round of ruthless competition with one another. While valuable in itself and regnant in its own limited domain, evolutionary biology and the allied sciences cannot encompass the entire scope of what is meaningfully human. The Pope taught that the human person enjoys a unique dignity based on the spiritual soul:

> With man, we find ourselves facing a different ontological order—an ontological leap, we could say. But in posing such a great ontological discontinuity, are we not breaking up the physical continuity which seems to be the main line of research about evolution in the fields of physics and chemistry? An appreciation for the different methods used in different fields of scholarship allows us to bring together two points of view which at first might seem irreconcilable. The sciences of observation describe and measure, with ever greater precision, the many manifestations of life, and write them down along the time-line. The moment of passage into the spiritual realm is not something that can be observed in this way—although we can nevertheless discern, through experimental research, a series of

> very valuable signs of what is specifically human life. But the experience of metaphysical knowledge, of self-consciousness and self-awareness, of moral conscience, of liberty, or of aesthetic and religious experience—these must be analyzed through philosophical reflection, while theology seeks to clarify the ultimate meaning of the Creator's designs.[42]

Failure to account for the distinctively spiritual dimension of human experience leads to de-humanizing policies and attitudes of the sort seen in support for euthanasia, cloning, and abortion.

Faith and reason

The principal thrust of John Paul II's encyclical *Fides et Ratio*, which summarizes his teaching on the relationship of faith and reason, is a plea that we not lose the search for ultimate truth. He writes, for instance: "She [the Church] sees in philosophy the way to come to know fundamental truths about human life ... I wish to reflect upon this special activity of human reason. I judge it necessary to do so because at the present time in particular the search for ultimate truth seems often to be neglected"[43]

In this search there are various ways of knowing and among them he contrasts philosophy with the natural sciences: "It may help, then, to turn briefly to the different modes of truth. Most of them depend upon immediate evidence or are confirmed by experimentation. This is the mode of truth proper to everyday life and to scientific research. At another level we find philosophical truth, attained by means of the speculative powers of the human intellect."[44] It is clear that philosophy and the natural sciences must each have their autonomy: "St. Albert the Great and St. Thomas were the first to recognize the autonomy which philosophy and the sciences needed if they were to perform well in their respective fields of research."[45]

Pope John Paul II described scientism as "the philosophical notion which refuses to admit the validity of forms of knowledge other than those of the positive sciences; and it relegates religious, theological, ethical and aesthetic knowledge to the realm of mere fantasy." Scientism is not based on the certainty of truth, but on ultimate faith in scientific techniques; it implicitly holds that man can create meaning and re-create himself. Since it rejects any "ethical judgment," the Pope continued, "the scientistic mentality has succeeded in leading many to think that if something is technically possible it is therefore morally admissible."[46]

Backing for a linear concept of history came from Pope John Paul II, when he proposed that the concept of nature "also expresses the meaning of history, which comes from God and advances towards its end, the return of all created things to God; therefore history cannot be understood as cyclical, for the Creator is also the God of salvation history".[47]

At the Jubilee for scientists in the year 2000, Pope John Paul II illustrated how scientific research investigates the cosmos and can draw the scientist closer to the Creator:

> Based on an attentive observation of the complexity of terrestrial phenomena, and following the object and method proper to each discipline, scientists discover the laws which govern the universe, as well as their interrelationship. They stand in wonderment and humility before the created order and feel drawn to the love of the Author of all things. Faith, for its part, is able to integrate and assimilate every research, for all research, through a deeper understanding of created reality in all its specificity, gives man the

> possibility of discovering the Creator, source and goal of all things. "Ever since the creation of the world his invisible nature, namely his eternal power and deity, has been clearly perceived in the things that have been made" (Rom 1:20).
>
> By increasing his knowledge of the universe, and in particular of the human being, who is at its centre, man has a veiled perception, as it were, of the presence of God, a presence which he is able to discern in the "silent manuscript" written by the Creator in creation, the reflection of his glory and grandeur. God loves to make himself heard in the silence of creation, in which the intellect senses the transcendence of the Lord of Creation. Everyone who seeks to understand the secrets of creation and the mysteries of man must be ready to open their mind and heart to the deep truth which manifests itself there, and which "draws the intellect to give its consent".[48]

Later in the same Jubilee Year, Pope John II remarked: "You, my dear friends who are involved in scientific research, must make universities 'cultural laboratories' in which theology, philosophy, human sciences and natural sciences may engage in constructive dialogue, looking to the moral law as an intrinsic requirement of research and a condition for its full value in seeking out the truth."[49]

On many occasions, Pope John Paul II insisted on the objective reality of what science investigates, despite the involvement of the observer in the scientific process:

> Analysis of the anthropological dimension of science raises above all else a precise set of epistemological questions and issues. That is to say, one wants to emphasize that the observer is always involved in the object that is observed. This is true not only in research into the extremely small,

> where the limits to knowledge due to this close involvement have been evident and have been discussed philosophically for a long time, but also in the most recent research into the extremely large, where the particular philosophical approach adopted by the scientist can influence in a significant way the description of the cosmos, when questions spring forth about everything, about the origins and the meaning of the universe itself.
>
> Truth, freedom and responsibility are connected in the experience of the scientist. In setting out on his path of research, he understands that he must tread not only with the impartiality required by the objectivity of his method but also with the intellectual honesty, the responsibility, and I would say with a kind of "reverence", which befit the human spirit in its drawing near to truth.[50]

This realist notion of the cosmos was reaffirmed in a message to astrophysicists at the Vatican Observatory:

> Your astrophysical research is not a luxury remote from the daily concerns of people and irrelevant to the building of a more humane world. What you do as scientists is important for all of us, especially when your empirically grounded vision of reality leads to an understanding of the human person as an integral element in the created universe, that is, when it leads to the wisdom which is at the heart of all genuine humanism.[51]

The Pope highlighted how a growth in scientific knowledge also assists philosophy and theology in their quest:

> This knowledge represents an extraordinary and profound value for the entire human family, and it is also of immeasurable significance for the disciplines of philosophy and theology as they continue along the path of *intellectus quaerens fidem* and of

> *fides quarens intellectum*, as they seek an ever more complete understanding of the wealth of human knowledge and of Biblical revelation. If philosophy and theology today grasp better than in the past what it means to be a human being in the world, they owe this in no small part to science, because it is science that has shown us how numerous and complex the works of creation are and how seemingly limitless the created cosmos is. The utter marvel that inspired the first philosophical reflections on nature does not diminish as new scientific discoveries are made. Rather, it increases with each fresh insight that is gained. The species capable of "creaturely amazement" is transformed as our grasp of truth and reality becomes more comprehensive, as we are led to search ever more deeply within the realm of human experience and existence.[52]

On the occasion of the fourth centenary celebrations for the Pontifical Academy of Sciences, Pope John Paul II once again illustrated this common quest for the truth:

> Our gatherings have also enabled me to clarify important aspects of the Church's doctrine and life relating to scientific research. We are united in our common desire to correct misunderstandings and even more to allow ourselves to be enlightened by the one Truth which governs the world and guides the lives of all men and women. I am more and more convinced that scientific truth, which is itself a participation in divine Truth, can help philosophy and theology to understand ever more fully the human person and God's Revelation about man, a Revelation that is completed and perfected in Jesus Christ. For this important mutual enrichment in the search for the truth and the benefit of mankind, I am, with the whole Church, profoundly grateful.[53]

The Pope has also treated the creativity of science and its relation to a participation in the activity of God the Creator:

> Revelation teaches that men and women are created in the "image and likeness of God" (cf. Gn 1:26) and thus possessed of a special dignity which enables them, by the work of their hands, to reflect God's own creative activity. In real way, they are meant to be "co-creators" with God, using their knowledge and skill to shape a cosmos in which the divine plan constantly moves towards fulfilment. This human creativity finds privileged expression in the pursuit of knowledge and scientific research. As a spiritual reality, such creativity must be responsibly exercised; it demands respect for the natural order and, above all, for the nature of each human being, inasmuch as man is its subject and end.[54]

This creativity is related to a realist perspective on the cosmos:

> Contemporary scientists, faced with the explosion of new knowledge and discoveries, frequently feel that they are standing before a vast and infinite horizon. Indeed, the inexhaustible bounty of nature, with its promise of ever new discoveries, can be seen as pointing beyond itself to the Creator who has given it to us as a gift whose secrets remain to be explored. In attempting to understand this gift and to use it wisely and well, science constantly encounters a reality which human beings "find". In every phase of scientific discovery, nature stands as something "given". For this reason, creativity and progress along the paths of discovery, as in all other human endeavours, are ultimately to be understood against the backdrop of the mystery of creation itself.[55]

> Despite the uncertainties and the labour which every attempt to interpret reality entails—not only in the sciences, but also in philosophy and theology—the paths of discovery are always paths towards truth. And every seeker after truth, whether aware of it or not, is following a path which ultimately leads to God, who is Truth itself.[56]

Notes

1 Pope John Paul II, *Discourse to teachers and university students in Cologne Cathedral* (15 November 1980).

2 Pope John Paul II, *Discourse to teachers and university students in Cologne Cathedral* (15 November 1980).

3 Pope John Paul II, *Discourse to the European Physical Society* (30 March 1979) in *IG* 2/1 (1979) p. 748. Cfr. also Gn 1:31.

4 Pope John Paul II, *Discourse to participants in a conference on the problem of the cosmos* (28 September 1979), in *IG* 2/2 (1979) p. 401.

5 S. W. Hawking, *A Brief History of Time* (London: Bantam Press, 1988), p. 55.

6 *Ibid.*, p. 136.

7 *Ibid.*, pp. 136–137.

8 *Ibid.*, pp. 140–141.

9 See Pope John Paul II, Encyclical *Evangelium Vitae*, 22.3.

10 Pope John Paul II, Encyclical *Sollicitudo rei socialis*, 34.2.

11 Pope John Paul II, Message for the World day of Peace, *Peace with God the Creator. Peace with all of creation*, 8.1.

12 Pope John Paul II, *Discourse at General Audience* (14 May 1986).

13 Pope John Paul II, *Discourse to the Pontifical Academy of Sciences* (31 October 1992), 14.

14 Pope John Paul II, *Discourse to Nobel Prize-Winners* (22 December 1980), in *IG* 3/2 (1980), p. 1784.

15 Pope John Paul II, *Discourse at General Audience* (12 March 1986).

16 Pope John Paul II, *Discourse to the Pontifical Academy of Sciences* (3 October 1981). See also Pope Pius XII, *Discourse to the Pontifical Academy of Sciences* (22 November 1951).

17 Hawking, *A Brief History of Time*, p. 120.

18 Pope John Paul II, *Discourse at General Audience* (10 July 1985), 1.

19 Pope John Paul II, *Discourse to the Pontifical Academy of Sciences* (28 October 1986), 3.

20 *Ibid.*, 7.

21 Pope John Paul II, *Discourse on the occasion of the tricentennial of Newton's* Principia Mathematica in *OR* 127/231 (27 September 1987), p. 5.

22 Pope John Paul II, *Message to the Reverend George V. Coyne, SJ, Director of the Vatican Observatory*, on the occasion of the publication of the Acts of the Congress for the tercentenary of the publication of Newton's *Principia Mathematica* in *IG* 11/2 (1988), p. 1706.

23 Pope John Paul II, *Discourse to the Pontifical Academy of Sciences* (29 October 1990), 3.

24 *Ibid.*

25 Pope John Paul II, *Discourse Address to the Symposium on* Science in the Context of Human Culture II (4 October 1991), 5.

26 *Ibid.*

27 *Ibid.*, 6. See Pope John Paul II, *Address at the European Centre for Nuclear Research* (15 June 1982), 4–5.

28 Pope John Paul II, *Discourse Address to the Symposium on* Science in the Context of Human Culture II (4 October 1991), 8.

29 *CCC* 2293.

30 *CCC* 2294.

31 *CCC* 283. Cf. Wis 7: 17–22.

32 *CCC* 284.

33 Pope John Paul II, *Discourse to the Pontifical Academy of Sciences* (31 October 1992), 10.

34 *Ibid*, 5.

35 *Ibid*, 7.

36 *Ibid*, 4.

37 *Ibid.*, 12. In English, Cardinal Baronius's quip indicates that the Bible "is intended to teach us how to go to heaven, not how the heavens go". Centuries earlier St Augustine had already written something similar: "We do not read in the Gospel that the Lord said, 'I will send the Paraclete to teach you the course of the sun and the moon', in fact He wanted to create Christians not mathematicians." (*De actis contra Felicem manichaeum*, 1.10.)

38 Pope John Paul II, *Discourse at General Audience* (29 January 1986).

39 Pope John Paul II, *Discourse at General Audience* (16 April 1986).

[40] Pope John Paul II, *Message to the Pontifical Academy of Sciences* (22 October 1996), 2. See also Leo XIII, *Providentissimus Deus.*

[41] *Ibid.*, 4. The English edition of the document at first translated the French original as: "Today, more than a half-century after the appearance of that encyclical, some new findings lead us toward the recognition of more than one hypothesis within the theory of evolution." The *Osservatore Romano* English Edition subsequently amended the text to that given, citing the translation of the other language editions as its reason. It should be noted that an hypothesis is the preliminary stage of the scientific method and the Pope's statement suggests nothing more than the concept that science has progressed beyond that stage.

[42] *Ibid.*, 6.

[43] Pope John Paul II, *Fides et Ratio,* 5.

[44] *Ibid.*, 30.

[45] *Ibid.*, 45.

[46] *Ibid.*, 88.

[47] Pope John Paul II, *Discourse to the Pontifical Academy of Sciences* (27 October 1998), 4.

[48] Pope John Paul II, *Discourse at the Jubilee for Scientists* (25 May 2000), 3. See St Albert the Great, *Commentary on John,* 6, 44.

[49] Pope John Paul II, *Discourse at the Jubilee for University Professors* (9 September 2000), 5.

[50] Pope John Paul II, *Discourse to the Pontifical Academy of Sciences* (13 November 2000), 2, 3.

[51] Pope John Paul II, *Message to the Participants in the Eighth Vatican Observatory School in Astrophysics* (6 July 2001)

[52] Pope John Paul II, *Discourse to the Pontifical Academy of Sciences* (11 November 2002).

[53] Pope John Paul II, *Discourse to the Pontifical Academy of Sciences* (10 November 2003).

[54] Pope John Paul II, *Discourse to the Pontifical Academy of Sciences* (8 November 2004), 2. See also Idem, *Laborem exercens,* 4; Vatican II, *Gaudium et spes,* 34.

[55] Pope John Paul II, *Discourse to the Pontifical Academy of Sciences* (8 November 2004), 3. See also Idem, *Laborem exercens,* 12.

[56] Pope John Paul II, *Discourse to the Pontifical Academy of Sciences* (8 November 2004), 4. See also Idem, *Fides et Ratio,* 16, 28.

9

Pope Benedict XVI and the Logos

Scientific research and the question of meaning, also in their specific epistemological and methodological physiognomy, spring from only one source, the Logos that presides over the work of creation and guides the intelligence of history.

Pope Benedict XVI, *Discourse on the visit to the Gemelli Hospital* (3 May 2012)

Early work

The starting point of this chapter is the monumental work of Professor Joseph Ratzinger, *Introduction to Christianity*, which reached its twelfth edition in a little more than thirty years. What are the relations between scientific thought and theology present in this work? The book is actually an exposition of faith in the context of scientific rationality, in the context of the environment addressed by the author. This specificity is not only expressed by the fact that Joseph Ratzinger has often cited scientists as well as philosophers, but also in the rigour and constant attention to reason with which ideas are proposed and developed. The style of this work enables the exposition of the Creed in a manner suited to an intellectual audience, accustomed to strict reasoning, and therefore also the man of science. In some pages of the work, Ratzinger also presents some ideas of Teilhard de Chardin, showing, with great balance, the potential for a re-reading of the cosmic relationship between anthropology and Christology.[1] It is clear that the author does not endorse the many ambiguous positions of Teilhard de Chardin.[2]

In the preface to the new edition of his *Introduction to Christianity* (2000), the then Cardinal Ratzinger indicated the consequences of forgetting God for today's technological society: a relationship between science and human life, where the human being is seen as a technical object and vanishes more and more as a human being. Rarely there are isolated horrified voices reacting to the news that in the laboratory embryos are "grown" as "material", from which to harvest the "stocks" of organs that could serve other humans.[3]

In his lectures, Professor Ratzinger dealt with the relationship between faith and science, particularly the theory of evolution. He asked to what extent faith is linked to the concept of the creation by God the of individual fundamental realities in the world. This way of posing the question, leads to a general problem that should represent the central issue of the whole problem: is the depiction of a world in the making reconcilable with the fundamental biblical idea of the creation of the world by the Word? Can the idea of being expressed in the Bible coexist with that of becoming proposed by the theory of evolution?[4]

Among these questions emerges another one, this time concerning fundamental theology: that of the relationship between the image of the world and faith in general. In this attempt to think at one and the same time in a creationist and a scientific evolutionary perspective, a world-picture is attributed to faith which is quite different from the image of the world that until now would have to be regarded as the true image of the world of faith. The crux of the whole of our reflections lies precisely in this process: faith has been robbed of its image in the world, which seemed even to be identified with her nature, and she has been given another world-picture. Can one do this without cancelling the identity of faith?[5] Cardinal Ratzinger concludes that belief in creation needs to understand faith in a world in becoming, made accessible empirically by science. He also clearly outlines the answer to the question about the creation of man: it is clear that the spirit is not a random product of the development of matter, but rather that the matter is a moment in the history of the spirit. But this is simply another way of expressing the fact that the spirit is created and not purely a product of development. Every person is more than a product of hereditary and environmental factors, nobody is only a result of calculable factors in the world; the mystery of creation is above all of us.[6]

This beautiful vision of the relationship between faith and science was further developed by Cardinal Ratzinger when he was Archbishop of Munich, in a series of homilies four homilies on creation in the Liebfrauenkirche, the cathedral church of Munich in Germany, preached in the spring of 1981.[7] He addressed, somewhat prophetically, the question of the relationship between creation and evolution:

> Through the reason of creation, God himself looks at us. Physics, biology, the natural sciences in general, have given us a new, unheard-of account of creation, with grandiose and new images, which enable us to recognize the face of the Creator and make us know again: Yes, in the beginning and deep down in every being is the Creator Spirit. The world is not the product of darkness and the absurd. It comes from an intelligence, from a freedom, from a beauty that is love. To acknowledge this, infuses in us the courage that enables us

> to live, that makes us capable of confidently facing life's venture.[8]

The Cardinal further specified the role of Holy Scripture in this regard:

> One answer was already worked out some time ago, as the scientific view of the world was gradually crystallizing ... It says that the Bible is not a natural science textbook, nor does it intend to be such. It is a religious book, and consequently one cannot obtain information about the natural sciences from it. One cannot get from it a scientific explanation of how the world arose; one can only glean religious experience from it.[9]

Cardinal Ratzinger then applied this clarification to the relationship between Creation and evolution:

> We cannot say: creation or evolution, inasmuch as these two things respond to two different realities. The story of the dust of the earth and the breath of God, which we just heard, does not in fact explain how human persons come to be but rather what they are. It explains their inmost origin and casts light on the project that they are. And, vice versa, the theory of evolution seeks to understand and describe biological developments. But in so doing it cannot explain where the "project" of human persons comes from, nor their inner origin, nor their particular nature. To that extent we are faced here with two complementary—rather than mutually exclusive—realities.[10]

The Cardinal delineated the respective spheres of competence which faith and science enjoy in the examination of this issue:

> It is the affair of the natural sciences to explain how the tree of life in particular continues to grow and

> how new branches shoot out from it. This is not a matter for faith. But we must have the audacity to say that the great projects of the living creation are not the products of chance and error. Nor are they the products of a selective process to which divine predicates can be attributed in illogical, unscientific, and even mythic fashion. The great projects of the living creation point to a creating Reason and show us a creating Intelligence, and they do so more luminously and radiantly today than ever before. Thus we can say today with a new certitude and joyousness that the human being is indeed a divine project, which only the creating Intelligence was strong and great and audacious enough to conceive of. Human beings are not a mistake but something willed; they are the fruit of love. They can disclose in themselves, in the bold project that they are, the language of the creating Intelligence that speaks to them and that moves them to say: Yes, Father, you have willed me.[11]

In 1990, the then Cardinal Ratzinger gave a talk at Parma on science and rationality. Some elements within the mass-media tried to misuse his comments to make it appear the Cardinal was against Galileo. Instead he simply called to mind a symptomatic case that highlights how far the question of modernity itself has influenced science and technology today. Today, the resistance of creation to manipulation by humanity has emerged as a new element in the overall cultural situation. The question of the limits of science, and the criteria which it must observe, has become unavoidable. Particularly emblematic, for Ratzinger, of this change of intellectual climate, is the different light in which the Galileo case is seen. This episode, which was little considered in the eighteenth century, was elevated to a myth of the Enlightenment in the century that followed. Galileo appeared as a victim of that medieval obscurantism that endures in the Church. Good and evil were sharply distinguished. On the one hand, the Inquisition is personified as a power that incarnates superstition, the adversary of freedom and conscience. On the other, there is natural science represented by Galileo: the force of progress and liberation of humanity from the chains of ignorance that kept it impotent in the face of nature. The star of modernity shines in the dark night of medieval obscurity.[12]

Today, things have changed, and not all exponents of modern thought are agreed with this caricature. Ratzinger indicated that, for Ernst Bloch, the heliocentric system—just like the geocentric—is based upon presuppositions that cannot be empirically demonstrated. Among these, an important role is played by the affirmation of the existence of an absolute space; an opinion which, in any event, has been cancelled by the Theory of Relativity. Curiously, it was precisely Bloch, with his Romantic Marxism, who was among the first to openly oppose the Galileo myth, offering a new interpretation of what happened. The advantage of the heliocentric system over the geocentric, Bloch suggested, does not consist in a greater correspondence to objective truth, but solely in the fact that it offers a greater ease of calculation. To this point, Bloch adds simply a modern conception of natural science. What is surprising, however, is the conclusion he draws:

> Once the relativity of movement is taken for granted, an ancient human and Christian system of reference has no right to interference in astronomic calculations and their heliocentric simplification; however, it has the right to remain faithful to its method of preserving the earth in relation to human dignity, and to order the world with regard to what will happen and what has happened in the world.[13]

If both the spheres of conscience are once again clearly distinguished among themselves under their respective methodological profiles, recognizing both their limits and their respective rights, then the synthetic judgment of the agnostic-sceptic philosopher P. Feyerabend appears much more drastic. He writes: "The Church at the time of Galileo was much more faithful to reason than Galileo himself, and also took into consideration the ethical and social consequences of Galileo's doctrine. Its verdict against Galileo was rational and just, and revisionism can be legitimized solely for motives of political opportunism."[14]

From the point of view of the concrete consequences of the turning point Galileo represents, however, C.F. Von Weizsacker takes another step forward, when he identifies a "very direct path" that leads from Galileo to the atomic bomb. To his great surprise, in a recent interview on the Galileo case, Cardinal Ratzinger was not asked a question like, "Why did the Church try to get in the way of the development of modern science?", but rather exactly the opposite, that is: "Why didn't the church take a more clear position against the disasters that would inevitably follow, once Galileo had opened Pandora's box?" It would be absurd, on the basis of these affirmations, to construct a hurried apologetics. The faith does not grow from resentment and the rejection of rationality, but from its fundamental affirmation and from being inscribed in a still greater form of reason.[15]

In his discussions with Professor Marcello Pera, Cardinal Ratzinger addressed the issue of the roots of rationality and the nature of science. First he proposes that modern science is a Western invention that has a universal value.[16] The Church, when she dialogues with science, should examine what is it that holds the world together. It is not matter which creates reason, nor chance that produces meaning.

Rather the intellect, the logos, and reason come first, so that reason, freedom and the good are already part of the principles that build reality.[17]

The Logos and the human person

From the beginning of his pontificate, Pope Benedict XVI affirmed: "We are not the random and meaningless product of evolution. Each of us is the result of a thought of God. Each of us is willed, each is loved, each is necessary."[18] He then examined this concept further. At the general audience of 9 November 2005, Pope Benedict XVI commented on a Homily of St. Basil and stated the presence of a clear evidence of purpose and design in the world and the full rationality of its recognition by man:

> I find the words of this fourth-century Father surprisingly up to date when he says: Some people, "deceived by the atheism they bore within them, imagined that the universe lacked guidance and order, at the mercy as it were of chance". How many these "some people" are today! Deceived by atheism they consider and seek to prove that it is scientific to think that all things lack guidance and order as though they were at the mercy of chance. The Lord through Sacred Scripture reawakens our reason which has fallen asleep and tells us: in the beginning was the creative Word. In the beginning the creative Word—this Word that created all things, that created this intelligent design which is the cosmos—is also love.[19]

The Pope later further developed this train of thought. In an address to the Pontifical Academy of Sciences and the Pontifical Academy of Social Sciences, he affirmed that the human person is at the heart of the whole social order.

In the words of St. Thomas Aquinas, the human person "signifies what is most perfect in nature".[20]

Human beings are part of nature and, yet, as free subjects who have moral and spiritual values, they transcend nature. This anthropological reality is an integral part of Christian thought, and responds directly to the attempts to abolish the boundary between human sciences and natural sciences, often proposed in contemporary society.

Understood correctly, this reality offers a profound answer to the questions posed today concerning the status of the human being. This is a theme which must continue to be part of the dialogue with science. The Church's teaching is based on the fact that God created man and woman in his own image and likeness and granted them a superior dignity and a shared mission towards the whole of creation (cf. Genesis 1 and 2). According to God's design, persons cannot be separated from the physical, psychological or spiritual dimensions of human nature. Even though cultures change over time, to suppress or ignore the nature that they claim to "cultivate" can have serious consequences. Likewise, individuals will only find authentic fulfillment when they accept the genuine elements of nature that constitute them as persons.

The concept of person continues to bring about a profound understanding of the unique character and social dimension of every human being. This is especially true in legal and social institutions, where the notion of "person" is fundamental. Sometimes, however, even when this is recognized in international declarations and legal statutes, certain cultures, especially when not deeply touched by the Gospel, remain strongly influenced by group-centered ideologies or by an individualistic and secularist view of society.[21]

In an address of Pope Benedict XVI to cardinals, archbishops, bishops and members of the Roman Curia in the traditional exchange of Christmas greetings, he proposed points of interest to the dialogue between faith and science. First of all, there was the invitation not to see the world that surrounds us solely as raw material with which we can do something, but to try to discover in it "the Creator's handwriting", the creative reason and the love from which the world was born and of which the universe speaks to us, if we pay attention, if our inner senses awaken and acquire perception of the deepest dimensions of reality. As a second element there is a further invitation: to listen to the historical revelation which alone can offer us the key to the interpretation of the silent mystery of creation, pointing out to us the practical way toward the true Lord of the world and of history, who conceals himself in the poverty of the stable in Bethlehem.[22]

Science and rationality

The Pope saw the relation of faith and science within the relationship between the Church and the world: "This relationship had a somewhat stormy beginning with the Galileo case. It was then totally interrupted when Kant described 'religion within pure reason'." Later, the natural sciences began to reflect more and more clearly their own limitations imposed by their own method, which, despite achieving great things, was nevertheless unable to grasp the global nature of reality.[23]

In a address for the Angelus on Trinity Sunday 2006, the Pope referred to the design in the universe as a manifestation of the Love of its Creator: "For those who have faith, the entire universe speaks of the Triune God. From the spaces between the stars to microscopic particles, all that exists refers to a Being who communicates himself in the multiplicity and variety of elements, as in an immense symphony."[24]

In his visit to Bavaria, the Pope stressed the rationality of creation.

> From the Enlightenment on, science, at least in part, has applied itself to seeking an explanation of the world in which God would be unnecessary. And if this were so, he would also become unnecessary in our lives. But whenever the attempt seemed to be nearing success—inevitably it would become clear: something is missing from the equation! When God is subtracted, something doesn't add up for man, the world, the whole universe. So we end up with two alternatives. What came first? Creative Reason, the Creator Spirit who makes all things and gives them growth, or Unreason, which, lacking any meaning, yet somehow brings forth a mathematically ordered cosmos, as well as man and his reason. The latter, however, would then be nothing more than a chance result of evolution and thus, in the end, equally meaningless. As Christians, we say: "I believe in God the Father, the Creator of heaven and earth"—I believe in the Creator Spirit. We believe that at the beginning of everything is the eternal Word, with Reason and not Unreason. With this faith we have no reason to hide, no fear of ending up in a dead end.[25]
>
> In his speech on the occasion of his visit in Verona, the Pope emphasized the rational foundations of science: Mathematics, as such, is a creation of our intelligence: the correspondence between its structures and the real structures of the universe—which is the presupposition of all modern scientific and technological developments, already expressly formulated by Galileo Galilei with the famous

> affirmation that the book of nature is written in mathematical language—arouses our admiration and raises a big question. It implies, in fact, that the universe itself is structured in an intelligent manner, such that a profound correspondence exists between our subjective reason and the objective reason in nature. It then becomes inevitable to ask oneself if there might not be a single original intelligence that is the common font of them both. Thus, precisely the reflection on the development of science brings us towards the creator *Logos.* The tendency to give irrationality, chance and necessity the primacy is overturned, also to lead our intelligence and our freedom back to it. Upon these bases it again becomes possible to enlarge the area of our rationality, to reopen it to the larger questions of the truth and the good, to link theology, philosophy and science between them in full respect for the methods proper to them and of their reciprocal autonomy, but also in the awareness of the intrinsic unity that holds them together. This is the task that is before us, a fascinating adventure that is worth our effort, to give a new thrust to the culture of our time and to restore the Christian faith to full citizenship in it.[26]

In the speech on his visit to the Pontifical Gregorian University, Pope Benedict XVI said:

> Here, I cannot forget the other human sciences which are encouraged at this famous University in the wake of the glorious academic tradition of the Roman College. The great prestige the Roman College acquired in the fields of mathematics, physics and astronomy is well known to all. It suffices to remember that the "Gregorian" Calendar, so-called because it was desired by my Predecessor, Gregory XIII, and currently in use

throughout the world, was compiled in 1582 by Fr Christopher Clavius, a Lecturer at the Roman College. It suffices also to mention Fr Matteo Ricci, who took to as far as distant China the knowledge he had acquired as a disciple of Fr Clavius, in addition to his witness to the faith. Today, the above-mentioned disciplines are no longer taught at the Gregorian University, but have been replaced by other human sciences such as psychology, the social sciences and social communications. Thus, man desires to be more deeply understood, both in his profound personal dimension and his external dimension as a builder of society in justice and peace, and as a communicator of the truth. For the very reason that these sciences concern the human being, they cannot set aside reference to God. In fact, man, both in his interiority and in his exteriority, cannot be fully understood unless he recognizes that he is open to transcendence. Deprived of his reference to God, man cannot respond to the fundamental questions that trouble and will always trouble his heart concerning the end of his life, hence, also its meaning. As a result, it is no longer possible to introduce into society those ethical values that alone can guarantee a coexistence worthy of man. Human destiny without reference to God cannot but be the desolation of anguish, which leads to desperation. Only in reference to God's Love which is revealed in Jesus Christ can man find the meaning of his existence and live in hope, even if he must face evils that injure his personal existence and the society in which he lives. Hope ensures that man does not withdraw into a paralyzing and sterile nihilism but opens himself instead to generous commitment within the society where he lives in order to improve it. This is the task that God entrusted to

> man when he created him in his own image and likeness, a task that fills every human being with the greatest possible dignity, but also with an immense responsibility.[27]

In a speech to the participants in the plenary of the Pontifical Academy of Sciences in 2006, Pope Benedict has delved into this subject of the responsibility of the human being:

> The increasing "advance" of science, and especially its capacity to master nature through technology, has at times been linked to a corresponding 'retreat' of philosophy, of religion, and even of the Christian faith. Indeed, some have seen in the progress of modern science and technology one of the main causes of secularization and materialism: why invoke God's control over these phenomena when science has shown itself capable of doing the same thing? Certainly the Church acknowledges that "with the help of science and technology..., man has extended his mastery over almost the whole of nature", and thus "he now produces by his own enterprise benefits once looked for from heavenly powers".[28]

The Pope continued:

> Science, however, while giving generously, gives only what it is meant to give. Man cannot place in science and technology so radical and unconditional a trust as to believe that scientific and technological progress can explain everything and completely fulfil all his existential and spiritual needs. Science cannot replace philosophy and revelation by giving an exhaustive answer to man's most radical questions: questions about the meaning of living and dying, about ultimate values, and about the nature of progress itself. For this reason, the Second

> Vatican Council, after acknowledging the benefits gained by scientific advances, pointed out that the "scientific methods of investigation can be unjustifiably taken as the supreme norm for arriving at truth", and added that "there is a danger that man, trusting too much in the discoveries of today, may think that he is sufficient unto himself and no longer seek the higher values".[29]

The scientific method itself, in its gathering of data and in the processing and use of those data in projections, has inherent limitations that necessarily restrict scientific predictability to specific contexts and approaches. Science cannot, therefore, presume to provide a complete, deterministic representation of our future and of the development of every phenomenon that it studies. Philosophy and theology might make an important contribution to this fundamentally epistemological question by, for example, helping the empirical sciences to recognize a difference between the mathematical inability to predict certain events and the validity of the principle of causality, or between scientific indeterminism or contingency (randomness) and causality on the philosophical level, or, more radically, between evolution as the origin of a succession in space and time, and creation as the ultimate origin of participated being in essential Being.

At the same time, there is a higher level that necessarily transcends all scientific predictions, namely, the human world of freedom and history. Whereas the physical cosmos can have its own spatial-temporal development, only humanity, strictly speaking, has a history, the history of its freedom. Freedom, like reason, is a precious part of God's image within us, and it can never be reduced to a deterministic analysis. Its transcendence vis-à-vis the material world must be acknowledged and respected, since it is a sign of our human dignity. Denying that transcendence in the name of a supposed absolute ability of the scientific method to predict and condition the human world would involve the loss of what is human in man, and, by failing to recognize his uniqueness and transcendence, could dangerously open the door to his exploitation.[30]

The Pope placed the relationship between faith and science in the context of faith and reason. He made a strong appeal against Deism:

> God is *Spiritus Creator,* he is *Logos,* he is reason. And this is why our faith is something that has to do with reason, can be passed on through reason and has no cause to hide from reason, not even from the reason of our age. But precisely this eternal, immeasurable reason is not merely a mathematics of the universe and far less, some *first cause* that withdrew after producing the *Big Bang*. This reason, on the contrary, has a heart such as to be able to renounce its own immensity and take flesh. And in that alone, to my mind, lies the ultimate, true greatness of our conception of God. We know that God is not a philosophical hypothesis, he is not something that *perhaps* exists, but we know him and he knows us. And we can know him better and better if we keep up a dialogue with him.[31]

The topic of creation and evolution came up again in one of those question and answer sessions with the clergy of Belluno-Feltre and Treviso in Italy.

> The big problem is that were God not to exist and were he not also the Creator of my life, life would actually be a mere cog in evolution, nothing more; it would have no meaning in itself. Instead, I must seek to give meaning to this component of being. Currently, I see in Germany, but also in the United States, a somewhat fierce debate raging between so-called "creationism" and evolutionism, pre-

sented as though they were mutually exclusive alternatives: those who believe in the Creator would not be able to conceive of evolution, and those who instead support evolution would have to exclude God. This antithesis is absurd because, on the one hand, there are so many scientific proofs in favour of evolution which appears to be a reality we can see and which enriches our knowledge of life and being as such. But on the other, the doctrine of evolution does not answer every query, especially the great philosophical question: where does everything come from? And how did everything start which ultimately led to man? I believe this is of the utmost importance. This is what I wanted to say in my lecture at Regensburg: that reason should be more open, that it should indeed perceive these facts but also realize that they are not enough to explain all of reality. They are insufficient. Our reason is broader and can also see that our reason is not basically something irrational, a product of irrationality, but that reason, creative reason, precedes everything and we are truly the reflection of creative reason. We were thought of and desired; thus, there is an idea that preceded me, a feeling that preceded me, that I must discover, that I must follow, because it will at last give meaning to my life. This seems to me to be the first point: to discover that my being is truly reasonable, it was thought of, it has meaning. And my important mission is to discover this meaning, to live it and thereby contribute a new element to the great cosmic harmony conceived of by the Creator. If this is true, then difficulties also become moments of growth, of the process and progress of my very being, which has meaning from conception until the very last moment of life.[32]

Science and the Logos

In the Encyclical *Spe Salvi*, Pope Benedict addressed the relationship between Christian hope and the scientific enterprise:

> That a new era emerged—through the discovery of America and the new technical achievements that had made this development possible—is undeniable. But what is the basis of this new era? It is the new correlation of experiment and method that enables man to arrive at an interpretation of nature in conformity with its laws and thus finally to achieve "the triumph of art over nature" (*victoria cursus artis super naturam*). The novelty—according to Bacon's vision—lies in a new correlation between science and praxis. This is also given a theological application: the new correlation between science and praxis would mean that the dominion over creation—given to man by God and lost through original sin—would be reestablished. Anyone who reads and reflects on these statements attentively will recognize that a disturbing step has been taken: up to that time, the recovery of what man had lost through the expulsion from Paradise was expected from faith in Jesus Christ: herein lay "redemption". Now, this "redemption", the restoration of the lost "Paradise" is no longer expected from faith, but from the newly discovered link between science and praxis. It is not that faith is simply denied; rather it is displaced onto another level—that of purely private and other-worldly affairs—and at the same time it becomes somehow irrelevant for the world. This programmatic vision has determined the trajectory of modern times and it also shapes the present-day crisis of faith which is essentially a crisis of Christian hope.[33]

The Pope concludes that it is not science that redeems man; man is redeemed by love and this truth applies even in terms of this present world.[34] Recalling that it is not science that redeems man, Benedict XVI warns us against the idea of a science that would rule by itself, regardless of an ethical law, as presupposed by mere faith in progress. It is the responsibility of ethics to lead the way to real progress that mankind, conscious of its dignity, is entitled to expect from science.[35]

In the speech that Pope Benedict XVI would have addressed during the visit to the University *La Sapienza* in Rome, scheduled for 17 January 2008, then cancelled on 15 January 2008, the Pope stressed the importance of the Middle Ages for the University and the scientific enterprise: "In medieval theology there was a detailed disputation on the relationship between theory and practice, on the proper relationship between knowledge and action—a disputation that we need not explore here. De facto, the medieval university with its four faculties expresses this correlation. Let us begin with the faculty which was understood at the time to rank as the fourth—the faculty of medicine. Even if it was considered more as an "art" than a science, the inclusion of medicine within the ambit of the *universitas* clearly indicated that it was placed within the realm of rationality, that the art of healing was under the guidance of reason and had been removed from the realm of magic."[36]

Pope Benedict wished to invite reason to set out ever anew in search of what is true and good, in search of God; to urge reason, in the course of this search, to discern the illuminating lights that have emerged during the history of the Christian faith, and thus to recognize Jesus Christ as the Light that illumines history and helps us find the path towards the future.[37]

The risk that humans can become an object of ideological manipulation or abuse was denounced once again by Benedict XVI, and so scientific progress must be able to resist the temptation to restrict human identity to technical parameters: "Whereas the exact, natural and human sciences have progressed prodigiously in the knowledge of man and his universe, there is a strong temptation to seek to isolate the identity of the human being and to enclose this identity in the knowledge that can derive from it. In order to avoid moving in this direction it is important to support anthropological, philosophical and theological research which allows the appearance and preservation in man of his own mystery, for no science can say who man is, where he comes from or where he is going."[38] The Pope stressed that it is important to recognize that the sciences, philosophy and theology can be mutually helpful for perceiving the human identity which is constantly developing.[39]

As a human person, man is never closed in on himself; he is always a bearer of otherness and from the very first moment of his existence interacts with other human beings, as the human sciences increasingly bring to light. How is it possible not to recall here the marvellous meditation of the Psalmist on the human being, knit together in the secret of his mother's womb and at the same time known in his identity and mystery to God alone, who loves and protects him (cf. Ps 139:1-16)? Man is neither the result of chance nor of a bundle of convergences nor of forms of determinism nor physio-chemical interaction; he is a being who enjoys freedom, which, while taking his nature into account, transcends it and symbolizes this mystery of otherness that dwells within him. Man bears within himself a specific capacity for discerning what is good and right. Affixed in him as a seal by the Creator, *synderesis* urges him to do good. Impelled by it, the human being is required to develop his conscience by forming and using it in order to direct his life freely based on the essential laws which are natural law and moral law. In our day, when the development of the sciences attracts and seduces with the possibilities they offer, it is more important than ever to educate the consciences of our contemporaries in order to prevent science from becoming the criterion of good and to ensure that man is respected as the centre of creation and not made the object of ideological manipulation, arbitrary decisions or the abuse of the weaker by the stronger. These are some of the dangers we have experienced in human history, especially during the twentieth century. Every scientific approach must also be a loving approach, called to be at the service of the human being and of humanity and to make its contribution to forming the identity of individuals.[40]

More recently, through new information technologies, globalization has often also resulted in disseminating in all cultures many of the materialistic and individualistic elements of the West. The formula *Etsi Deus non daretur* is increasingly becoming a way of living that originates in a sort of arrogance of reason—a reality nonetheless created and loved by God—that deems itself self-sufficient and closes itself to contemplation and the quest for a superior Truth. The light of reason, exalted but in fact impoverished by the Enlightenment, has radically replaced the light of faith, the light of God.[41]

The Pope has always stressed the importance of a fruitful dialogue between science and faith, which has been long awaited by the Church but also by the scientific community.

> Through it, faith implies reason and perfection, and reason, enlightened by faith, finds the strength to rise to the knowledge of God and spiritual

> realities. In this sense secularization does not foster the ultimate goal of science which is at the service of man, "imago Dei". May this dialogue continue in the distinction of the specific characteristics of science and faith. Indeed, each has its own methods, contexts and subjects of research, its own aims and limitations, and must respect and recognize the other's legitimate possibility of exercising autonomy in accordance with its own principles; both are called to serve man and humanity, encouraging the integral development and growth of each one and all.[42]

Pope Benedict has also indicated how science and philosophy are increasingly related in today's world: "In our own day, scientists themselves appreciate more and more the need to be open to philosophy if they are to discover the logical and epistemological foundation for their methodology and their conclusions. For her part, the Church is convinced that scientific activity ultimately benefits from the recognition of man's spiritual dimension and his quest for ultimate answers that allow for the acknowledgement of a world existing independently from us, which we do not fully understand and which we can only comprehend in so far as we grasp its inherent logic. Scientists do not create the world; they learn about it and attempt to imitate it, following the laws and intelligibility that nature manifests to us. The scientist's experience as a human being is therefore that of perceiving a constant, a law, a logos that he has not created but that he has instead observed: in fact, it leads us to admit the existence of an all-powerful Reason, which is other than that of man, and which sustains the world. This is the meeting point between the natural sciences and religion. As a result, science becomes a place of dialogue, a meeting between man and nature and, potentially, even between man and his Creator." Noteworthy here is the Pope's stress on a realist perspective.[43]

The doctrine of the Logos has features many times in the addresses of Pope Benedict and he sees that this lies at the basis of the fertile European root of culture and progress. This fertile root involved the search for the absolute—the *quaerere Deum*— and included the need to study further the natural sciences.[44] The Pope added:

> In fact, scientific research and the question of meaning, also in their specific epistemological and methodological physiognomy, spring from only one source, the Logos that presides over the work of creation and guides the intelligence of history. An essential techno-practical mentality generates a risky imbalance between what is technically possible and what is morally good, with unforeseeable consequences.[45]

A religion of the *Logos*, Christianity does not relegate faith to the realm of the irrational, but attributes the origin and meaning of reality to a creative Reason, which in the crucified God manifested itself as love and which invites us to undertake the path of the *quaerere Deum*: "I am the Way, the Truth and the Life."[46] Pope Benedict pointed out that lived in its integrality, research is illumined by science and faith, and from these two "wings" it draws impulse and outburst, without ever losing the rightful humility, the sense of its own limit. In this way the search for God becomes fecund for the intelligence, ferment of culture, promoter of true humanism, a search that does not stop on the surface.[47]

Reason needs to be completed by love for science to be fully human. It is in fact the love of God, which shines in Christ, which renders acute and penetrating the look of research and to grasp what no research is able to grasp. It belongs to man's nature to read in others the image of God-love and his imprint on creation. Without love, science also loses its nobility. Love alone guarantees the humanity of research.[48]

In the context of a study carried out by the Pontifical Academy of Sciences concerning complexity in the cosmos, Pope Benedict XVI pointed out how the concept of analogy is important:

> Such an interdisciplinary approach to complexity also shows too that the sciences are not intellectual worlds disconnected from one another and from reality but rather that they are interconnected and directed to the study of nature as a unified, intelligible and harmonious reality in its undoubted complexity. Such a vision has fruitful points of contact with the view of the universe taken by Christian philosophy and theology, with its notion of participated being, in which each individual creature, possessed of its proper perfection, also shares in a specific nature and this within an ordered cosmos originating in God's creative Word. It is precisely this inbuilt "logical" and "analogical" organization of nature that encourages scientific research and draws the human mind to discover the horizontal co-participation between beings and the transcendental participation by the First Being. The universe is not chaos or the result of chaos, rather, it appears ever more clearly as an ordered complexity which allows us to rise, through comparative analysis and analogy, from specialization towards a more universalizing viewpoint and vice versa. While the very first moments of the cosmos and life still elude scientific observation, science nonetheless finds itself pondering a vast set of processes which reveals an order of

> evident constants and correspondences and serves as essential components of permanent creation.
>
> It is within this broader context that I would note how fruitful the use of analogy has proved for philosophy and theology, not simply as a tool of horizontal analysis of nature's realities, but also as a stimulus to creative thinking on a higher transcendental plane. Precisely because of the notion of creation, Christian thought has employed analogy not only for the investigation of worldly realities, but also as a means of rising from the created order to the contemplation of its Creator, with due regard for the principle that God's transcendence implies that every similarity with his creatures necessarily entails a greater dissimilarity: whereas the structure of the creature is that of being a being by participation, that of God is that of being a being by essence, or *Esse subsistens*. In the great human enterprise of striving to unlock the mysteries of man and the universe, I am convinced of the urgent need for continued dialogue and cooperation between the worlds of science and of faith in the building of a culture of respect for man, for human dignity and freedom, for the future of our human family and for the long-term sustainable development of our planet. Without this necessary interplay, the great questions of humanity leave the domain of reason and truth, and are abandoned to the irrational, to myth, or to indifference, with great damage to humanity itself, to world peace and to our ultimate destiny.[49]

In 2011, in his Epiphany sermon, Pope Benedict turned once again to the truth of a rational universe, not guided by chance: "But, as sages, the Magi also knew that it is not with any kind of telescope but rather with the profound eyes of reason in search of the ultimate meaning of reality and with the desire for God, motivated by faith, that it is possible to meet him, indeed, becomes possible for God to come close to us."

Pope Benedict insisted that the universe is not the result of chance, as some would like to make us believe. In contemplating it, we are asked to interpret in it something profound; the wisdom of the Creator, the inexhaustible creativity of God, his infinite love for us. We must not let our minds be limited by theories that always go only so far and that—at a close look—are far from competing with faith but do not succeed in explaining the ultimate meaning of reality. We cannot but perceive in the beauty of the world, its mystery, its greatness and its rationality, the eternal rationality; nor can we dispense with its guidance to the one God, Creator of Heaven and of earth.[50]

As we have seen, the relationship between faith and science in the thought of Joseph Ratzinger, and later, Pope Benedict XVI is modulated according to the parameters of faith and reason with particular emphasis on the Logos of rationality and love. In its turn, the relationship between faith and reason is placed in the context of divine revelation given by Jesus Christ and its reception in human culture.

Notes

1 Cfr. J. Ratzinger, *Introduction to Christianity* (San Francisco: Ignatius Press, 2004), pp. 236–238.

2 See ibid., p. 236, where Ratzinger gently chides Teihard de Chardin for his "not entirely unobjectionable tendency toward the biological approach". See also my book, *Creazione e creatività scientifica* (Leominster: Gracewing, 2009), pp. 272, where I stated that the theological problem in the vision of Teilhard de Chardin is that his concept of creation is no longer applied in the biblical sense, and the transcendence of God is therefore not expressed with

sufficient clarity. In his vision, the natural and the supernatural are confused, and matter and spirit are not distinct enough. In addition, the mystery of evil is neglected and the angelic world seems to have no place in this system. The freedom of God in Creation is not clear and so the cosmos may seem necessary rather than contingent. Man's freedom is also not evident. Cfr. *L'Osservatore Romano,* 1 July 1962 (N. 148) which refers to the *Monitum* directed to P. Teilhard de Chardin as found in *AAS* 54 (1962), p. 166.

3 Ratzinger, *Introduction to Christianity,* Introductory Essay to the new 2000 edition, p. 17.

4 J. Ratzinger, Lecture «Fede nella creazione e teoria dell'evoluzione», which is part of a collection of essays entitled o *Wer ist das eigentlich—Gott?* (München 1969). Italian transaltion by *Il foglio quotidiano* (23 dicembre 2005).

5 *Ibid.*

6 *Ibid.*

7 J. Ratzinger, *'In the Beginning...': A Catholic Understanding of the Story of Creation and the Fall,* (Grand Rapids: William. B. Eerdmans Publishing Co., 1995).

8 *Ibid.*, 25.

9 *Ibid.*, p. 5.

10 *Ibid.*, p. 50.

11 *Ibid.*, p. 56.

12 Cfr. J. Ratzinger, *Discorso a Parma su Galileo* (15 marzo 1990) in Idem, *Svolta per l'Europa? Chiesa e modernità nell'Europa dei rivolgimenti* (Roma: Paoline, 1992), pp. 76–79.

13 Cfr. *ibid.* See also E. Bloch, *Das Prinzip Hoffnung* (Frankfurt/Main, 1959), p. 920f.; F. Hartl, *Der Begriff des Schopferischen. Deutungsversuche der Dialektik durch E. Bloch und F. v. Baader,* (Frankfurt/Main 1979), p. 111.

14 Cfr. J. Ratzinger, *Discorso a Parma su Galileo*. See also P. Feyerabend, *Wider den Methodenzwang* (FrankfurtM/Main 1976, 1983), p. 206.

15 Cfr. J. Ratzinger, *Discorso a Parma su Galileo*, pp. 76–79.

16 Cf. M. Pera, J. Ratzinger, *Without Roots. The West, Relativism, Christianity, Islam* (New York: Basic Books, 2006), p. 2.

17 Cf. *ibid.*, p. 127.

18 Papa Benedict XVI, *Homily at the beginning of his Petrine ministry* (24 April 2005).

[19] Pope Benedict XVI, *Discourse at General Audience* (9 November 2005). Cfr. St Basil the Great, *On Genesis*, 1, 2, 4.

[20] St Thomas Aquinas, *Summa Theologiae* I, q.29, a.3.

[21] See Pope Benedict XVI, *Discourse to the Pontifical Academy of Social Sciences and to the Pontifical Academy of Sciences* (21 November 2005).

[22] Pope Benedict XVI, *Discourse to the Roman Curia on the occasion of the exchange of Christmas Greetings* (22 December 2005).

[23] *Ibid.*

[24] Pope Benedict XVI, *Angelus Discourse* (11 June 2006).

[25] Pope Benedict XVI, *Homily during the Mass at Islinger Feld*, Regensburg (12 September 2006).

[26] Pope Benedict XVI, *Address to the Participants at the Fourth National Congress of the Italian Church* (19 October 2006).

[27] Pope Benedict XVI, *Address to the Pontifical Gregorian University* (3 November 2006).

[28] Pope Benedict XVI, *Discourse to the Pontifical Academy of Sciences* (6 November 2006). See also Vatican II, *Gaudium et spes*, 33.

[29] Pope Benedict XVI, *Discourse to the Pontifical Academy of Sciences* (6 November 2006). See also Vatican II, *Gaudium et spes*, 57.

[30] Pope Benedict XVI, *Discourse to the Pontifical Academy of Sciences* (6 November 2006).

[31] Pope Benedict XVI, *Discourse at the conclusion of the meeting with the Swiss bishops* (9 November 2006).

[32] Pope Benedict XVI, *Meeting with the Clergy of the Dioceses of Belluno-Feltre and Treviso* (24 July 2007).

[33] Pope Benedict XVI, Enciclical *Spe Salvi*, 16–17. Cfr. also F. Bacon, *Novum Organum* I, 117, 129.

[34] Pope Benedict XVI, Enciclical *Spe Salvi*, 26.

[35] Cfr. Cardinal G. Cottier, "Le pretese salvifiche della scienza moderna" in *L'Osservatore Romano* (11 April 2008).

[36] Pope Benedict XVI, *Address for the meeting with the university of Rome "La Sapienza"* (17 January 2008).

[37] *Ibid.*

[38] Pope Benedict XVI, *Address to the participants in the Inter-Academic Conference sponsored by the Académie des Sciences in Paris and the Pontifical Academy of Sciences* (28 January 2008).

[39] *Ibid.*

[40] *Ibid.*

[41] Pope Benedict XVI, *Address to the participants in the plenary*

assembly of the Pontifical Council for Culture (8 March 2008). Cfr. Pope Benedict XVI, *Address for the meeting with the university of Rome "La Sapienza"* (17 January 2008). The same expression *etsi Deus non daretur* was treated in J. Ratzinger, Introductory Essay to the new 2000 edition of *Introduction to Christianity*, p. 16. The Latin phrase, *etsi Deus non daretur*, was coined by the famous Dutch international lawyer Hugo Grotius. It was the key concept by which God was removed from natural law which, in turn, became itself "autonomous." Once autonomous, subject only to our own consciousness, we could fashion it as we pleased in principle. From hence forward, ominously, we had "natural rights" which were not based in anything but human will.

[42] Pope Benedict XVI, *Address to the participants in the plenary assembly of the Pontifical Council for Culture* (8 March 2008). Cfr. Vatican II, *Gaudium et spes*, 36.

[43] Pope Benedict XVI, *Discourse to the Pontifical Academy of Sciences* (28 October 2010),

[44] Pope Benedict XVI, *Discourse on the visit to the Gemelli Hospital*, Rome, (3 May 2012). See also Idem, Address to the College of Bernardins of Paris (12 September 2008).

[45] Pope Benedict XVI, *Discourse on the visit to the Gemelli Hospital*, Rome, (3 May 2012).

[46] *Ibid.*

[47] *Ibid.*

[48] See *ibid.*

[49] Pope Benedict XVI, *Discourse to the Pontifical Academy of Sciences* (8 November 2012).

[50] Pope Benedict XVI, *Sermon* (6 January 2011).

10

Pope Francis and the Periphery

The Church has no wish to hold back the marvellous progress of science. On the contrary, she rejoices and even delights in acknowledging the enormous potential that God has given to the human mind. Whenever the sciences—rigorously focused on their specific field of inquiry—arrive at a conclusion which reason cannot refute, faith does not contradict it. Neither can believers claim that a scientific opinion which is attractive but not sufficiently verified has the same weight as a dogma of faith. At times some scientists have exceeded the limits of their scientific competence by making certain statements or claims. But here the problem is not with reason itself, but with the promotion of a particular ideology which blocks the path to authentic, serene and productive dialogue.

Pope Francis, *Evangelii gaudium*

Early life

Pope Francis was born in Buenos Aires on 17 December 1936, the son of Italian immigrants, and baptised Jorge Mario Bergoglio. His father Mario was an accountant employed by the railways and his mother Regina Sivori was a committed wife dedicated to raising their five children. When Jorge Mario Bergoglio was a young man, he graduated from technical school as a chemical technician. He then earned his Masters degree in chemistry from the University of Buenos Aires. Only afterwards did he follow the path of the priesthood, entering the Diocesan Seminary of Villa Devoto. On 11 March 1958 he entered the novitiate of the Society of Jesus. He went to Casa Loyola in Chile in 1958 to start his juniorate, studying languages, liberal arts, and basic human sciences geared toward ministry. He completed his studies of the humanities in Chile and returned to Argentina in 1963 to graduate with a degree in philosophy from the Major Seminary of San José in San Miguel. From 1964 to 1965 he taught literature and psychology at Immaculate Conception College in Santa Fé and in 1966 he taught the same subject at the College of El Salvador in Buenos Aires. From 1967–1970 he studied theology and obtained a degree from the Major Seminary of San José.

On 13 December 1969 he was ordained a priest by Archbishop Ramón José Castellano. From 1970 to 1971 he completed the third probation at Alcala de Henares, Spain, and on 22 April 1973, pronounced his perpetual vows, including the final fourth vow (obedience to the pope) in the Society of Jesus. Back in Argentina, he was novice master from 1972 to 1973 at Villa Varilari, San Miguel where he was also professor of theology.

He made a pilgrimage to Jerusalem in 1973, shortly after being named Provincial Superior, but his stay was shortened by the outbreak of the Yom Kippur War. On 31 July 1973 he was appointed Provincial of the Jesuits in Argentina, an office he held for six years. From 1980 to 1986 he was rector of the Philosophical and Theological Faculty of San Miguel as well as pastor of the Patriarca San Jose parish in the Diocese of San Miguel. In March 1986 he went to Sankt Georgen Graduate School of Philosophy and Theology in Frankfurt, Germany, to start a doctoral thesis on Romano Guardini; it seems the project did not come to fruition. In Augsburg, Germany, he saw the painting of Mary, Untier of Knots, and brought a copy of the image back to Argentina where it has become an important Marian devotion. His superiors then sent him to the College of El Salvador and then to Cordoba where he served as a confessor and spiritual director. Cardinal Antonio Quarracino, Archbishop of Buenos Aires wanted Fr Bergoglio as a close collaborator. So, on 20 May 1992 Pope John Paul II appointed him titular Bishop of Auca and Auxiliary of Buenos Aires. On 27 May he received episcopal ordination from the Cardinal in the cathedral. He chose as his episcopal motto, *miserando atque eligendo,* and on his coat of arms inserted the IHS, the symbol of the Society of Jesus.

He gave his first interview as a bishop to a parish newsletter, *Estrellita de Belém.* He was immediately appointed Episcopal Vicar of the Flores district and on 21 December 1993 was also entrusted with the office of Vicar General of the Archdiocese. Thus it came as no surprise when, on 3 June 1997, he was raised to the dignity of Coadjutor Archbishop of Buenos Aires. Scarcely nine months had passed when, upon the death of Cardinal Quarracino, he succeeded him on 28 February 1998, as Archbishop, Primate of Argentina and Ordinary for Eastern-rite faithful in Argentina who have no Ordinary of their own rite.

Three years later, at the Consistory of 21 February 2001, Pope John Paul II created him Cardinal, assigning him the title of San Roberto Bellarmino. Bergoglio asked the faithful not to come to Rome to celebrate his creation as Cardinal but rather to donate to the poor what they would have spent on the journey. As Grand Chancellor of the Catholic University of Argentina, he is the author of the books:

Meditaciones para religiosos (1982), *Reflexiones sobre la vida apostólica* (1992) and *Reflexiones de esperanza* (1992).

In October 2001 he was appointed General Relator to the tenth Ordinary General Assembly of the Synod of Bishops on the Episcopal Ministry. This task was entrusted to him at the last minute to replace Cardinal Edward Michael Egan, Archbishop of New York, who was obliged to stay in his homeland because of the terrorist attacks on 11 September. At the Synod he placed particular emphasis on "the prophetic mission of the bishop", his being a "prophet of justice", his duty to "preach ceaselessly" the social doctrine of the Church and also "to express an authentic judgement in matters of faith and morals".

All the while Cardinal Bergoglio was becoming ever more popular in Latin America. Despite this, he never relaxed his sober approach or his strict lifestyle, which many have defined as "ascetic". In this spirit of poverty, he declined to be appointed as President of the Argentine Bishops' Conference in 2002, but three years later he was elected and then, in 2008, reconfirmed for a further three-year mandate. Meanwhile, in April 2005 he took part in the Conclave in which Pope Benedict XVI was elected.

As Archbishop of Buenos Aires—a diocese with more than three million inhabitants—he conceived of a missionary project based on communion and evangelization. He had four main goals: open and brotherly communities, an informed laity playing a lead role, evangelization efforts addressed to every inhabitant of the city, and assistance to the poor and the sick. He aimed to re-evangelize Buenos Aires, "taking into account those who live there, its structure and its history". He asked priests and lay people to work together. In September 2009 he launched the solidarity campaign for the bicentenary of the Independence of the country. Two hundred charitable agencies are to be set up by 2016. And on a continental scale, he expected much from the impact of the message of the Aparecida Conference in 2007, to the point of describing it as the "*Evangelii Nuntiandi* of Latin America".

Following the abdication of Pope Benedict XVI on 28 February 2013, a papal conclave elected Cardinal Jorge Mario Bergoglio as his successor on 13 March. He chose Francis as his papal name in honour of Saint Francis of Assisi. Francis is the first Jesuit Pope, the first Pope from the Americas, the first Pope from the Southern Hemisphere and the first non-European Pope since Pope Gregory III in 741.

The periphery

The Church is experiencing the extraordinary impact of Pope Francis following his election to the See of Peter. Through his genuine kindness and easy familiarity with people of every religious viewpoint and attitude, she is witnessing various renewed aspects and expressions of the Petrine office. The Church is embracing a servant leader who, inspired by the *Poverello* of Assisi, has cast aside the trappings of the papal court. A recurring theme of the thought of Pope Francis is what he calls "the periphery". In a pre-conclave speech to his fellow cardinals, that may well have influenced his election, he provided an insight into his agenda for the Church.

> When the Church does not come out of herself to evangelize, she becomes self-referential and then gets sick ... The evils that, over time, happen in ecclesial institutions have their root in self-referentiality and a kind of theological narcissism. In Revelation, Jesus says that He is at the door and knocks. Obviously, the text refers to His knocking from the outside in order to enter but I think about

> the times in which Jesus knocks from within so that we will let Him come out. The self-referential Church keeps Jesus Christ within herself and does not let Him out.[1]

In the encyclical *Evangelii Gaudium*, Francis writes that "Each Christian and every community must discern the path that the Lord points out, but all of us are asked to obey His call to go forth from our own comfort zone in order to reach all the 'peripheries' in need of the light of the Gospel."[2] Francis also adopts the concept of existential peripheries. In his address to the bishops of Latin America Pope Francis wrote: "That is why I like saying that the position of missionary disciples is not in the centre but at the periphery: they live poised towards the peripheries … including the peripheries of eternity, in the encounter with Jesus Christ … The disciple is sent to the existential peripheries."[3] In an address to the diocese of Rome he also stated:

> The Gospel is for everyone! This reaching out to the poor does not mean we must become champions of poverty or, as it were, "spiritual tramps"! No, no this is not what it means! It means we must reach out to the flesh of Jesus that is suffering, but also suffering is the flesh of Jesus of those who do not know it with their study, with their intelligence, with their culture. We must go there! I therefore like using the expression "to go toward the outskirts", the outskirts of existence. All the outskirts, from physical and real poverty to intellectual poverty, which is also real. All the peripheries, all the crossroads on the way: go there. And sow there the seed of the Gospel with your words and your witness.[4]

On another occasion, the Pope said that in priestly ministry, "the light of witness can be obscured or hidden under a bushel if there is a lack of missionary spirit, of the wish to go out to the peripheries, with an ever-renewed missionary conversion to seek or encounter those who await Christ's Good News."[5]

In a philosophical sense too, he cautions against seeing the world through the lens of one narrow ideological scheme. Flexibility is all. A wise thinker, he says, needs to see things from multiple perspectives, from the edges:

> I am convinced of one thing: the great changes in history were realized when reality was seen not from the centre but rather from the periphery. It is a hermeneutical question: reality is understood only if it is looked at from the periphery, and not when our viewpoint is equidistant from everything. Truly to understand reality we need to move away from the central position of calmness and peacefulness and direct ourselves to the peripheral areas. Being at the periphery helps to see and to understand better, to analyze reality more correctly, to shun centralism and ideological approaches ... It is not a good strategy to be at the centre of a sphere. To understand we ought to move around, to see reality from various viewpoints. We ought to get used to thinking ... This is really very important to me: the need to become acquainted with reality by experience, to spend time walking on the periphery in order really to become acquainted with the reality and life-experiences of people. If this does not happen we then run the risk of being abstract ideologists or fundamentalists, which is not healthy.[6]

Like many recent Biblical scholars from the Global South, Francis bases his "peripheral" principles in the life of Jesus:

> The fulfilment of the evangelical command "Go to the whole world and proclaim the Gospel to every creature" (Mk 16:15) can be accomplished with this hermeneutical key shifted to the existential and

> geographical periphery. It is the most concrete way of imitating Jesus, who went toward all the peripheries. Jesus went to all, really all. I would not really feel uncomfortable going to the periphery: you should not feel uncomfortable in reaching out to anyone.[7]

But what is actually meant by the periphery? One could look at various groups and decide whether they occupy the periphery in societal terms, or ecclesial terms, or both. Migrant workers, undocumented persons and street people seem to be situated both at the socio-economic and ecclesial periphery. In Western Europe and North America, divorced and remarried Catholics experience virtually no social stigma but often find themselves relegated to the periphery of Church life. One could reverse the equation. Devout Catholics who publicly oppose abortion and same-sex marriage occupy a kind of ecclesial centre in terms of their adherence to magisterial teaching, but their views are increasingly at odds not only with civil society, but even with a significant number of self-identified Catholics. Traditionalist Catholics as well share an ecclesial experience of marginalization.

Pope Francis' approach to the periphery needs to be interpreted in light of another closely related message. In an audience for journalists only days after his election, he set forth his agenda in the clearest possible terms: "And how I would like a Church that is poor and for the poor."[8] It seems that poverty, heretofore the province of consecrated men and women, has been extended by Francis to the Church as a whole. Further, the intended periphery now comes into focus: he is calling the Church (including his fellow bishops and religious superiors!) to discard the trappings of wealth and identify with those who are materially poor.

Pope Francis' embrace of poverty at the periphery was particularly evident in two symbolic gestures. On Holy

Thursday 2013 he celebrated the Mass of the Lord's Supper in the Casal del Marmo juvenile detention facility and washed the feet of several young offenders including a young Muslim woman. Later in July 2013, his first trip outside of Rome took him to the Mediterranean island of Lampedusa, situated only 110 km from the Tunisian coast. Hundreds of African and Middle-Eastern migrants had died in those waters attempting to reach the European periphery and escape the chaos of the Arab spring. In his homily at Lampedusa, he lamented what he called the anaesthesia of the heart: "We are a society which has forgotten how to weep, how to experience compassion—'suffering with' others; the globalization of indifference has taken from us the ability to weep!"[9]

The periphery provides a spiritual antidote to the stultifying effects of worldviews and ideologies turned in on themselves. The periphery can awaken one to the wonder of the Kingdom of God rather than the merely comfortable! In the periphery we learn that contrary to the dictates of the economy we do not have to substitute competition and rivalry for living together in friendship. In the periphery we realize that the true history of the world often runs hidden and deep rather than in the illusion of the stages of the rich and powerful. In the periphery hope can be found, take root and grow.

Francis' call for us to embrace the periphery is explicitly Christocentric. In a meeting at the Jesuit Refugee Centre in Rome, he chastised communities who were creating tourist "bed and breakfasts" from strategically-located former religious houses: "Empty convents don't belong to you; they are for the flesh of Christ, the refugees. The Lord calls us to welcome them courageously and generously into empty communities, religious houses and convents."[10] Pope Francis has identified a new and startling sacramentality in our engagement with the poor who are transfigured into Christ's own flesh. It calls to mind the invitation of Pope Paul VI of almost forty years ago. His Apostolic Exhortation *Evangelii Nuntiandi* indicated the importance of proclamation and teaching, but more forcefully identified Christian witness as a key constituent in evangelization.

It is therefore primarily by her conduct and by her life that the Church will evangelize the world, in other words, by her living witness of fidelity to the Lord Jesus—the witness of poverty and detachment, of freedom in the face of the powers of this world, in short, the witness of sanctity.[11]

Faith, science and the periphery

Now how can this concept of the periphery be applied to the question of faith and science? One way is to consider how the relation between faith and reason as expressed in the relation between faith and science sometimes implies that science is an area of spiritual poverty, because of its great concentration on the material realm. Pope Francis expressed his hopes for this dialogue in his encyclical *Lumen Fidei*:

> Nor is the light of faith, joined to the truth of love, extraneous to the material world, for love is always lived out in body and spirit; the light of faith is an incarnate light radiating from the luminous life of Jesus. It also illumines the material world, trusts its inherent order and knows that it calls us to an ever widening path of harmony and understanding. The gaze of science thus benefits from faith: faith encourages the scientist to remain constantly open to reality in all its inexhaustible richness. Faith awakens the critical sense by preventing research from being satisfied with its own formulae and helps it to realize that nature is always greater. By stimulating wonder before the profound mystery

> of creation, faith broadens the horizons of reason to shed greater light on the world which discloses itself to scientific investigation.[12]

Then there is also the problem that scientific results often only benefit the more prosperous sectors of humanity, whereas science should be a more shared activity. Scientists in developing countries have access to only a tiny fraction of the information they need, and their own contribution to science is hardly noticed by others. It is important that these countries strengthen their scientific research and that their scientists become fully integrated members of the worldwide network of science.[13] Pope Francis explored a basis for such sharing again in his encyclical *Lumen Fidei*:

> Faith, on the other hand, by revealing the love of God the Creator, enables us to respect nature all the more, and to discern in it a grammar written by the hand of God and a dwelling place entrusted to our protection and care. Faith also helps us to devise models of development which are based not simply on utility and profit, but consider creation as a gift for which we are all indebted; it teaches us to create just forms of government, in the realization that authority comes from God and is meant for the service of the common good. Faith likewise offers the possibility of forgiveness, which so often demands time and effort, patience and commitment. Forgiveness is possible once we discover that goodness is always prior to and more powerful than evil, and that the word with which God affirms our life is deeper than our every denial. From a purely anthropological standpoint, unity is superior to conflict; rather than avoiding conflict, we need to confront it in an effort to resolve and move beyond it, to make it a link in a chain, as part of a progress towards unity.[14]

Speaking to a group of young astronomers studying on a summer school at the Vatican Specola, Pope Francis stated: "It is only right that men and women everywhere should have access to research and scientific training. The hope that one day all peoples will be able to enjoy the benefits of science is one which spurs all of us on, scientists in particular."[15] The Vatican Observatory School in Astrophysics is thus a place where young people the world over can engage in dialogue and collaboration, helping one another in the search for truth, which in this case is concretized in the study of galaxies. This simple and practical initiative shows how the sciences can be a fitting and effective means for promoting peace and justice.[16]

Pope Francis has clearly stated that a dialogue between faith and science belongs to the domain of evangelization: "Dialogue between science and faith also belongs to the work of evangelization at the service of peace."[17] the Pope indicates how positivism and scientism are obstacles to this dialogue, since they refuse to admit the validity of forms of knowledge other than those of the positive sciences. The Church proposes another path, which calls for a synthesis between the responsible use of methods proper to the empirical sciences and other areas of knowledge such as philosophy, theology, as well as faith itself, which elevates us to the mystery transcending nature and human intelligence. Faith is not fearful of reason; on the contrary, it seeks and trusts reason, since the light of reason and the light of faith both come from God and cannot contradict each other. Evangelization is attentive to scientific advances and wishes to shed on them the light of faith and the natural law so that they will remain respectful of the centrality and supreme value of the human person at every stage of life.[18]

The Church's commitment to dialogue with the sciences is based upon the light provided by faith: it is her conviction that faith is capable of both expanding and enriching the horizons of reason.[19] In this dialogue, the Church rejoices in the marvellous progress of science, even as a mother rejoices and is rightly proud as her children grow "in wisdom, and age and grace" (Lk 2:52).[20]

The Church thus encourages scientific progress, but is careful to distinguish between science and ideology:

> The Church has no wish to hold back the marvellous progress of science. On the contrary, she rejoices and even delights in acknowledging the enormous potential that God has given to the human mind. Whenever the sciences —rigorously focused on their specific field of inquiry— arrive at a conclusion which reason cannot refute, faith does not contradict it. Neither can believers claim that a scientific opinion which is attractive but not sufficiently verified has the same weight as a dogma of faith. At times some scientists have exceeded the limits of their scientific competence by making certain statements or claims. But here the problem is not with reason itself, but with the promotion of a particular ideology which blocks the path to authentic, serene and productive dialogue.[21]

This extrapolation from science to ideology appears sometimes among evolutionists: "Care must be taken to distinguish between hard scientific fact (obtained in an *a posteriori* manner) in the theory of evolution and an unjustified a priori extrapolation of this theory to form an atheist ideology."[22]

One area in which Pope Francis has expressed some important consequences for sharing in science lies in the care for creation and ecology. He explained how the vocation of being a protector of creation is not just something involving Christians alone; it also has a prior dimension which is simply human, involving everyone. It means protecting all creation, the beauty of the created world, as the Book of Genesis tells us and as Saint Francis of Assisi showed us. It means respecting each of God's creatures and respecting the environment in which we live. To protect creation, to protect every man and every woman, to look upon them with tenderness and love, is to open up a horizon of hope; it is to let a shaft of light break through the heavy clouds; it is to bring the warmth of hope![23]

Nurturing and cherishing creation is a command God gives not only at the beginning of history, but to each of us. It is part of his plan; it means causing the world to grow responsibly, transforming it so that it may be a garden, a habitable place for everyone. This task entrusted to us by God the Creator requires us to grasp the rhythm and logic of creation. But we are often driven by pride of domination, of possessions, manipulation, of exploitation; we do not "care" for it, we do not respect it, we do not consider it as a free gift that we must care for. However "cultivating and caring" do not only entail the relationship between us and the environment, between man and creation. They also concern human relations. The popes have spoken of a human ecology, closely connected with environmental ecology. We are living in a time of crisis; we see it in the environment, but above all we see it in men and women. The human person is in danger today, hence the urgent need for human ecology! And the peril is grave, because the cause of the problem is not superficial but deeply rooted. It is not merely a question of economics but of ethics and anthropology.[24]

Saint Francis of Assisi bears witness to the need to respect all that God has created and as he created it, without manipulating and destroying creation; rather to help it grow, to become more beautiful and more like what God created it to be. And above all, Saint Francis witnesses to respect for everyone, he testifies that each of us is called to protect our neighbour, that the human person is at the centre of creation, at the place where God—our Creator—willed that we should be. Not at the mercy of the idols we have created! Pope Francis warned however that Franciscan peace is not a kind of pantheistic harmony with forces of the cosmos: "It is not Franciscan, but a notion that some people have invented!"[25]

We human beings are not only the beneficiaries but also the stewards of other creatures. Thanks to our bodies, God has joined us so closely to the world around us that we can feel the desertification of the soil almost as a physical ailment, and the extinction of a species as a painful disfigurement. Let us not leave in our wake a swath of destruction and death which will affect our own lives and those of future generations. The Pope cited the touching and prophetic lament voiced some years ago by the bishops of the Philippines:

> An incredible variety of insects lived in the forest and were busy with all kinds of tasks ... Birds flew through the air, their bright plumes and varying calls adding colour and song to the green of the forests ... God intended this land for us, his special creatures, but not so that we might destroy it and turn it into a wasteland ... After a single night's rain, look at the chocolate brown rivers in your locality and remember that they are carrying the life blood of the land into the sea... How can fish swim in sewers like the Pasig and so many more rivers which we have polluted? Who has turned the wonderworld of the seas into underwater cemeteries bereft of colour and life?[26]

The human family has received from the Creator a common gift: nature. The Christian view of creation includes a positive judgment about the legitimacy of interventions on nature if these are meant to be beneficial and are performed responsibly, that is to say, by acknowledging the "grammar" inscribed in nature and by wisely using resources for the benefit of all, with respect for the beauty, finality and usefulness of every living being and its place in the ecosystem. Nature, in a word, is at our disposition and we are called to exercise a responsible stewardship over it. Yet so often we are driven by greed and by the arrogance of dominion, possession, manipulation and exploitation; we do not preserve nature; nor do we respect it or consider it a gracious gift which we must care for and set at the service of our brothers and sisters, including future generations.[27]

Pope Francis explained that the gift of knowledge, imparted by the Holy Spirit, leads us to grasp, through creation, the greatness and love of God and his profound relationship with every creature. The gift of knowledge helps us not to fall into attitudes of excess or error. The first error lies in the risk of considering ourselves the masters of creation. Creation is not some possession that we can lord over for our own pleasure; nor, even less, is it the property of only some people, the few: creation is a gift, it is the marvellous gift that God has given us, so that we will take care of it and harness it for the benefit of all, always with great respect and gratitude. "We must protect creation for it is a gift which the Lord has given us, it is God's present to us; we are the guardians of creation. When we exploit creation, we destroy that sign of God's love. To destroy creation is to say to God: 'I don't care'. And this is not good: this is sin."[28]

The Pope added that custody of creation is precisely custody of God's gift and it is saying to God: "thank you, I am the guardian of creation so as to make it progress, never to destroy your gift". Pope Francis recounted how once he was in the countryside and he heard a saying from a simple person who had a great love for flowers and took care of them. The person said: "We must take care of the beautiful things that God has given us! Creation is ours so that we can receive good things from it; not exploit it, but protect it. God forgives always, we men forgive sometimes, but creation never forgives and if you don't care for it, it will destroy you."[29]

The second erroneous attitude is represented by the temptation to stop at creatures, as if these could provide the answer to all our expectations. With the gift of knowledge, the Holy Spirit helps us not to fall into this error.

> The outpouring of the Holy Spirit enlightens the thoughts of artists, poets, and scientists. Their great minds receive from You prophetic insights into Your laws, and reveal to us the depth of Your creative wisdom. Unwittingly, their works speak of You; how great You are in all You have created, how great You are in man!
> Glory to You, showing your unfathomable might in the laws of the universe!
> Glory to You, for all nature is permeated by Your laws,
> Glory to You for what You have revealed to us in Your goodness,
> Glory to You for all that remains hidden from us in Your wisdom,
> Glory to You for the inventiveness of the human mind,
> Glory to You for the invigorating effort of work,
> Glory to You for the tongues of fire which bring inspiration,
> Glory to You, O God, from age to age.[30]

Notes

1 Cardinal Jorge Bergoglio, *Address to the pre-conclave General Congregation of the Cardinals*, March 2013. As found on en.radiovaticana.va/storico/2013/03/27/bergoglios_intervention_a_diagnosis_of_the_problems_in_the_church/en1-677269.

2 Pope Francis, *Evangelii Gaudium*, 20.

3 Pope Francis, *Address to the Leadership of the Episcopal Conferences of Latin America during the General Coordination Meeting* (28 July 2013).

4 Pope Francis, *Address to Participants in the Ecclesial Convention of the Diocese of Rome* (17 June 2013).

5 Pope Francis, *Address to Polish bishops* (7 February 2014).

6 A. Spadaro, "Wake up the World: Conversation with Pope Francis about the Religious Life" in *La Civiltà Cattolica* (2014/I), pp. 3–17.

7 *Ibid.*

8 Pope Francis, *Address to members of the communications media* (16 March 2013): "E come vorrei una Chiesa povera e per i poveri!"

9 Pope Francis, *Homily* (8 July 2013).

10 Pope Francis, *Address on his visit to the Centro Astalli for Refugees* (10 September 2013).

11 Pope Paul VI, *Evangelii Nuntiandi* (1975), 41.

12 Pope Francis, *Lumen Fidei*, 34.

13 See S. Arunachalam, "Science on the Periphery: Bridging the Information Divide" in H. F. Moed, W. Glänzel, U. Schmoch, *Handbook of Quantitative Science and Technology Research* (Springer: 2005), pp. 163–183.

14 Pope Francis, *Lumen Fidei*, 55.

15 Pope Francis, *Address to young astronomers participating in the Vatican Observatory's School of Astrophysics' Summer Course* (26 June 2014).

16 See *ibid.*

17 Pope Francis, *Evangelii Gaudium* (2013), 242.

18 *Ibid.*

19 See Pope Francis, *Address to young astronomers participating in the Vatican Observatory's School of Astrophysics' Summer Course* (26 June 2014). See also Idem, *Evangelii Gaudium*, 238.

20 See Pope Francis, *Address to young astronomers participating in the Vatican Observatory's School of Astrophysics' Summer Course* (26 June 2014).

[21] Pope Francis, *Evangelii Gaudium*, 243.

[22] P. Haffner, *Mystery of Creation* (Leominster: Gracewing, 2010), p. 253.

[23] Pope Francis, *Homily for the Beginning of the Petrine Ministry of the Bishop of Rome* (19 March 2013).

[24] Pope Francis, Address at General Audience (5 June 2013).

[25] Pope Francis, *Homily in Assisi* (4 October 2013).

[26] Pope Francis, *Evangelii Gaudium*, 215. See also The Catholic Bishops' Conference of the Philippines, Pastoral Letter *What Is Happening to Our Beautiful Land* (29 January 1988).

[27] Pope Francis, *Message for the World Day of Peace 2014* (8 December 2013), 9.

[28] Pope Francis, *Address at General Audience* (21 May 2014).

[29] See *ibid.*

[30] Metropolitan Tryphon, *An Akathist in Praise of God's Creation*, Ikos 7.

Bibliography

AA. VV., *Papal Addresses to the Pontifical Academy of Sciences 1917–2002 and to the Pontifical Academy of Social Sciences 1994–2002. Pontificiae Academiae Scientiarum Scripta Varia: Vol. 100* (Vatican City: Pontificial Academy of Sciences, 2003).

Brown, N. M., *The abacus and the cross: The story of the Pope who brought the light of science to the Dark Ages* (New York: Basic Books, 2010).

Consolmagno, G., *Brother astronomer: Adventures of a Vatican scientist* (New York: McGraw-Hill, 2000).

Idem, *God's mechanics: How scientists and engineers make sense of religion* (San Francisco: Jossey-Bass, 2008).

Idem, *The heavens proclaim: Astronomy and the Vatican* ([Huntington, IN]: Our Sunday Vistor; [Rome, Italy] : Vatican City State; Vatican Observatory Publications, 2009).

Idem, *The new physics and the old metaphysics* (Regina (Canada): Campion College at the University of Regina, 2012).

Coyne, G. V., Hoskin, M. A., & Pedersen, O., *Gregorian reform of the calendar: Proceedings of the Vatican Conference to commemorate its 400th anniversary, 1582–1982* (Città del Vaticano, Europe: Pontificia Academia Scientiarum; Specola vaticana, 1983).

Crombie, A. C., *Robert Grosseteste and the origins of experimental science, 1100–1700* (Oxford: Clarendon-Press, 1953).

Idem, *Science, optics, and music in medieval and early modern thought* (London, Ronceverte, WV, USA: Hambledon Press, 1990).

Idem, *Styles of scientific thinking in the European tradition: The history of argument and explanation especially in the mathematical and biomedical sciences and arts* (London: Duckworth, 1994).

Idem, *The history of science from Augustine to Galileo* (New York: Dover Publications, 1995).

Idem, *Science, art, and nature in medieval and modern thought* (London, Rio Grande, Ohio: Hambledon Press, 1996).

Egan, J., *The Godless Delusion: Dawkins and the limits of human sight* (Oxford, New York: Peter Lang, 2009).

Ferngren, G. B., *Medicine & health care in early Christianity* (Baltimore: Johns Hopkins University Press, 2009).

Flusche, A. M., *The life and legend of Gerbert of Aurillac: The organbuilder who became Pope Sylvester II* (Lewiston, NY: Edwin Mellen Press, 2006).

Gargantini, M., *I Papi e la scienza: Antologia del magistero della Chiesa sulla questione scientifica da Leone XIII a Giovanni Paolo II . Già e non ancora: Vol. 122* (Milano: Jaca Book, 1985).

Grant, E., *The foundations of modern science in the Middle Ages: Their religious, institutional, and intellectual contexts*. Cambridge history of science (Cambridge: Cambridge University Press, 1996).

Guerrini, L., *The "Accademie dei Lincei" and the New World. Preprint / Max-Planck-Institut für Wissenschaftsgeschichte: Vol. 348* (Berlin: Max-Planck-Institut für Wissenschaftsgeschichte, 2008).

Haffner, P. (Ed.), *Discourses of the popes from Pius XI to John Paul II to the Pontifical Academy of Sciences, 1936–1986. Pontificiae Academiae Scientiarum scripta varia: Vol. 66* (Vatican City: Pontificia Academia Scientiarum, 1986).

Idem, *The Mystery of Reason* (Leominster: Gracewing, 2001).

Idem, *Creation and scientific creativity: A study in the thought of Stanley L. Jaki* (2nd edition) (Leominster: Gracewing, 2009).

Hannam, J., *The genesis of science: How the Christian Middle Ages launched the scientific revolution* (Washington, DC, New York: Regnery Publishing, 2011).

Hodgson, P. E., *The roots of science and its fruits: The Christian origin of modern science and its impact on human society* (London: Saint Austin Press, 2002).

Idem, *Theology and modern physics. Ashgate science and religion series* (Aldershot, Hants, England; Burlington, VT: Ashgate, 2005).

Idem, *Faith, science, and society* (Ave Maria, FL: Sapientia Press, 2008).

Horn, S. O., Wiedenhofer, S., & Schönborn, C. von, *Creation and evolution: A conference with Pope Benedict XVI in Castel Gandolfo* (San Francisco: Ignatius Press, 2008).

Jaki, S. L., *The road of science and the ways to God* (Chicago: University of Chicago Press, 1978).

Idem, *The origin of science and the science of its origin* (South Bend: Regency/Gateway, 1979).

Idem, *Cosmos and creator* (Edinburgh: Scottish Academic Press, 1980).

Idem, *Angels, apes, and men* (La Salle, Ill: S. Sugden, 1983).

Idem, *Angels, apes, and men* (La Salle, Il: Sherwood Sugden, 1983).

Idem, *Uneasy genius: The life and work of Pierre Duhem. Archives internationales d'histoire des idées: Vol. 100* (The Hague, Lancaster: Nijhoff, 1984).

Idem, *Chance or reality and other essays* (Lanham, Md, London: University Press of America, 1986).

Idem, *Brain, mind and computers* (3rd ed) (Washington, D.C: Regnery Gateway, 1989).

Idem, *God and the cosmologists* (Edinburgh: Scottish Academic Press, 1989).

Idem, *Cosmos in transition: Studies in the history of cosmology. Pachart history of astronomy series: v. 5* (Tucson: Pachart, 1990).

Idem, *Science and creation: From eternal cycles to an oscillating universe* (Lanham, M.D: University Press of America, 1990).

Idem, *The Virgin birth and the birth of science* (Front Royal, Va: Christendom Press, 1990).

Idem, *The relevance of physics* (New ed) (Edinburgh: Scottish Academic Press, 1992).

Idem, *Is there a universe?: The forwood lectures for 1992* (Liverpool: Liverpool University Press, 1993).

Idem, *Bible and science* (Front Royal, Va: Christendom Press, 1996).

Idem, *Means to message: A treatise on truth* (Grand Rapids, Mich: Eerdmans Pub, 1999).

Idem, *Scientist and Catholic: An essay on Pierre Duhem* (Front Royal, VA: Christendom Press, 1991).

Kermit, H., *Niels Stensen, 1638-1986* (Leominster: Gracewing, 2003).

Kneller, K. A., & Jaki, S. L., *Christianity and the leaders of modern science: A contribution to the history of culture during the nineteenth century* (Michigan: Real-View-Books, 1995).

Kort, J. J. M. A. de, *Astronomical appreciation of the Gregorian calendar*. Ricerche astronomiche: vol. 2, n. 6 (Città del Vaticano: Specola Vaticana, 1949).

Lattin, H. P., *The peasant boy who became pope: Story of Gerbert* (London: Abelard-Schuman, 1958).

Lindgren, U., *Gerbert von Aurillac und das Quadrivium: Unters. zur Bildung im Zeitalter d. Ottonen. Sudhoffs Archiv: Beihefte: Vol. 18* (Wiesbaden: Steiner, 1976).

Madrid, P., & Hensley, K., *The Godless Delusion: A Catholic challenge to modern atheism* (Huntington, IND: Our Sunday Visitor, 2010).

Maffeo, S., *The Vatican Observatory: In the service of nine popes* (Vatican City State: Vatican Observatory Publications, 2001).

Mascall, E. L., *Christian theology and natural science: Some questions on their relations. Bampton lectures: Vol. 1956* (London: Longmans Green, 1956).

Morghen, R., *L'Accademia nazionale dei Lincei nel CCCLXVIII anno della sua fondazione, nella vita e nella cultura dell'Italia unita* (Roma: Accademia nazionale dei Lincei, 1972).

Nuvolone, F. G., *Gerberto d'Aurillac–Silvestro II, linee per una sintesi: Atti del Convegno internazionale, Bobbio, Auditorium di S. Chiara, 11 settembre 2004, sotto la presidenza del prof. Pierre Racine. Archivum Bobiense Studia: Vol. 5* (Bobbio (Piacenza): Associazione culturale Amici di Archivum bobiense, 2005).

Pedersen, O., *The book of nature* (Vatican City State, Notre Dame, IN: Vatican Observatory Publications; University of Notre Dame Press, 1992).

Russell, R. J., *John Paul II on science and religion: Reflections on the new view from Rome. Vatican Observatory publications* (Notre Dame IN, Città del Vaticano: University of Notre Dame Press; Libreria Editrice Vaticana, 1990).

Scruton, R., *The soul of the world* (Princeton: Princeton University Press, 2014).

Sobiech, F., *Herz, Gott, Kreuz: Die Spiritualität des Anatomen, Geologen und Bischofs Dr. med. Niels Stensen (1638-1686). Westfalia sacra: Vol. 13* (Münster: Aschendorff, 2004).

Stark, R., *The Victory of Reason: How Christianity Led to Freedom, Capitalism, and Western Success* (New York: Random House Trade Paperbacks, 2006).

Idem, *How the West won: The neglected story of the triumph of modernity* (Wilmington, DE: Intercollegiate Studies Institute, 2014).

Trascancos, S., *Science Was Born of Christianity: The Teaching of Fr. Stanley L. Jaki* (Titusville, FL: Habitation of Chimham Publishing, 2014).

Treanor, P. J., *The Vatican Observatory* (Città del Vaticano: Specola Vaticana, 1969).

Turek, J., *Georges Lemaître and the Pontifical Academy of Sciences. Vatican Observatory publications: v. 2, no. 13* (Città del Vaticano: Specola Vaticana, 1989).

Walsh, J. J., *The Popes and Science: The history of papal relations to science during the middle ages down to our own time* (New York: Fordham University Press, 1915).

Walsh, M. J., *The sixteenth century Gregorian reform of the Julian calendar: An historical and mathematical examination of the reform* (Dublin: University College Dublin, 2005).

www.ingramcontent.com/pod-product-compliance
Ingram Content Group UK Ltd.
Pitfield, Milton Keynes, MK11 3LW, UK
UKHW041842190726
13854UKWH00002B/674

9 780852 448601